The Complete Book of Electronic Security

Bill Phillips

McGraw-Hill

New York   Chicago   San Francisco   Lisbon   London
Madrid   Mexico City   Milan   New Delhi   San Juan   Seoul
Singapore   Sydney   Toronto

Cataloging-in-Publication Data is on file with the Library of Congress.

McGraw-Hill

A Division of The McGraw·Hill Companies

1 2 3 4 5 6 7 8 9   DOC/DOC   0 7 6 5 4 3 2 1

ISBN 0-07-138018-3

The sponsoring editor for this book was Shelley Carr, the editing supervisor was Caroline Levine, and the production supervisor was Sherri Souffrance. It was set in Century Schoolbook by Kim Sheran, Victoria Khavkina, Wayne Palmer, and Vicki Hunt of McGraw-Hill Professional's Hightstown, N.J. composition unit.

Printed and bound by R. R. Donnelley & Sons Company.

McGraw-Hill books are available at special quantity discounts to use as premiums and sales promotions, or for use in corporate training programs. For more information, please write to the Director of Special Sales, Professional Publishing, McGraw-Hill, Two Penn Plaza, New York, NY 10121-2298. Or contact your local bookstore.

 This book is printed on recycled, acid-free paper containing a minimum of 50% recycled de-inked fiber.

To Janet Lynn Griffin

Contents

1-22-03
SC

About the Contributors

The following security professionals have contributed to this book:

Allan B. Colombo, a highly respected security industry journalist and book author. He's the technology editor for *Security Distributing & Marketing* magazine. In this capacity, and through his Websites at *http://www.ssmagazine.com,* he strives to educate and inform security professionals on existing and oncoming techniques, trends, and technologies related to all aspects of electronic security and surveillance.

John "Jack" Fay, CPP, a security consultant in Atlanta, Georgia, and author and editor of many books, including *Butterworth's Security Dictionary*; *Encyclopedia of Security Management*; *The Police Dictionary and Encyclopedia*; and *Approaches to Criminal Justice Training*.

Francis Gallagher, Senior Security Systems Engineer with TECHMARK Security Integration, Inc. in Pembroke, Massachusetts.

Richard P. Grassie, CPP, President and Principal Consultant for TECHMARK Security Integration, Inc. in Pembroke, Massachusetts. He is an author of many articles on security design and integration and countermeasures development for security trade journals, and coauthor of U.S. Department of Justice publications on crime analysis, criminal warrant service, and the Integrated Criminal Apprension Program (ICAP).

Tab Hauser, Vice President of Tane Alarm Products, Floral Park, New York.

Jerry Jacobson, Ph.D., Director of Marketing for Fiber Optics in Bohemia, New York, formerly Manager of Corporate Communications at Vicon Industries, and author of many electronic security technical articles.

Kenneth Kirschenbaum, Esq., an attorney with Kirschenbaum & Kirschenbaum, P.C. in Garden City, New York. He specializes in security issues and is a columnist for *Security Dealer* magazine.

Karl Pararndjuk, Vice President of Marketing for Ivex in Norcross, Georgia, and formerly director of advanced systems planning at Scientific-Atlanta. He has over 13 years of experience developing and marketing high technology products and services. He holds an MBA in marketing from Georgia State University and a B.A. in physics from the State University of New York at Potsdam.

Robert Pearson, PE, manager of corporate electronic security for Raytheon/TI in Dallas, Texas, and technical editor for *Security Technology & Design.*

Charlie Pierce, President of LRC Electronics Company and LTC Training Center in Davenport, Iowa. He is one of the world's foremost authorities on CCTV, and the author of many books and articles on CCTV.

Rudy Prokupets, Chief Technology Officer and Executive Vice President of R & D for Lenel Systems International, Inc., in Fairport, New York.

Robert A. Wimmer, President of Video Security Consultants in Landisville, Pennsylvania and technical editor for *Security Technology & Design.*

Introduction

In the Foreword to one of my books, *Home Mechanix,* editor-in-chief Michael Chotiner wrote: "Bill is an experienced security professional and a widely published writer in his fields of expertise. While his credentials and hands-on experience are impressive . . . the text provides both general and specific information on the latest equipment, including alarm systems, locks, safes, fire sprinklers, lighting devices, and video and intercom systems designed to enhance security. Through the clear instructions and detailed illustrations in this book, you can learn to install and use this equipment properly."

The same can be said for this book, except this one is bigger and better. I give more practical, in-depth information on more topics. In addition to being useful as a self-study guide or textbook, this book is designed to be a comprehensive reference source that you'll turn to many times. To make it as authoritative and useful as possible, I include contributions from over a dozen leading electronic security professionals—including technical editors and columnists from all the major electronic security trade journals.

Contributors include Al Colombo, technology editor for *Security Distributing & Marketing* and author of several security books; John "Jack" Fay, CPP, a security consultant, former professor, and author of many notable security books; Charlie Pierce, one of the world's foremost authorities on closed-circuit television systems, President of LTC Training Center, and a regular contributor to many trade journals; Kenneth Kirschenbaum, a practicing attorney who specializes in security issues and a columnist for *Security Dealer* magazine; Robert A. Wimmer, President of Video Security Consultants and technical editor for *Security Technology & Design*; and Jerry L. Jacobson, Ph.D., of Fiber Options.

Some topics covered in this book include:

- Installing and servicing wireless and hardwired alarms
- Understanding and installing closed-circuit television systems
- Low-voltage wiring
- Using coaxial and fiber optics cable
- Installing security lighting

- Smart homes and home automation systems
- Understanding access control and systems integration
- Installing vehicle alarms
- Getting licensed and certified as an alarm systems technician (sample certification test is included)
- Finding a job and negotiating a great salary
- Starting, running, and expanding an electronic security business

This book also includes helpful resources, such as a glossary, state licensing laws, and lists of suppliers, manufacturers, and training and certification programs with website and email addresses.

To help you quickly get the information you want, each chapter is divided into two parts. The first part covers the basics of a topic. It's for anyone who needs a general and easy to understand overview of the chapter. The second part is more pratical and detailed and is especially useful for the professional installer or security dealer. If you don't have a good understanding of Part 1 of a chapter, you won't be able to follow Part 2. That's why I've included review questions at the end of each Part 1, to let you check right away if you need to read Part 1 first.

I'm not trying to downplay the Part 1s, because even a seasoned professional may learn something new from them or find them to be great for review. You'll get the most out of this book by reading it straight through, but I'm offering the two-part chapters to make it more useful for busy people. That makes it easier to skip around. Parts 1 and 2 of a chapter are separated by a stair step drawing to illustrate a stepping up in detail.

After you've read *The Complete Book of Electronic Security,* let me know what you think. And tell me what you'd like to see in the next edition. Send your comments and questions to:

Bill Phillips
Box 2044-E
Erie, PA 16512-2044

Or send email to: billphillips@iahssp.org.

Acknowledgments

There are many people who helped with this book in some way, far more than I'm able to list here. But I'd like to mention a few.

I'm especially grateful to the security industry experts who unselfishly shared their knowledge in the pages of this book. I have great respect for each of them and was honored by their participation. Special thanks to John J. Fay, CPP, a security consultant and author of many security books (several of which I own); Francis Gallagher and Richard P. Grassie, CPP, of Techmark Security Integration Inc.; Jerry Jacobson, Ph.D., of Fiber Optics; Kenneth Kirschenbaum, Esq., of Kirschenbaum & Kirschenbaum, PC (who really seems to love the law, especially with respect to the security industry); Karl Parandjuk of Ivex Corporation; Robert Pearson, PE, of Raytheon/TI; Charlie Pierce, President of LTC Training Center (an expert's expert on closed-circuit television); Rudy Prokupets, Chief Technology Officer of Lenel Systems International; and Robert A. Wimmer of Video Security Consultants.

Many fine companies were also helpful, including: Ademco Security Group; A.W. Sperry Instruments Inc.; Black Widow Vehicle Security Systems; George Risk Industries (G.R.I.); Highpower Security Products, LLC; Ivex Corporation; Napco Security Systems; Ultrak, Inc.; Visonic; and Winsted Corporation.

Special thanks to Patricia Bruce, M.S.S.A.; Jonathan Dupree "Jayrock" Gavin; and Ricky "Sabian" Smith for their help with photographs. Thanks also to my sons Danny and Michael for being my inspiration for this and every book.

I was fortunate to have worked with a talented and hardworking group at McGraw-Hill, including Carol Levine, the supervising editor who made my writing readable; Margaret Webster-Shapiro who worked on the book's cover; and Shelley Carr, my acquisitions editor, who helped me shape and sell the idea. I thank all of them and their assistants for their patience, good nature, and professionalism.

Electronic Security: Past and Present

Part 1 of this chapter traces the development of some of the most important electronic security systems and services. Part 2 is an overview of the size and scope of the industry today throughout the world, along with industry projections and forecasts.

Part 1: Electronic Security Development

Benjamin Franklin was a pioneer in the study of electricity. As the story goes, in 1752 during a thunderstorm he flew a kite with a key tied to the tail. That experiment symbolically tied security to electricity early on. Today much of security involves electricity—intruder alarms, closed-circuit television, access control systems, smoke and heat detectors, and other fire and crime prevention products and services.

Security and fire safety haven't always been combined in the same industry. Today's technology and safety regulations help make fire and crime prevention systems integral. If you install security systems, laws require you to take fire codes into consideration. Also, because many fire and security products can easily be installed together, it makes good business sense to be able to install both types in the same installation.

Alarms and Central Stations

The first electric burglar alarm (or intruder alarm) was invented by Edwin Thomas Holmes and Thomas Watson, contemporaries of Alexander Graham Bell, in 1858. The alarm had a spring that was released when a door or window was opened. An electric circuit was completed by the spring's making contact with the wires. In those days alarms were used for protecting bank vaults and safe cabinets. A more sophisticated system included a clock that automatically turned off the alarm in the morning to avoid false alarms.

1

Fast Fact

When Holmes formed the Holmes Protection Group in 1858, it was the first
company of its kind in the United States and then Canada. Today it's the oldest
electronic security company, and it offers many commercial and residential
security products and services, including access control, closed-circuit television,
interactive video, fire detection, sprinkler supervision, and vehicle tracking.

Making noise is effective to alert occupants and others nearby, but alarms
can be more effective if they also contact someone at a remote location. That
was the idea behind the first *central station* (or *monitoring company*) concept for a company to monitor and respond to alarm systems. (For more on
central station monitoring today, see Chapter 17.) In 1852 Boston's fire
alarm center became the first central station. In 1856 similar installations
were made in Philadelphia and St. Louis. Although the idea for central stations was well developed for fire alarm use in the 1860s, it wasn't used for
intruder alarms until the 1870s. E. A. Calahan introduced the concept to
the intruder alarm industry.

In 1871 Calahan conceived a *district messenger service* in which the city of
New York was divided into several areas. Each area had a call box connected to
a central station that let subscribers call for a messenger. The American District
Telegraph (now called ADT) Company of New York was organized in 1871 to
commercially develop Calahan's inventions. By 1874, the ADT Company was
operating 12 central stations in Manhattan. By 1887 there were about 20 companies in cities such as Baltimore, Chicago, and Philadelphia (see Figure 1.1).

At that time, Holmes was developing more sophisticated alarm systems for
homeowners and businesses. In 1872, Holmes developed an electrically wired
cabinet to store jewelry. The cabinet was lined with current-carrying foil, and
the doors were equipped with detector switches. Holmes wired the cabinet to
a central office, allowing men, on duty 24 hours per day, to be dispatched in
response to any alarm condition.

Early alarm central stations were crucial in promoting the telephone during
its early days. Alexander Graham Bell patented the first telephone in 1876. The
first major telephone exchange was 700 of Alexander Graham Bell's telephones,

---

Fast Fact

In 1918, Dominion Messenger purchased Holmes Protection of Canada, and
later it became Dominion Electric Protection Company. Within a few years the
all-Canadian enterprise became Canada's largest full-service alarm company.
In 1956, ADT Security Systems gained controlling interest. Today ADT Canada
is the largest commercial and residential security firm in Canada.

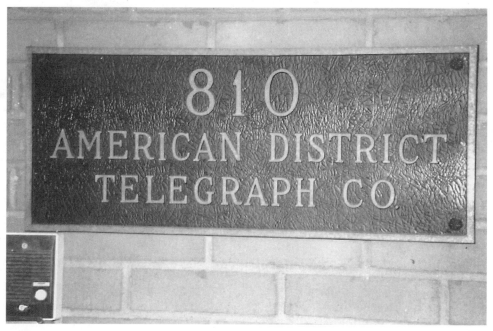

Figure 1.1 "American District Telegraph" is the oldest central station; its offspring companies are called "ADT."

which were connected to his central station, being leased by Edwin T. Holmes. The telephones were soon introduced to police and fire stations, enabling the first telephone alarm dispatches. Eventually, the Holmes family sold its telephone side of the business. By then the telephone was emerging as one of the most important devices for the upcoming twentieth century.

Computers

Another major invention that revolutionized the alarm industry, and the twentieth century in general, was the computer. The first analog computer was invented by Vannevar Bush in the 1930s. In 1968 Burroughs produced the first computers to use integrated circuits. Such companies as Smith Alarm Systems, Denver Intruder Alarms, Wells Fargo, Honeywell, and ADT pioneered work with digital computers in the alarm industry.

Computers greatly improved the ability to keep accurate records of the type of alarm received from actual break-ins, accidental triggers by nature or people, etc. The computer also greatly increased the number of accounts that could be monitored, and the telephone line made the distance between the central station and the point of signal activation irrelevant. Today computer networks and the Internet (which is a network of networks) are being used to aid in security system monitoring.

The early communicators used tape dialers, which had been invented in 1896. When an alarm was activated, a loop tape would send a prerecorded message to the police or fire department or whomever it was set to call. Tape dialers resulted in many false alarms, and often they malfunctioned. The tape would often start the message in mid-sentence or get locked in an infinite loop. Digital communicators solved that problem by sending binary information to a digital computer. Today tape dialers are used mostly in older and low-cost do-it-yourself alarm systems.

Many businesses today do their own monitoring in-house, and when trouble arises, they either dispatch their own guards or call for help. Figure 1.2 shows a setup for in-house monitoring.

Questions for review

1. Where was the first fire alarm station?
2. Who installed the first intruder alarm?
3. When were central stations used to monitor intruder alarms?
4. Why do intruder alarm installers need to know about fire safety?
5. What major twentieth-century invention revolutionized the electronic security industry?

Figure 1.2   Some companies find it more cost-effective to monitor their own premises (Courtesy of Winsted Corp.).

Part 2: Today's Electronic Security Market

Although there was a lot of activity in the electronic security industry during the late nineteenth and twentieth centuries, all indications are that this decade will be unprecedented in profits earned and the use of new technology. Today the electronic security industry's scope is broader than ever. It includes companies that sell, service, and install intrusion and fire alarm systems, closed-circuit television systems, access control systems, home automation systems, electronic article surveillance (EAS), and vehicle security systems, as well as companies that provide central station monitoring services. Few companies do all these things. (For manufacturer contact information, see Appendix A.)

Because there's so much diversity in the industry, it is not always easy to accurately compare industry statistics. If you search the Internet or read the trade journals, you'll find a lot of numbers tossed around about industry size and projections. To make much sense of them, however, you need to know exactly what fields and countries the reports cover and how the information was obtained. I looked at reports from some of the best-known market researchers.

The World

According to *World Security Services,* a report from the Freedonia Group, a market research firm, the global market for private security services will grow 8.4 percent annually through 2004, approaching $100 billion. Big gains are expected in central station services. Rapid growth is expected in Africa, Asia, eastern Europe, Latin America, and the Middle East.

North America

According to the Frost and Sullivan report *North American Markets for Fire and Smoke Detection Devices,* the demand for fire safety devices will continue to show moderate growth through 2005. By 2005, the market is expected to reach $643.9 million compared to $548.8 million for 2001. The report says that the smoke and heat detector market is strongly driven by building codes, new construction, and renovation of buildings.

The United States

The United States is the world's largest electronic security market. In 2000, U.S. security dealer firm revenues reached more than $18.1 billion, according to an annual reader survey conducted by *Security Distributing & Marketing* magazine. One reason for that is that, except for minor regional differences, the U.S. products sold in one part of the country can almost always be used by the rest of the country.

The U.S. demand for passive electronic components is forecast to advance nearly 4 percent per year to $21.4 billion in 2005, according to the *Passive Components* study conducted by the Freedonia Group. (See Table 1.1.) Above-average advances in certain end-user applications, particularly wireless and fiber-optic communications, combined with an improved outlook for the defense and aerospace sector, will support increases. Rising electronics content in motor vehicles will continue to benefit the passive components industry. Growth through 2005 represents a significant slowdown from increases over the past decade, which is reflected in reduced growth in demand for passive device–containing original equipment, particularly electronic equipment. Continuing competition from integrated passive devices combined with dramatic price increases for capacitors will also limit gains to some degree.

> **Fast Fact**
>
> Tyco International Ltd.'s Fire and Security Services unit, which includes ADT Security Systems and Thorn Security, is the world's largest manufacturer, installer, and servicer of fire protection and life safety systems and services.

TABLE 1.1 Passive Component Demand Forecast

(million dollars)

Item	1990	2000	2005	Percent of annual growth 90/00	05/00
Passive component demand	9,881	17,850	21,370	6.1	3.7
Connectors	3,741	6,540	7,500	5.7	2.8
Capacitors	1,349	3,195	3,870	9.0	3.9
Inductance devices	1,413	2,850	3,610	7.3	4.8
Resistors	1,046	1,480	1,635	3.5	2.0
Other	2,332	3,785	4,755	5.0	4.7

Connectors represent the largest segment of the passive components industry, accounting for more than 35 percent of the total in 2000. Despite below-average increases due to the presence of a number of mature products, connectors will remain the largest segment of the industry for the foreseeable future. Microwave components and inductance devices have the best prospects through 2005. Both of these products will benefit from the continued strength in the cellular and wireless communications market and expected increased defense spending. The large capacitor market will also see above-average growth, despite expected price decreases.

Europe

The European market is fragmented into distinct countries, with differing languages and regulations. The lack of standardization makes it harder to sell a single product to all the countries. Even if European countries were combined, the market for Europe wouldn't be as big as that for the United States.

United Kingdom

The UK market for electronic security systems is believed to have grown continuously between 1994 and 1998. Market Strategies for Industry (MSI) projects that the market will increase by 7 percent in real terms in 1998.

The intruder alarms sector has accounted for the largest proportion of the UK market for electronic security systems between 1994 and 1998. However, growth in the demand for intruder alarms has slowed due to the mature nature of the sector. MSI projects that the intruder alarms sector will increase by 3 percent in real terms in 1998.

The introduction of the Association of Chief Police Officers' false-alarms policy in 1995 has had significant implications for various sectors of the UK electronic security systems market, including the intruder alarms and central station monitoring service sectors. Indeed, MSI believes the policy has been a key factor contributing to the increase in the market for central station monitoring services in recent years. The central station services sector is projected to increase by 10 percent in real terms in 1998.

According to MSI, the UK market for access control systems increased by 54 percent between 1994 and 1997. Increased public acceptance of the use of access control has stimulated demand for the systems. Furthermore, the rate of technological advancement has served to expand the market for access control.

The closed-circuit television sector is believed to have increased by 59 percent between 1994 and 1997, with real growth of 17 percent expected to occur in 1998. MSI believes that the high profile of closed-circuit television in the media is a factor, which has stimulated demand in the market.

The level of competition in the UK electronic security industry has increased the importance of being competitively priced. Furthermore, it's important for install its various components, and on how your customer uses it. If you make bad selection or installation choices, or your customer doesn't properly use the system, the system will seem to overreact (give false alarms) or react too slowly (overlook real problems).

Let your customer know that blaming the alarm system for a false alarm is like blaming a trained dog for sitting when you accidentally say "sit," instead of what you meant to say. That will help your customer appreciate the importance of spending a little time with you to learn how to properly use the system.

It's your job to provide a system that the end user will be able to easily operate. No matter how technologically advanced a system may be, if the customer finds it too frustrating to use regularly, it won't be of much value. That's why it's important for you to know about the many options that are available. If your customer has poor vision, for instance, he or she might prefer a system that talks or responds to voice commands, or perhaps a large backlit English (or other language) screen on the control panel. You also need to consider other special needs, such as whether there are children or pets in a home. If you take the time to get to know your customer's needs, instead of taking a "cookie cutter" approach, you can avoid most false alarms and have happy customers.

System Components

A basic alarm system consists of a controller, an annunciator, and at least one detection device. The control panel (or controller or control box) is the brain of the system. This is where someone arms and disarms the system and programs it to react to various alarm conditions. Someone might set it to wait a bit after receiving an intruder signal from a certain door before it starts the sirens blaring, for example. A little delay gives a person time to come through the door, set down the bags, and disarm the system. An alarm that sounds right away every time a door opens is not only annoying, but also like the boy who cried wolf. Neighbors and police will start ignoring the alarm (but alert burglars will be attracted to it).

In a hardwired system, the control panel is a box (usually metal) with a circuit board and terminal screws to connect wiring that has been run to and from the various detection devices, annunciators, and other components. A hardwire control panel is shown in Figure 2.1. The control panel in a wireless system is smaller, because you don't need to run wires from all the components into it. As Figure 2.2 shows, a wireless control panel looks like a keypad. Some control panels are mostly wireless, but have one or more hardwired zones. That affords the advantages of wireless, while giving you the option of hardwiring certain components.

Although the control panel decides what to do (based on how it's programmed), the detection devices give it the data. Detection devices (or *sensors*) are the eyes, ears, and nose of the system. They notice when something isn't right (such as unexpected movement, sound, heat, or smoke), and they pass that information on to the control panel. After quickly analyzing the informa-

suppliers to be aware of the strong purchasing power of some end users, such as in the retail sector, which can have a relatively high degree of influence on price.

Another factor that seems to be critical to the success of companies in the electronic security market is accreditation by one of the recognized bodies in the industry, such as the National Approval Council for Security Systems, to satisfy end users that they are receiving high-quality products and services. The importance of being accredited by regulatory bodies has also been influenced by insurance companies. Many require insured electronic security systems to consist of regulatory body–approved equipment and to be installed by accredited installers.

How Alarm Sy

For a good basic understanding of alarm systems, this may be the mos
important chapter in this book. Part 1 of this chapter describes the main
of alarm systems and components, tells the pros and cons of each, shows
to thwart the tricks that burglars use to defeat them, and tells how to insta
alarms. Part 2 focuses on the special alarm concerns of the security manager.

Part 1: Types of Alarm Systems

Introduction

In movies, superspies and master criminals often defeat the most sophisticated security systems. Those systems include items such as retina scanners, fingerprint readers, closed-circuit televisions, and strategically placed ultrasensitive body heat, movement, and sound sensors. Usually the systems are based on real technology—as you'll find throughout this book—but the techniques the actors use to defeat them are fantasy and created for dramatic effect.

In the movie *Entrapment,* for example, while wearing a tight leather body suit, Catherine Zeta-Jones shimmied along the floor and used sensual dancelike movements to maneuver around an invisible web of protective beams to bypass a state-of-the-art security system. That may have been the most talked about scene of the movie (it was my favorite). Other movies and television shows later used a similar scene. The fact that you can't really defeat an even halfway decent system that way doesn't make the scene less exciting to watch. But if you install a security system that someone can dance past, you better have good liability insurance.

Modern alarm systems (even low-cost ones) are pretty reliable. They can be as sensitive as you want them to be, and they seldom do anything for no reason. So-called false alarms are usually the result of a system doing what it's set to do. How intelligently your system reacts depends on how well you choose and

Figure 2.1   Because the control panel is the central command unit of an alarm system, it needs to be installed in a safe place and kept locked. (*Courtesy of Visonic.*)

Figure 2.2   A wireless control panel looks like a keypad. (*Courtesy of Visonic.*)

tion, the control panel may trigger one or more annunciators. An annunciator is a signaling device, such as a siren (see Figure 2.3), bell, or flashing lights. For convenience, many alarm systems have one or more keypads near entrances (see Figure 2.4). Keypads allow people with the proper code to arm and disarm the system without having to walk to the control panel. (When a system uses keypads, the control panel is often called the *master controller.*)

Annunciators

The most common annunciators in alarms systems are bells, sirens, and strobe lights. Many annunciators used in fire alarm systems combine a siren with a strobe light.

Some annunciators are made to be installed indoors. More rugged and weather-resistant models are made for outdoor installations. Installation may be hidden or in the open. Hidden installations are common in residential applications. In commercial applications, annunciators are generally highly visible.

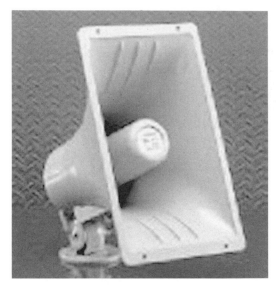

Figure 2.3 Sirens are popular annunciators in alarm systems. (*Courtesy of Ademco.*)

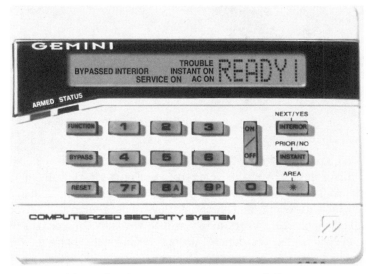

Figure 2.4 A keypad makes it convenient to arm and disarm a system. (*Courtesy of Napco Security Group.*)

To install an annunciator, find a mounting location that is out of easy reach (typically about 12 feet high) and easy to hear, but not directly exposed to precipitation or temperature extremes. Don't mount it directly above heating vents. If you install a siren outside, it should point downward, to avoid collecting rain and moisture.

Using the wire size recommended by the alarm system's manufacturer, you route the wiring from the control panel to the siren and make the terminal connections. Run separate wires to each annunciator. Protect the wiring by running it inside walls or through conduit and then connecting it directly to the annunciator without exposing wire. If you don't protect the wiring, someone may be able to defeat the system by cutting the wire. Unless the siren or bell is concealed, also use a bell box that has a tamperproof switch.

Detection devices

To design an effective system and to keep false alarms to a minimum, you need to choose the right detection devices. There are many types for monitoring different conditions. Heat, cold, moisture, noise, and vibrations in an area are all considerations in choosing the best detection devices for that area. Other considerations include cost and aesthetics.

Most detection devices fall within two broad categories: *perimeter* and *interior* (or *space*). Perimeter devices are designed to protect a door, wall, or window. They are designed to detect an intruder before he or she gets into a room or building. Interior devices detect an intruder who has entered a room or building. These two types of detection devices are often used together to supplement each other.

Perimeter devices.   Three of the most popular perimeter devices are foil, magnetic switches, and glass-break detectors.

Foil.   You've probably seen foil on storefront windows. It's a thin, metallic, lead-based tape of varying grades, usually $^1/_2$ to 1 inch wide, that's applied to glass windows and doors. Figure 2.5 shows foil in use. Sometimes foil is used on walls. Like wire, foil acts as a conductor to make a complete circuit in an alarm system (see Chapter 4 for more information about circuits). When someone breaks the window (or wall or door), the fragile foil breaks, creating a short circuit and triggering an alarm condition.

Usually foil comes in long, adhesive-backed strips and is applied along the perimeter of a sheet of glass or drywall. With practice you can learn to run it straight to make the installation look neat. Some installers make attractive designs with foil. Each end of a run must be connected to the control panel with connector blocks and wire. Foil is popular for stores because it costs only a few cents per foot, and it lets would be intruders know right away that the premises are protected.

There are three major drawbacks to foil:

1. It can be tricky to install properly.
2. It breaks easily when the glass is being washed.
3. Many people consider it unsightly.

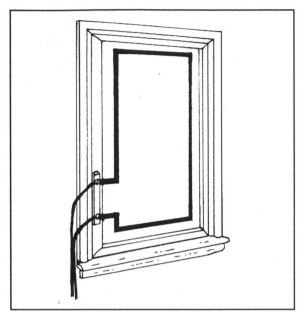

Figure 2.5 Although not so popular today, foil is still
sometimes used for commercial applications on windows
and doors.

Magnetic switches. The most popular perimeter device is the magnetic contact
(or magnetic switch). It's used for protecting doors and windows that open.
Figure 2.6 shows an installed magnetic contact. Magnetic contacts are reliable, inexpensive, and easy to install. They come in surface-mounted and
recessed (or *flush*) styles. Recessed models can be a little trickier to install,
because you need to be more precise. When properly installed, however,
they're barely visible. Both styles work the same way. Surface models are used
more often on windows. Recessed models are found more often on wooden
doors.

As the name implies, a magnetic contact consists of two small parts: a magnet and a switch. Each part is housed in a matching case and is often covered
by a matching cover (usually the case and cover are plastic). (See Figure 2.7.)
Surface-mounted styles come in rectangular cases; recessed styles are cylin-
drical. Figure 2.8 shows a recessed magnetic contact. With either style, the
switch contains two electrical contacts and a metal spring-loaded bar that
moves across the contacts when magnetic force is applied. That bridges the
contacts, completing the circuit. When magnetic force is removed, the bar lifts
off one of the contacts, breaking the circuit and creating an alarm condition. A
similar break occurs when an intruder opens a door or window, which moves
the magnet away from the switch (see Figure 2.9).

It's important to understand that the break in the circuit does not occur simply because the magnet is away from the switch. The break occurs because

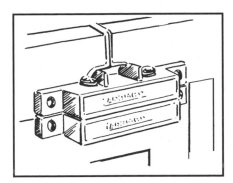

Figure 2.6 A magnetic contact is commonly used on doors and windows that open. (*Courtesy of Ademco.*)

Cover

Switch

Magnet

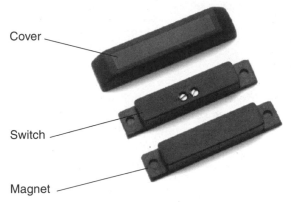

Figure 2.7 A magnetic contact consists of a switch and magnet, each of which is usually housed under a matching cover. (*Courtesy of George Risk Industries, Inc.*)

Figure 2.8 Recessed magnetic contacts are designed to be snugly installed in small recessed cavities. (*Courtesy of George Risk Industries, Inc.*)

inside the switch there's a pole (or *arm*) that moves to make or break the connection. The magnet is simply one means of making the pole keep the connection. It is important to understand that fact, because thieves can try to find other ways to keep the switch's pole in place while the door or window is being opened. Use of a strong magnet from outside a door or window near the switch can defeat some magnetic contacts. Placing a wire across the terminal screws of the switch and jumping the contacts (which keeps the circuit closed and doesn't create an alarm condition even though the door is opened) can defeat other models.

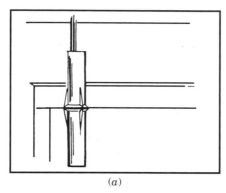
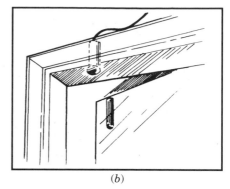

Figure 2.9   When a closed door or window (*a*) is opened, the magnet separates from the switch (*b*), breaking the electric circuit and creating an alarm condition. (*Courtesy of Ademco.*)

"Wide-gap" reed switches can be used to solve those problems. Because reed switches use a small reed instead of a metal bar, they're less vulnerable to being manipulated by external magnets. The wide-gap feature allows a switch to work properly even if the switch and magnet move from 1 to 4 inches apart.

Other high-security magnetic contacts are UL-listed, have metal housings, have a tamper switch to prevent removal, and are available with concealed cable or stainless-steel cable. Those features make a magnetic contact highly resistant to jumping and other attempts to tamper with them (see Figure 2.10).

Before you install a magnetic contact, confirm its operating gap—the working distance between the switch and the magnet. Otherwise, you might install them too far apart and get unwanted alarms. You can use a multimeter to check the gap distance.

In a typical installation, the magnet is mounted on a door or window, and the switch is aligned about $\frac{1}{2}$ inch away on the frame. When an intruder pushes the door or window open, the magnet is moved out of alignment. Although the switch and magnet are often installed parallel to each other, adjacent configurations can also be used. See Figure 2.11 for examples of such configurations. The main thing to keep in mind is that the magnet needs to be close enough to the contact to reliably affect the switch.

Glass-break detectors.   The two most common types of glass-break detectors are shock sensors and audio discriminators. *Shock sensors* have adhesive (or a suction cup), so you can stick them to a window. (See Figure 2.12.) They respond to the vibrations of someone striking the glass.

Audio discriminators trigger alarms when they sense the sound of breaking glass, at about 150 kHz (see Figure 2.13). The devices are very effective and easy to install, usually on a window frame or ceiling. According to a survey by *Security Dealer* magazine, more than 50 percent of professional installers favor audio discriminators over all other forms of glass-break protection.

By strategically placing audio discriminators in a protected area, you can protect several large windows at once. Some models can be mounted on a wall up to 50 feet away from the protected windows. Other models equipped with

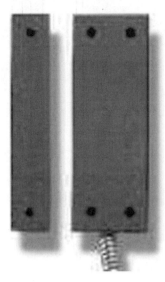

Figure 2.10 High-security magnetic contacts have special covers and are designed to thwart attempts at defeating them. (*Courtesy of Ademco.*)

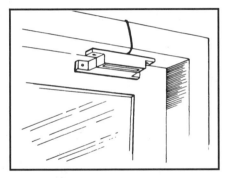 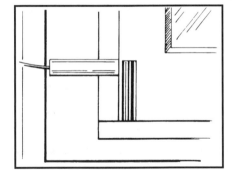

Figure 2.11 Magnetic contacts can be installed in various configurations, as long as the magnetic is close enough to the switch. (*Courtesy of Ademco.*)

Figure 2.12 A shock sensor reacts to vibrations of glass being hit. (*Courtesy of Ademco.*)

Figure 2.13 An audio discriminator responds to the sound of breaking glass. (*Courtesy of Napco Security Group.*)

an *omnidirectional pickup pattern* can monitor sounds from all directions and are designed to be mounted on a ceiling for maximum coverage.

A problem with many audio discriminators is that they confuse certain high-pitched sounds, such as jingling keys, with the sound of breaking glass and so produce false alarms. Better models require both the sound of breaking glass and shock vibrations to trigger an alarm condition. That feature greatly reduces the incidence of false alarms.

Another problem with audio discriminators is that they recognize an alarm condition only after the glass is broken. That allows an intruder to bypass the detector by cutting a hole through the glass and climbing through, or by forcing open a window sash. Audio discriminators work best when used with magnetic switches or other detectors.

Interior devices.   The five most common interior devices are ultrasonics, micro-waves, passive infrareds, quads, and dual-technology devices.

Ultrasonic detectors.   Ultrasonic detectors transmit high-frequency sound waves to sense movement within a protected area. The sound waves, usually at a frequency over 30,000 cycles per second, are inaudible to humans but can be annoying to dogs. Some models have a transmitter that's separate from the receiver; others combine the two in one housing.

In either type, the sound waves are bounced off the walls, floor, and furniture in a room until the frequency is stabilized. Thereafter, the movement of an intruder will cause a change in the waves and create an alarm condition.

A drawback to ultrasonic detectors is that they don't work well in rooms with wall-to-wall carpeting and heavy draperies because those soft materials absorb sound.

Another drawback is that ultrasonic detectors do a poor job of sensing fast or slow movements and movements behind objects. At least in theory, an intruder could defeat such a detector by moving slowly and hiding behind furniture. Ultrasonic detectors are prone to false alarms caused by noises such as a ringing telephone or jingling keys. Newer models have an *anti-masking* feature that signals if any object has been placed too close to the unit. That feature prevents a mask from being placed over the face of the detector. Although they were popular a few years ago, ultrasonic detectors are a poor choice for most homes today. Other types of interior devices are more cost-effective.

Microwave detectors. Microwave detectors work like an ultrasonic detector, but they send ultrahigh-frequency radio waves instead of sound waves. Unlike ultrasonics, microwaves can go through walls and monitor areas of various configurations. Microwave detectors are easy to hide because they can be placed behind solid objects. When properly adjusted, they aren't susceptible to loud noises or air movement.

The big drawback to microwave detectors is that their extreme sensitivity makes them hard to adjust properly. Because the waves penetrate walls, a passing car can cause a false alarm. An alarm condition can also be triggered by fluorescent lights and radio transmissions.

Passive infrared detectors. Passive infrared (PIR) detectors became popular in the 1980s. Today they are among the most popular and cost-effective type of interior devices (see Figure 2.14.). PIR detectors sense rapid changes in temperature within a protected area by monitoring infrared radiation (energy in the form of heat). They use less power, are smaller, and generally are more reliable than either an ultrasonic or a microwave detector.

The PIR detector is effective because all living things give off infrared energy. If an intruder enters a protected area, the device senses a rapid change in heat. When properly positioned and adjusted, the detector ignores all gradual fluctuations of temperature caused by sunlight, heating systems, and air conditioners. A typical PIR detector can monitor an area of about 20 × 30 feet or a narrow hallway about 50 feet long. It doesn't penetrate walls (or anything else), so a PIR detector is easier to adjust than microwave detectors and it doesn't respond to radio waves, sharp sounds, or sudden vibrations. Figure 2.15 shows some detection patterns. A PIR detector is passive, meaning it doesn't emit anything. It just monitors whatever infrared energy is present.

The biggest drawback to a PIR detector is that it can't "see" an entire room or area. Rather than provide blanketed protection (like sound waves filling a room), it has a detection pattern much like long invisible fingers, pointing in various directions. The spaces outside of and between the "fingers" are outside the detection areas. The detection pattern depends on the PIR detector lens design and how the sensor is installed.

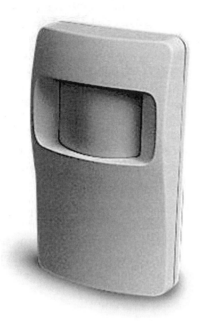

Figure 2.14   A PIR detector is the most popular type of interior sensor. (*Courtesy of Visonic.*)

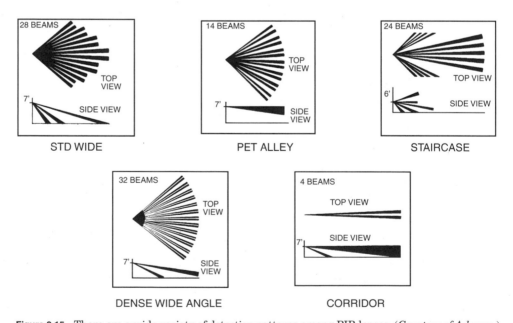

Figure 2.15   There are a wide variety of detection patterns among PIR lenses. (*Courtesy of Ademco.*)

PIR detectors come in wall-mounted and ceiling-mounted designs (see Figure 2.16). The wall-mounted styles are more common and generally less expensive. Ceiling-mounted models are disk-shaped and cover a 360° area. They're unobtrusive and can look like a light fixture. Another shortcoming of wall-mounted models is that they prevent you from using a lot of space, because they need to be free of obstructions. They may prevent you from pushing tall furniture against a wall, for instance.

Which detection pattern is best for you will depend on where and how you're using the PIR detector. Many models have interchangeable lenses that offer a wide range of pattern choices. Some patterns, called *pet alleys,* are several feet above the floor to allow pets to move about freely without triggering the alarm.

A useful feature of PIR devices is *signal processing* (also called *event verification*). This high-technology circuitry can reduce false alarms by distinguishing between large and small differences in infrared energy.

Another common feature to help reduce false alarms is *pulse count.* If you could watch through an oscilloscope while an intruder walked through a PIR detector's coverage pattern, you'd see the PIR device register a series of pulses—about one each time the intruder entered a twin leg of a protective field. Pulse count helps filter out false alarms by not registering an alarm condition until at least two pulses are counted (see Figure 2.17).

Alternate-polarity pulse count (or *signature analysis*) is a special kind of pulse count found on quad and standard PIR devices. It gives an extra layer of false-alarm protection by considering polarity in addition to the number of

Figure 2.16 A ceiling-mounted PIR device provides a conical detection pattern (as viewed from floor to ceiling). (*Courtesy of Visonic.*)

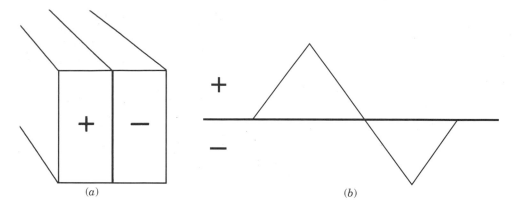

Figure 2.17 (a) Because an intruder walks horizontally through a zone, (b) the intruder will virtually always create a pattern of alternating positive and negative pulses. (*Courtesy of Ademco.*)

pulse counts. Standard PIR detectors are more susceptible to electronic disturbances that create a series of positive or negative pulses (see Figure 2.18). A PIR device that just counts pulses would sound an alarm under such conditions. But a real intruder would cause alternating-polarity pulse count, which is why alternating pulse count PIR devices are more reliable. Figure 2.19 shows what a series of alternating pulses would look like.

Quads. A quad PIR device (or quad, for short) consists of two dual-element sensors in one housing. Like most other sensors, quads come in a variety of shapes, colors, and styles, to match many decors. Figure 2.20 shows one quad design. Each sensor of a quad has its own processing circuitry. The device gives a high level of protection against false alarms because it basically has two alarm channels, and both must simultaneously detect an alarm condition before it triggers an alarm. That prevents the alarm from activating in response to, say, insects or mice, because they're too small to be detected by the fingers of protection of two alarm channels at once. A mouse would cross channels one at a time, which wouldn't create an alarm condition. Figure 2.21 illustrates how the dual channels work. Likewise, electronic disturbances and internally generated noise are likely to affect no more than one channel at a time.

Quads are especially useful for harsh environments, such as warehouses. The most reliable quad is an alternate-polarity quad. An alternate-polarity quad only triggers an alarm in response to opposite signals on its two alarm channels (see Figure 2.22).

Dual-technology devices. Detection devices that incorporate two different types of sensor technology into one housing are called dual-technology devices (or "dual techs"). A dual tech triggers an alarm only when both technologies sense an intrusion. Dual techs are available for commercial and residential use, but because they're more expensive than other types of detection devices, they're more often used by businesses. The most effective

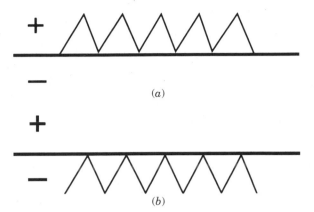

(a)

(b)

Figure 2.18 Some types of electronic disturbances look like (*a*) a series of positive pulses or (*b*) a series of negative pulses. (*Courtesy of Ademco.*)

Figure 2.19 Because a real intruder causes alternating-polarity pulses, an alternate-polarity pulse count feature filters out many electronic disturbances. (*Courtesy of Ademco.*)

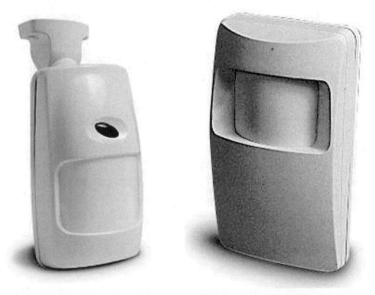

Figure 2.20 A quad PIR device can be as stylish as a standard PIR detector. (*Courtesy of Visonic.*)

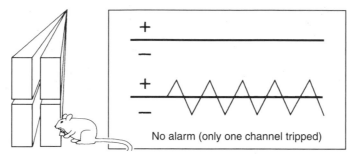

Figure 2.21 A quad PIR detector has two alarm channels that filter out things too small to be an intruder. (*Courtesy of Ademco.*)

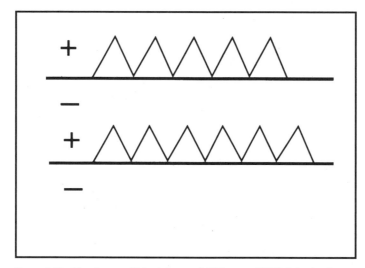

Figure 2.22 No alarm will be triggered if the quad PIR detector has alternate-polarity pulse count. (*Courtesy of Ademco.*)

type of dual tech for homes is one that combines PIR detector and microwave technology (see Figure 2.23).

For this type of dual tech to trigger an alarm, a condition must exist that simultaneously triggers both technologies. The presence of infrared energy alone, or movement alone, would not trigger the alarm. Movement outside a wall that would ordinarily trigger a microwave, for example, won't trigger the dual tech because the PIR element would fail to simultaneously sense infrared energy.

Types of alarm systems

There are three basic kinds of alarm systems: wireless, hardwired, and self-contained. Wireless systems rely mainly on radio waves, instead of wire, to communicate between the control panel and detection devices. With the hardwired ones you have to run wire from the control panel to each of the detection

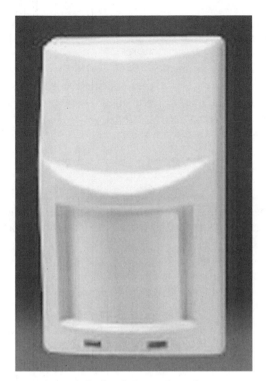

Figure 2.23   A dual tech is two detection technologies in one housing. (*Courtesy of Ademco.*)

devices and annunciators. A self-contained alarm is a single unit, often shaped like a VCR, with all or most of its components in one housing.

Self-contained alarms.   Two advantages of a self-contained unit are portability and ease of installation. You can take it with you when you travel. Installation is usually just a matter of positioning it on a sturdy table or shelf and plugging it into an electric outlet. A disadvantage is that the unit can monitor only one small area at a time. Some self-contained units allow you to attach an external siren and various detection devices. By expanding the system that way, it becomes a hardwired or wireless system.

Wireless alarms.   Wireless models are easier to install than hardwired systems and are popular among do-it-yourselfers. (Chapter 7 tells how to install and troubleshoot wireless alarms.) Until recently, a big problem with low-cost wireless alarms was that they weren't "supervised"—only expensive high-technology models included supervising circuitry. A supervised alarm is one that regularly checks its detection devices to confirm that they're communicating properly with the controller. That lets you know immediately if a detection device is broken, if a battery is low, or if a protected door or window has been left open. Perhaps the biggest problem with wireless systems is that their components are much more expensive than their hardwired counterparts.

Hardwired alarms.   In addition to having lower-cost equipment, hardwired systems are more reliable and easier to troubleshoot than wireless systems. The big drawback to hardwired systems is that running wire in aesthetically pleasing and effective ways can be time-consuming and costly. (Chapter 7 tells how to install and troubleshoot hardwired systems.)

Monitoring the system

The easiest and least expensive way to have an alarm call for help is to use a telephone dialer. When the alarm is triggered, the dialer calls one or more pre-programmed numbers and gives a recorded message. The idea is that someone will get the message and check things out, or call the police. But if the phone line is busy, or no one answers, or someone answers but doesn't want to be bothered, then the dialer isn't of much use. Instead of pestering friends, you can sometimes program a dialer to call the police directly. Many municipalities either don't allow dialer connections to police or charge hefty fines when a dialer reports a false alarm.

What makes tape dialers so annoying is there's no way to know if the system was activated by an intruder or is a false alarm. Even if you were to quickly call the police back to say the alarm went off by accident, the police wouldn't know who was calling. For all they know, you could be the burglar.

A more reliable way of calling for help is to use the monitoring services of a central station. When the alarm is triggered, the central station quickly receives a signal and then calls you to verify there's a problem. If you don't give the right code word, even if you have a great excuse for not giving it, they immediately call the police. The code word is how they know you're not a burglar or being held up. That service involves paying a monthly fee, usually to the alarm installation company. Some installation companies do the monitoring directly, but most use the services of a third-party firm. Monitoring requires special training, takes a lot of time (24 hours per day), and has a lot of potential legal liability.

Not all central stations are alike. Make sure yours has more than one telephone line and isn't being run by someone out of his or her bedroom. The alarm installation company who contracts with a shoddy central station could be held liable for mistakes the central station makes. It's best to use a central station that's listed with Underwriters Laboratories (UL) or is a member of the Central Station Alarm Association (CSAA).

To get a UL listing, a central station must have adequate equipment and software to handle its accounts. Its building must be fire-resistant and must have sprinklers, a dual generator system, and a backup battery system. That helps ensure that the monitoring service won't be interrupted. The CSAA is more than 50 years old. To join, a monitoring company must be UL-listed or meet comparable standards. And CSAA has professional standards for its members and provides members with continuing education. For more details on offering monitoring services, see Chapter 17.

Appendix B contains contact information on central stations and alarm system suppliers.

Questions for review

1. What is meant by the term *supervised alarm,* and what is an advantage of a supervised model over a nonsupervised one?

2. What service does a central station offer?

3. What is a quad PIR device? How does it differ from a dual tech?

4. What is required of a central station before it qualifies for UL certification?

5. What is a drawback to microwave detectors for most residential applications?

Part 2: Alarm Management Is Key Ingredient in Effective Security Management Operations*

Security managers acquire and install security management systems to accomplish risk management objectives. What happens when those systems, upon installation, actually increase a company's risk of harm or loss? Consider the following examples of two fictitious companies that have just completed similar projects, each with decidedly opposite results.

Company A Company A has just completed the installation of a companywide security management system for its new headquarters building complex (three connected buildings plus a five-story open garage) consisting of 590,000 square feet of office, manufacturing, and storage areas. The company utilized the services of a knowledgeable outside security consultant to work closely with its security manager and architectural firm by designing and specifying all security-related systems during all phases of building design and construction.

The new security management system consists of integrated access control, intrusion detection, and closed-circuit television (CCTV) subsystems operating over its own network with five separate personal computer (PC) workstations located at critical entry monitoring points throughout the buildings. The consultant took great care to design and specify the technical system requirements for protecting the company's facility assets; the consultant also painstakingly detailed the facility operational requirements for the system integrator's eventual programming of system points to coincide with the company's day-to-day facility operations. Three weeks after completing the endurance test and the final test and after turnover of the complete system to company A, assigned monitoring operators are experiencing very few, if any, alarms from false or nuisance sources.

Company B Company B also has just completed the installation, testing, and turnover of a brand new corporate security management system with integrated

---

*This article was contributed by Francis J. Gallagher and Richard P. Grassie.

access control, intrusion detection, and CCTV subsystems for its new corporate headquarters (480,000 square feet) and four-story employee parking garage. Company B decided to use the same manufacturers of the security systems previously installed in the old corporate headquarters building. Consequently, company B saw no need to utilize the services of an outside security consultant to work with its architect on the new building. Rather, company B called upon its captive systems integrator to provide systems design services as part of the complete systems installation package.

Three weeks after turnover of the complete system to company B, assigned monitoring operators are experiencing 500 to 1000 spurious alarms weekly. These alarms are from various sources throughout the new facilities, especially false and nuisance alarms due to what is suspected to be poorly installed, misapplied, or incorrectly programmed alarm points. Operators are so currently overloaded with alarms at all times of the day and evening from repeat, multiple sources that they are simply ignoring most alarms on the screen until the systems administrator clears them the following day from the file server. Essentially the system is worthless, and the company's security risk after installation has actually increased.

Security managers must recognize the increasing use of automated, PC-based technologies to perform critical security and facility monitoring and control functions. This has created a totally new discipline in the security field called *alarm management*—the process of integrating electronic security technologies in a security management system with a company's operational environment.

Installed security management systems provide the technological tools necessary to make security incident monitoring, display, and response more effective. When these systems are designed, installed, and programmed correctly, a company's risk management program is the principal beneficiary. Effective alarm management is the key function, and this responsibility is ultimately shared by the user's security manager and the integrator installer, with expert technical design and integration support of the security consultant.

A security manager's effectiveness in controlling facility risks is determined by four critical security design and integration decision-making functions: (1) the relevance and completeness of the initial and continuing risk and requirements analyses upon which facility security requirements are based; (2) the completeness and degree of applicability of the security system design in relation to security and facility operational requirements; (3) the quality of selected systems and their effective installation; and (4) the manner in which applied systems control perceived risks, promote the business, and facilitate daily operations.

Alarm management principally applies to the fourth function but is directly affected by the quality and completeness of all critical decision-making functions. To maximize the utility of the investment in the security management system, great care must be taken to ensure that control room operators do not become complacent in their alarm-monitoring duties as a result of responding to a variety of alarms from nuisance, false, or other spurious sources. The effectiveness of security operators is dependent upon both operator quality and effective security systems design, installation, and alarm management. However efficient your individual security operators are, they will be only marginally effective if the security design, systems installation, and alarm management functions have not been satisfactorily completed.

Described below are the steps that security managers should take to implement a formal alarm management program.

Alarm Management Recommendations

To identify nuisance alarms and their sources, it is recommended that the alarm history file be periodically examined to determine what areas are sending alarms, the times, and the frequency. Based on this analysis, adjustments can be made to the security management system or security policies and procedures.

For example, if an alarm associated with a loading dock door is constantly being received, this alarm point should be reprogrammed within the system so that it is shunted during normal business hours. If alarms from mechanical or utility rooms are being received because maintenance personnel require access to a particular area, a policy should be implemented to notify the security control room that work will be performed in a certain area for a specific time, allowing the security systems operator to temporarily shunt the particular alarm point.

It is important to be able to correlate the time and location of an alarm, so its possible source can be identified prior to full implementation of a security response. For example, if it is determined that a facility access-controlled interior door alarm point is transmitting an alarm signal, these are the most likely scenarios:

- The door has been propped open by an employee.
- The door was held open by an employee.
- The door failed to close properly upon an employee's entering or exiting an access-controlled area.
- The door was forced open.

It is imperative that the causes of these alarms be identified so that proper alarm mitigation strategies can be employed to reduce or eliminate these alarms.

Alarm point definition

The first step in any alarm management program is to define the alarm points that will be connected to the security management system. Analysis of company assets, threats, vulnerabilities, and risks will reveal specific security requirements. Those requirements, in turn, are used to identify and select appropriate countermeasures to achieve a desired level of protection for a given asset or collection of assets. Next, a security concept of operations should be developed. This will detail the location of each countermeasure and its intended function within the context of risk management and facility operations. For example, it will take into account the need to define specific times at which select countermeasures are active and when they are shunted. Some countermeasures (access controls for doors, door contacts, etc.) will be active at all times. Other countermeasures will be shunted during normal business hours. The end result is a complete alarm point definition that must be factored into the security system design, as summarized below.

- Determine how and when the facility operates, both interior and exterior, from the standpoint of facility users and facility owners.
- Identify assets, threats, vulnerabilities, risks, and security requirements.
- Select and validate appropriate security countermeasures based on requirements.
- Determine how facility security procedures will complement selected countermeasures and impact facility operations.
- Develop a security concept of operations.
- Integrate the concept of operations with facility operations.
- Define and program alarm point active/inactive times.

Following is a partial example of a security concept of operations developed for a facility complex similar to that described for companies A and B.

Concept of Operations—Building A   The main entrance to building A, the side entrance to building A near the pavilion, and the loading dock door must be access-controlled. A proximity card reader (surface-mounted), an electric lock, a recessed door contact, and a request-to-exit device should be provided for these doors, which will be locked at all times. Employees requiring access to building A will be required to present a card credential to the reader. If a valid credential is presented, the door will unlock. If an invalid credential is presented, an alarm signal will be sent to the security management system. Visitors will be required to enter through the revolving door and check in at the reception desk.

The revolving door and the single-leaf door, located at the main entrance to building A and not access-controlled, should be fitted with door contacts. The contacts should be shunted during normal business hours (8 a.m. to 6 p.m.). After that, the alarm points should be armed and the revolving door and single-leaf door secured. During normal business hours the single-leaf door will be locked from the outside, but individuals may freely leave the facility through this door. After hours, individuals must egress through the access-controlled door. The reception desk should be provided with a duress button.

Non-access-controlled exterior doors should be provided with door contacts. The door contacts should be active at all times, although the contact for the loading dock door should be shunted during normal business hours. The door leading to the roof of building A should be fitted with a door contact.

Developing Effective Response Procedures

Once individual alarm points have been identified and their integration with other protection or automated response devices has been verified, the next step is to develop response procedures specifically tailored to each alarm point. These procedures should aid the operator in responding to the alarm; therefore, what is displayed on the monitoring screen should be concise and unambiguous. Regardless of the type of alarm, the format of the displayed alarm response procedures should be consistent. Although there are many alarm points potentially being monitored by a security management system (SMS), most likely fewer than 10 types of devices are being monitored. Therefore, a majority of the response procedures will be similar to one another, which aids in keeping the format consistent.

To maintain consistency, the criticality and type of alarm should be displayed above the response procedures. Depending upon the level of integration associated with the alarm point, additional procedures should be displayed. A sample response procedure is shown here:

Priority. High

Alarm type. Door forced open

The main entrance door has been forced open. Check camera 1 for suspicious activity. In the event of suspicious activity, dispatch patrol officer to alarm location.

Note that the response procedure is very brief and specific, which leads to complete understanding by the operator and an effective response. These are some guidelines for developing response procedures:

- Response procedures should be concise and unambiguous.
- Response procedures should be tailored to each specific alarm point.
- The format must be consistent.
- There should be an area within the response procedure window where operators input their response to the alarm.
- Operators should be allowed to acknowledge an alarm using an icon embedded in the response procedure window of the SMS.

Alarm Displays

One of the most critical decisions that security organization can make at the installation integration stage is the choice of what types of alarms will be displayed on the alarm monitoring screen. Some security organizations choose to display all alarms and access transactions. Since the security officer is there to monitor the system, company managers incorrectly assume that the more transactions the officer is responsible for monitoring, the greater value the officer will have. But with so many access transactions taking place in a typical building, the real alarms are lost in a series of access-granted transactions or alarm reset messages, even though there is a color distinction between them.

The most effective way to optimize the performance of a security management system response and to increase operator efficiency is to display *exceptions only* or incoming alarms only. The primary task of the operator is to monitor and respond to alarms. This is the security system's risk management function at its best. Therefore, the SMS should display only changes from a secure state to an alarm state. Where applicable, the SMS also can display facility management alarms and SMS trouble alarms. There is no need for the operator to receive any other routine transactions. However, certain operators at reception desks do utilize the access transaction screen to visually verify cardholders. If this is a desired function, it is recommended that the operator be given the ability to turn on/off access transactions on the screen when this type of activity is desired. Otherwise, exceptions-only monitoring should be the norm.

Consideration now should be given to what additional information should be provided to the operator to aid in the assessment and response to the alarm. Alarm response procedures and a map indicating the location of the alarm should be provided. Providing a graphic map of the alarm point can speed up operator response to the alarm. Furthermore, the graphic can act as a training aid, allowing the operator to become more familiar with locations of alarm points within each facility.

Alarm Analysis

The core of effective alarm management is alarm analysis, the only effective way we have found to clear a monitoring screen of unneeded alarms. Simply changing shunt times or increasing/decreasing door-held-open times without proper investigation of the source of the problem(s) is too risky, and the result may be to increase a company's risk of loss or harm.

The first step is to obtain a printout of the alarm history file and export it to a spreadsheet program. The file will display all alarms received at a particular location for a specified time. The data should be closely scrutinized. Sort the alarms by location. Are there multiple entries for a single alarm point? If so, identify the alarm point type, the time, and the date each alarm was received, and determine their frequency. Next, classify these alarms. Are they hold-open alarms, door-ajar alarms, etc.? Is one device constantly sending alarms? If so, the shunt time of the device may need to be adjusted; it could be malfunctioning, or it may be a nuisance alarm that requires some type of procedural solution. Of course, the alarm signal always could represent a breach in security; so when you are reviewing the alarm history data, be mindful of any incidents that may have occurred in the given facility. If there is a camera associated with a problem alarm point, utilize the capabilities of the video system to review the cause of the alarm.

Obtain the alarm history file for the next month, and analyze the alarm data as noted. Furthermore, compare the current month's alarms with the previous ones. Were there more or fewer alarms? Have any problem alarm points in last month's analysis reappeared? Over the course of the year, compare the number of alarms received at the end of the year to the number received at the beginning. If the number of alarms has been drastically reduced, your alarm mitigation strategies are effective. Of course, the amount of alarms will plateau at a certain level. Once a plateau is reached, you have successfully implemented an alarm management program.

Alarm Mitigation Strategies

Based on the results of the alarm analysis, adjustments to certain alarm shunt times or policies and procedures may be required. For doors that present a variety of mechanical problems, signage can be used to instruct employees: "Be sure the door closes behind you." Also, during routine patrols, facility perimeter doors should be checked to ensure they are secure. If doors are found to be ajar, they should be secured and the patrol officer should notify the security operator thereof.

Another way to reduce nuisance alarm sources is to ensure that door hardware is properly maintained. Often the cause of a nuisance alarm is not employees propping open doors, but faulty hardware, such as a defective door closer. An effective maintenance program, coupled with proactive patrols and alarm reviews, is the best way of managing and mitigating nuisance alarms. Security managers should review the alarm history to identify nuisance alarms, their frequency, and when they occur. If a pattern emerges (i.e., an overhead door is sending an alarm during normal business hours), then the alarm point shunt time should be adjusted.

Training

Another critical aspect of alarm monitoring is ensuring that the operators responsible for monitoring security systems are sufficiently trained. Ideally, they should not be intimidated by technology. On the contrary, they should be most comfortable with the use of a computer or demonstrate a willingness and capability to learn basic computer skills associated with security management systems monitoring. Below are recommended areas in which security officers responsible for alarm monitoring should be trained.

Initial orientation.   The basic monitoring functions are as follows:

- Operators must perform basic alarm monitoring tasks.

- Operators must be able to access the on-screen alarm response procedures.

- Operators must be trained in how to acknowledge and respond to alarms.

- Operators must be able to retrieve and view an employee's cardholder record, if the operator is allowed this level of access.

- Operators must be able to retrieve and view an employee's photograph from the photograph ID database.

- Operators must remotely unlock an access-controlled door, using the features available in the software.
- Operators must be familiar with the system management functions associated with the graphical maps.
- Training on other system functions should be provided as necessary.

Conclusions

When new security management systems are installed, the task is not complete until the systems are properly programmed, operators trained, and procedures promulgated. Even then, misapplied technologies or applications resulting from improper designs can turn a well-intentioned capital investment into a nightmare for some security managers. Planning for and implementing sound alarm management strategies can mean the difference between extracting optimum value from a new security management system or becoming mired in the mundane struggle to prove the value of security to the company.

3

Fire Safety

Whenever you install an intruder alarm, you should take fire safety into account. Many times, the National Electrical Code (NEC) and local codes and regulations require you to. In addition to providing your customer with extra safety, incorporating fire safety components can be a good way to increase your revenues. Having a basic understanding of the nature of fire and of fire safety devices will help you in choosing and selling such equipment. Part 1 of this chapter is a primer on fires and fire safety devices. Part 2 shows how to install some of the devices.

Part 1: Fires and Fire Safety Devices

Fire is the chemical reaction that occurs when heat, fuel, and oxygen are present at the same time under the right conditions. The combination is often represented by the *fire triangle*, which illustrates that if any one of the three is not present, then there can be no fire. (See Figure 3.1.) There must be enough heat to raise the material to its ignition temperature. In some cases, once a fire gets started, it will generate its own heat to keep it going. Fuel for a fire is any combustible or flammable material, whether solid, liquid, or gas. There must be enough oxygen to sustain combustion. About 21 percent of the air we breathe is oxygen; 16 percent (or more) is needed to sustain a fire. By removing any of the three elements, you can prevent (or put out) a fire.

Anatomy of a Building Fire

A fire can begin from one well-placed spark hitting paint or a dust ball on a wall. The more fuel the fire consumes, the larger it grows and the more fuel it goes after. That process causes gases to be released, which the fire uses as more fuel. The fire needs a continuous supply of oxygen. Because heated air rises, so do fires (hence the phrase "it burned up"). The more fuel and oxygen a fire uses,

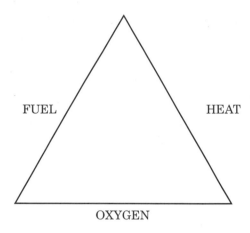

Figure 3.1 Each side of the fire triangle represents what must be present in sufficient amount before fire can exist.

the hotter the surrounding air gets. At the ceiling the temperature can reach 1000°F—nearly 4 times the temperature of boiling water. If conditions allow, as heated air rises, a fresh supply of cool oxygen-rich air rushes in near the base of the fire. That creates a type of windstorm that helps the fire grow.

Within a short time, a once-small fire can engulf a building in smoke and flames. The heated air gathers at the ceiling, and when enough of that superhot air collects, the temperature of the room reaches the flashover point. At that point everything in the room is combustible and will instantly burst into flames—even if the flames had been confined to one side of the room. As the fire grows, the room fills with thick, black smoke, making it impossible for someone to see even a few inches away. (This is contrary to the television and movie portrayals of fire, where rooms are filled with light; perhaps they do it that way because real blazing fire conditions don't film well.)

> **Fast Fact**
>
> Ninety percent of fire deaths are due in whole or in part to smoke and gas.

Fire follows the path of *least resistance*. If the doors are closed, fire may race down a hallway without ever going into a room.

Often long before you see flames or smell smoke, a fire will have released deadly gases. One of those gases—*carbon monoxide*—is clear and odorless. That's why someone can drop cigarette ashes in the couch or chair and fill the house with enough poisonous gases to kill everyone sleeping upstairs.

Once a fire is started, it can only be stopped by removing one of the three elements in the fire triangle.

Most fires can be traced to smoking, cooking, heating equipment, and electric appliances. In homes, smoking-related fires are the biggest cause of death. Ashes that fall onto a mattress or couch cushion may smolder for hours before bursting into flames. The number one cause of home fires is heating equipment, such as space heaters, fireplaces, and wood stoves. The kitchen is where most fires start, sometimes through flammable liquids, spilled grease, or unsafe cooking habits.

Heat rises toward the ceiling of a room, spreads across the ceiling, and then goes back down the walls. There's a dead airspace between where the ceiling and wall meet, which is about a 4-inch gap. That's why smoke detectors shouldn't be installed where the ceiling and wall meet. Instead, they should be installed on the ceiling about 6 to 8 inches away from the wall.

Smoke detectors are critical because usually it isn't the flames that kill, but the smoke and poisonous gases. The odorless carbon monoxide makes you dizzy before knocking you out and then killing you. The heat can also kill you. A breath of the hot air can sear your lungs.

Classes of fire

There are four classes of fire, denoted by A, B, C, and D. Different types are caused, monitored, and put out in different ways. Class A fires are fueled by such things as wood, paper, and cloth, and they can be put out with water or a foam solution of aluminum sulfate and bicarbonate of soda. Class B fires are fueled by oil, lubricants, and petroleum, and they can be extinguished with a similar foam solution. But water can be more harmful than helpful in putting out a class B fire. Class C fires are caused by electric motors, generators, and transformers. Dry chemical can be used to help put out a class C fire, but you also need to be able to automatically shut down the burning devices. Class D fires are fueled by flammable metals, such as magnesium, potassium, and sodium, and they are extinguished with a dry powder. Using water on a class D fire can cause an explosion.

Fire Control Panel

Fire safety components can be connected to fire circuits of a fire/intruder alarm panel or to a fire control panel (see Figure 3.2). A fire control panel, like many external devices of a fire system, is bright red.

Manual Pull Station

A manual pull station lets someone initiate a fire alarm, which activates lights and sirens. (See Figures 3.3 and 3.4.) If it's zoned properly, a pull station will signal where the fire signal is coming from.

Smoke Detector

A smoke detector is the single most important (and most cost-effective) fire safety device, because it provides an early-warning signal that helps save people and property. (See Figure 3.5.) Reports from the National Fire Protection Association (NFPA) suggest that homes with working smoke detectors have a 50 percent increased chance of surviving a fire. Most fatal home fires occur between midnight and 4:00 a.m., when residents are asleep. Without a smoke detector, a family may not wake up during a fire, because poisonous gases from smoke can put people into a deeper sleep.

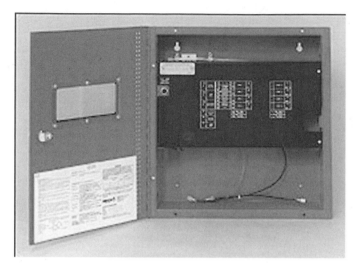

Figure 3.2   A fire alarm control panel is the brain of a fire alarm system. (*Courtesy of Napco Security Group.*)

Figure 3.3   A fire pull station can trigger an alarm to alert occupants and show firefighters where someone activated the alarm.

Figure 3.4 Fire alarm sirens often include a flashing light to help guide people during a fire.

Figure 3.5 A test button is a useful feature to let you quickly make sure the detector is working. (*Courtesy of Napco Security Group.*)

More than 90 percent of U.S. homes (including apartments, nursing homes, dormitories, etc.) have a smoke detector, according to the U.S. Fire Department. However, this country has one of the highest fire death rates in the industrialized world, followed by Canada. Each year, fire kills more Americans than all natural disasters combined. About 80 percent of fire deaths take place in homes not equipped with working smoke detectors.

Most smoke detectors don't work because their batteries are dead or missing. Some people never change the batteries, or they remove them for use in a radio or some other device. Another problem is that people remove the battery to silence a "false alarm" (such as when too much smoke builds up in the kitchen while cooking). For practical purposes, a smoke detector that doesn't work is the same as no smoke detector. Battery-powered models are most common because they're inexpensive and easy to install. Typically they're installed with just a screwdriver.

Smoke detectors powered by alternating current (ac) run off the building's electric current and need to be wired. (See one in Figure 3.6.) They cost more than battery-powered models, but they can be interconnected to other wired components in a security/fire system. Some fire codes require ac-powered models in new construction.

Smoke detector types

There are two basic types of smoke detectors: *ionization* and *photoelectric*. They work on different principles and have advantages and disadvantages. An

Figure 3.6 An ac-powered smoke detector is tied into a building's electrical system.

ionization smoke detector uses ions, or electrically charged particles, to detect smoke. When smoke particles enter the sensing chamber, they create an electrical imbalance. When that imbalance reaches a preset level, the smoke detector activates.

Ionization types respond more quickly to small smoke particles, such as those produced by flames. An ionization sensor responds to microscopic combustion particles. It won't react to dust or steam, but will notice the invisible ions from a fire even when no smoke is present. It may be sensitive to normal cooking.

A photoelectric smoke detector uses a beam of light and sensor. In its untriggered state, the light doesn't hit the sensor; but when smoke enters the chamber, the smoke deflects the light, causing light to hit the sensor. The more smoke that enters the chamber, the more light that's deflected to the sensor. When enough light hits the sensor, based on a preset level, the smoke detector is activated.

Photoelectric types respond more quickly than ionization types to large smoke particles, such as those produced by smoldering fires. Photoelectric sensors are only good for indoor use, and they are more likely to react to such things as woodworking dust, steam from a hot shower, and cooking smoke—which makes them not quite as good for use near a kitchen or bathroom.

Special features

Some smoke detectors have special features that can be helpful. One feature lets you check the detector just by shining a flashlight at it, which can be easier than trying to reach the standard test button. Another special feature is an override button that turns the alarm off for about 15 minutes. That's better than removing the batteries. Some detectors also have a security light to help mark escape routes.

Fire Sprinkler Systems

From 1852 to 1885, perforated pipe systems were used in textile mills throughout New England as a means of fire protection. However, they were not automatic systems—they did not turn on by themselves. The first automatic sprinkler system patented in the United States was developed by Philip W. Pratt in 1872 in Abington, Massachusetts. Parmalee improved upon Pratt's design. In 1874 Parmalee installed his fire sprinkler system into the piano factory that he owned.

Until the 1940s, sprinklers were installed almost exclusively to protect commercial buildings, whose owners were generally able to recoup their expenses with savings in insurance costs. Over the years, fire sprinklers have become mandatory safety equipment, and they are required by building codes to be placed in hospitals, schools, hotels, and other public buildings. A fire sprinkler is shown in Figures 3.7 and 3.8.

Studies by the U.S. Fire Administration indicate that the installation of quick-response fire sprinkler systems in homes could save thousands of lives,

Figure 3.7   A commercial sprinkler head connected to pipe.

Figure 3.8   A close-up of a sprinkler head.

prevent a large portion of fire-related injuries, and eliminate hundreds of millions of dollars of property loss each year.

Sprinklers are the most reliable and effective fire protection devices, because they operate immediately and don't rely on the action of people in the building. Sprinklers have been used by businesses for more than a century, but most homeowners haven't considered installing them because of common misconceptions.

One misconception about residential sprinklers is that if a fire occurs, all will be activated at once, dousing the entire house. In reality, only the sprinkler directly over the fire will go off, because each sprinkler head is designed to react individually to the temperature in that particular room. A fire in the kitchen, for example, won't activate a sprinkler head in the bedroom.

Another misconception is that fire sprinklers are prohibitively expensive. A home sprinkler system can cost less than 1 percent of the cost of a new home. The additional cost may be minimal when spread out over the life of the mortgage. In some cases, a home sprinkler system will virtually pay for itself in homeowner insurance savings. Some insurers give up to 15 percent premium discounts for homes with sprinkler systems.

Questions for review

1. What are the two basic types of smoke detectors, and how do they differ?

2. How long have sprinklers been in use by businesses?

3. What is one common misconception about residential sprinklers?

4. What is a manual pull station?

5. What is a major reason for smoke detectors not working?

Part 2: Installing Fire Safety Devices

Installing Smoke Detectors

Smoke detectors should be installed on every level of a home, including the basement. A detector should be placed directly outside each sleeping area. Unless manufacturer's instructions say otherwise, install it on the ceiling or 6 to 8 inches below the ceiling on walls. Keep it away from air vents. Because smoke and deadly gases rise, it's important to install smoke detectors at the right position to give the earliest warning.

Battery-powered detectors

Usually installing a battery-powered smoke detector is just a matter of mounting the baseplate with two screws, installing the battery, and snapping the cover in place. Use a 10-year lithium battery, so your customer won't have to keep changing the battery all the time. To keep the detector in good working order, periodically clean it during your regular system maintenance check. A small vacuum can be great for that, as shown in Figure 3.9.

AC-powered detectors

An ac-powered detector can be plugged directly into a wall outlet or hardwired. If you plug it into an outlet, use a plug retainer to make sure no one accidentally unplugs it.

Before you hardwire a detector, turn off the power at the circuit board. Connect the detector's black lead to the black wire in the circuit cable, and the white lead to the white wire. Twist the wire ends together to make the connections, cover with wire caps, and then tape the caps together. If the detector can be wired to sound simultaneously with other hardwired detectors, it will

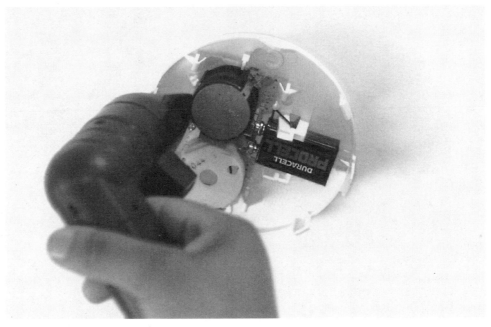

Figure 3.9   Use a small vacuum to clean a smoke detector.

also have a yellow lead, which needs to be connected by a different conductor that you'll need to install.

Don't tie an ac-powered smoke detector into a wall switch circuit. It needs to be on an unswitched circuit so that it can't be accidentally turned off, and you'll know immediately if it loses power.

Electricity Basics

This chapter covers the minimum you need to know about electricity to install electronic security systems. Part 1 focuses on electricity. Part 2 deals with electronics. To help you with complex systems, some of the information is expanded on later in the book. If you've never installed a hardwired system (or if you have, but it didn't work), read this chapter.

Part 1: Electricity

Types of Electricity

There are three types of electricity: static, alternating current (ac), and direct current (dc). Static electricity happens in one place, instead of flowing through wires. An example is when you rub your shoes across a carpet and then get a shock when you touch someone. You can also see it at work by rubbing a balloon on your hair and then sticking the balloon to a wall. The most dangerous form of static electricity is lightning. For our purposes, the main concern about static electricity is preventing it from damaging electronic components.

Direct current comes from batteries. And, of course, alternating current comes from electrical outlets in a building. Both types work by following a continuous loop from the power source through conductors (usually wires) to a load (*L*)—such as an alarm controller or other electrical device—and back again. Current from batteries flows directly from the negative terminal back to the positive. Alternating current, on the other hand, is more erratic; it "alternates" back and forth, first in one direction and then in another along the circuit.

Alternating current is generated at a power plant and then transmitted many miles through a network of high-voltage power lines. Along the route, the electricity may be more than 750,000 volts. When it gets to the substation nearest you, a transformer is used to step down the electricity to between 5000 and 35,000 volts. Another step-down transformer on a nearby utility pole further reduces it to about 240 volts, and that's carried to your building in a cable with two separate 120-volt lines. Typically, buildings are wired so the two 120-volt lines work together at some outlets to provide 240 volts. The 120-volt circuits are for televisions, table lamps, and other small appliances. The 240-volt outlets are for large appliances, such as washing machines, clothes dryers, and refrigerators. (Some older homes have only one 120-volt incoming line.)

Most electronic security components are low-voltage; they require much less than 120 volts. For those, you use the transformer that comes with them. You connect the component to the transformer, and then plug the transformer into a 120-volt outlet. That reduces the 120 volts going into the transformer to an amount that's right for the electronic device. The use of low-voltage transformers makes installing electronic security systems very safe.

Types of Circuits

For electricity to do useful work, it needs to flow through a circuit. A circuit is the pathway, or route, of electric current. A *series* circuit has only one pathway; it has no branches. If multiple devices are wired in series, the current flows through each in turn, and a break at any device stops the flow for all the devices. An example is the old-style Christmas tree lights: When one goes out, they all go out. Figure 4.1 depicts a series circuit. A *parallel* circuit has two or more pathways for electricity to move through. If multiple devices are wired in parallel, each is wired back to the power source so that each has its own current. See Figure 4.2. A *combination* circuit has both series and parallel portions.

How a circuit works

The three basic parts of a circuit are a power source, conductors, and a load. The cord for an appliance has at least two wires. When you plug it into an elec-

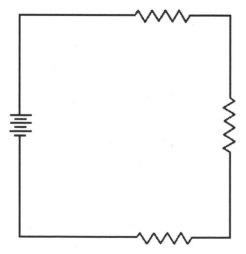

Figure 4.1   A series circuit has just one path.

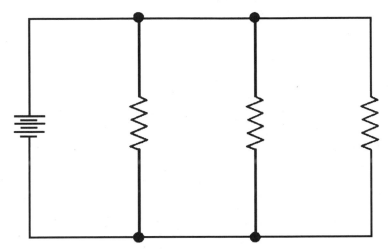

Figure 4.2 A parallel circuit has two or more paths.

tric outlet, electricity flows from the outlet through the incoming wire (conductor) to the appliance (load) and then returns through the outgoing wire back to the outlet. It continues that loop until the circuit is broken.

You could turn off an appliance by using a pair of scissors and cutting one of the wires through which electricity flows (of course, that could be dangerous). You would be breaking the circuit. When you wanted to turn the appliance back on, you would need to splice the wires back together. A safer and more convenient way of breaking a circuit is to use a switch. Whether it's a light switch, car ignition switch, or alarm controller key switch, it opens and closes or redirects one or more circuits. From the outside, an installed switch doesn't look like much—just a little toggle, pushbutton, or turnkey. But if you look at the back of a switch, you'll find one or more tiny metal poles that move into position to complete or break circuits. The poles are little conductors that are part of the circuit. When you flip on a light switch, for example, a pole closes, to allow current to flow; when you flip it to the off position, the pole moves a little to prevent current flow.

Controlling current flow

Controlling the path of electricity is only part of the battle. You also need to control the current flow. If there is too little current, your components won't work correctly. Too much current, and you have to buy new components.

A common way of describing how electricity is controlled uses the analogy of water flowing through a pipe (or hose). I don't like it much, but I see it in other books, and I was taught it in alarm systems school. So I feel obliged to pass it on to you. Then I'll tell you another way to think about the matter that might make more sense.

Water is measured in gallons and electricity in amperes (or "amps"), symbolized by *I*. Water pressure is measured in pounds per square inch. Electrical pressure is measured in volts, symbolized by E. Imagine you have a 1000-foot hose attached to your kitchen faucet, and you turn on the water. When you finally stretch the hose all the way out, you notice that the water isn't running out very fast. To make it run faster, you could plug the hose into a fire hydrant (not recommended) for more water pressure. Or you could use a shorter hose.

Electric current can be controlled in similar ways. You can vary the pressure (voltage), and you can change the length and width of the conductors. Changing the conductor size is one way of changing *resistance,* symbolized by *R,* to current flow.

Going back to the water hose, you could increase or decrease resistance by adding kinks to or removing them from the hose. To further add resistance you could push a bunch of rocks into the hose. (I don't know why anyone would do that. I'm just trying to make a point.) Resistance, measured in ohms, symbolized by Ω, is anything that slows the flow.

All conductors offer resistance to current flow, but some resist more than others. Copper, silver, and aluminum are good conductors, because they offer little resistance. Some materials, called *insulators,* are poor conductors. Examples include glass, dry wood, and plastic. Because it's a flexible insulator, plastic is used to sheathe cable and wire to keep current from being misdirected, and to help keep you from getting shocked. Electrical tape, another insulator, is used to cover breaks in the plastic insulation. Plastic connectors are used to join and insulate bare ends of wire.

Here's another way of looking at current flow. Imagine that you won $1 million but have to drive 10 miles to pick it up. That money (or rather, your desire for it) is the force pushing you to jump in your car, much as voltage pushes current. As you drive along, you are like current flowing. Various obstacles, such as bad weather, red lights, and police cars, are resistance—they slow you down. The fewer obstacles there are, the faster you'll go (or flow). Suppose, instead of winning $1 million, you won only $100. That would be less motivating force, so you wouldn't drive as fast (or go as far) for it. Your speed and the distance you'll travel will vary depending on your motivation and the obstacles you face. The same is true of electricity.

Ohm's Law

Having a general concept of how voltage, current, and resistance relate to one another is good, but you need to know how to put it to practical use. It would be a big hassle if every time you began an installation, you had to use trial and error to figure out what size power supply and what material, length, and diameter of conductors to use. Fortunately, you don't have to, because of a formula called *Ohm's law,* created by the German physicist Georg Ohm.

The formula is remarkable. It's like a simple equation that lets you calculate how fast a person will drive if he wins $1 million and has to go 10 miles in bad weather to get it, and how fast he'll drive if he wins $100,000 and has to go 50 miles in good weather. As incredible as the formula is, you don't need a degree in mathematics to use it. In a couple of minutes you'll have a good working knowledge of Ohm's law.

In short, Ohm's law says 1 volt can push 1 ampere through 1 ohm of resistance. Or 2 volts can push 2 amperes through 1 ohm of resistance. Or 3 volts can . . . —you get the idea. That means if the resistance stays constant and you double or triple the voltage, the current also doubles or triples.

A common written form of Ohm's law is $E = IR$, meaning voltage in volts equals current in amperes times resistance in ohms. (The multiplication sign $\times$ generally isn't used in these kinds of equations because it can be confused with the letter X, which has another meaning in mathematics.) If you know the values of any two of the variables, you can find the value of the third. Variations of Ohm's law include $I = E/R$, or current equals voltage divided by resistance; and $R = E/I$, or resistance equals voltage divided by current. Figure 4.3 shows a helpful picture form of the equations.

Try these examples:

1. If you're using a 6-volt battery in a 3-ampere circuit, how much resistance is in the circuit? To find resistance, just divide the volts by current: $E/I = 6/3$, or $R = 2$ ohms. If a circuit has 10 ohms of resistance and 5 amperes of current, how much voltage is present? To find voltage, multiply current times resistance: $E = 50$ volts.

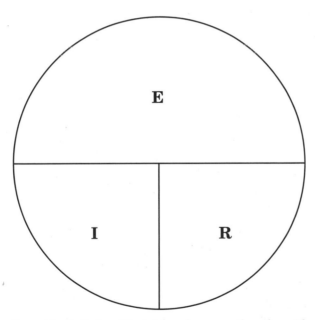

Figure 4.3 To find an Ohm's law value, cover the value with your finger and calculate the remaining two. To find voltage, for example, cover the E. The I and R remain on the same line, which means you multiply them to get the voltage. To find amperage, cover the I, and what remains is E over R. That means you divide E by R.

2. If you have a 6-volt power source connected to a 4-ohm conductor, how much current is flowing through the conductor? To find current, divide voltage by resistance: $I = E/R$, so $E = 1.5$ amperes. (If you answered 0.666 ampere, you made the mistake of dividing resistance by voltage.)

3. If you have an appliance with 15 ohms of resistance plugged into a 120-volt outlet, how much current will it draw? Since $I = E/R$, we know that $I = 8$ amperes. (If you answered 0.125 ampere, you divided resistance by voltage. Try again.)

Power

Now that you've mastered Ohm's law, you'll have no trouble figuring out the power P, which is usually measured in watts (abbreviated W). This is the last formula I'm going to give you, so bear with me for just a moment longer. Power is the amount of electricity that you're using or referring to. To find power in watts, just multiply the number of amperes a device consumes by the amount of voltage in the power supply: $P = IE$.

If you have the power and one of the other values from Ohm's law, you can find either of the other two values. Let's say you know the power and the voltage, for example; to find the current, you divide power by voltage: $I = P/E$.

Questions for review

1. What does *amperage* mean?

2. What is Ohm's law?

3. In what ways can electric current be controlled?

4. How many pathways does a series circuit have?

5. How does alternating current get to homes?

Part 2: Basics of Electronics

Understanding common schematic drawings will help you read electrical drawings of architects, electrical designers, and security equipment manufacturers. You'll often find the drawing used in installation manuals.

Schematic Symbols

Hundreds of *circuit components* may go into an electronic device. To make it easier to show what components are in a device, each component is represented by a symbol or letter, number, or both. Although not every electronic technician uses the same symbols, their differences are so slight that if you understand one symbol for a component, you're not likely to get confused when seeing another symbol for the same component.

Connecting wires (used as conductors in the circuit) are always shown as straight solid lines. They bend at sharp angles, usually 90°. They rarely curve, except when crossing lines would make it unclear whether the wires are electrically connected. When there's no electrical connection between crossing lines, sometimes a half circle will be drawn in the top line to show it jumping over the bottom line. That's the best way to do it. But some people do make straight lines cross each other when the wires aren't meant to be electrically connected. When you see a straight line crossing another, you need to find out what convention is being used.

Resistors

A resistor is one of the most common components used in electronics. It restricts the flow of electric current and produces a voltage drop. Its value is color-coded by four bands, based on the standard of the Electronics Industries Associated (EIA). As Table 4.1 shows, the meaning of each band depends on its position and color. The band closest to the end of the resistor represents the first position number, depending on its color. The second band represents the second position number, depending on its color. The third number represents the multiplier. The fourth band is used to show the tolerance of the resistor. For example, say you have a band that's marked, from the position closest to the end, red, violet, orange, and silver. Using Table 4.1 you can see that the first number is 2 and the second is 7, which are the first and second position numbers, respectively. That means the number is 27. The third position color, red, means the multiplier is 1000. When you multiply the 27 by 1000, you get the nominal resistor value of 27,000 ohms. The resistor manufacturing process isn't perfect, and there's always some tolerance. The last color band tells how much above or below the nominal resistor value the actual value may be. The silver band in the last position means the actual resistor value is in the range of ±10 percent of the nominal value. That doesn't necessarily mean the resistor is more or less than its nominal value; it could be exactly the same value. (See Figure 4.4.)

There are several types of resistors. *Fixed resistors* have a fixed value in ohms. *Variable resistors* (also called *rheostats* or *potentiometers*) can be adjusted from zero to their full value to alter the amount of resistance in a circuit.

TABLE 4.1   Position and Color of Resistor Bands

Color	Band 1	Band 2	Band 3	Band 4
Black	0	0	1	—
Brown	1	1	10	1%
Red	2	2	100	2%
Orange	3	3	1,000	3%
Yellow	4	4	10,000	4%
Green	5	5	100,000	—
Blue	6	6	1,000,000	—
Violet	7	7	10,000,000	—
Gray	8	8	100,000,000	—
White.	9	9	—	—
Gold	—	—	0.1	5%
Silver	—	—	0.01	10%
No color	—	—	—	20%

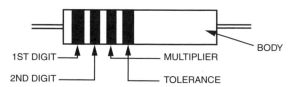

Figure 4.4 The stripes on a resistor are coded based on their colors and positions.

Tapped resistors are a cross between a fixed and variable resistor. Like a variable resistor, they can be adjusted. Once adjusted, however, tapped resistors become like a fixed resistor and cannot be adjusted anymore. The schematic drawing for both types of resistors is shown in Figure 4.5.

Resistance is also shown by the letter *R*, and sequential numbers if there are multiple resistors. For example, *R*1, *R*2, and *R*3 might appear at various points along a circuit diagram near schematic drawings of resistors, indicating that they're the first, second, and third resistors listed on the schematic diagram. Sometimes a resistance value will also be shown on a diagram, using the Greek letter omega (Ω). You might see "30 kΩ" near a schematic symbol for a resistor, for instance. See Figure 4.6.

Capacitors

Like resistors, capacitors are among the most common components used in electronics. The capacitor stores electricity and acts as a filter. It allows alternating current to flow while blocking direct current. It consists of two metal plates or electrodes separated by some kind of insulation, called the *dielectric,*

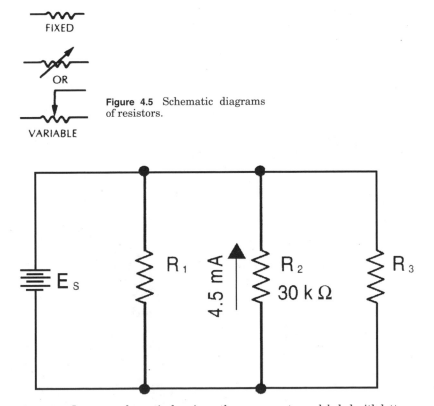

Figure 4.5 Schematic diagrams of resistors.

Figure 4.6 In many schematic drawings, the components are labeled with letters, numbers, and symbols.

such as air, glass, mica, polypropylene film, and titanium acid barium. The type of dielectric used affects how much capacitance can be obtained relative to the size of the capacitor, and in which applications they can be best used.

There are two types of capacitors: *fixed* and *variable.* The tuning dial of a radio is generally attached to a fixed capacitor. When you turn the dial, you're changing its frequency. There are many schematic symbols for identifying different types of capacitors. The letter *C* is used for referring to all types of capacitors, however. A whole number next to the letter *C* shows there are multiple capacitors and which one is within the circuit. For instance, C15 means the fifteenth capacitor listed for the circuit. The value, or *capacitance,* of the capacitor, shown in microfarads (abbreviated as μF or mfd or mF), may also be shown near the schematic symbol.

Switches

One way to turn off a light is to cut a wire that's part of its circuit. You could then turn the light back on by reconnecting that wire. That action of disconnecting and reconnecting the circuit is basically what a switch does, except that using a switch is more convenient and less dangerous. Whenever you turn on a light or start your car or turn on your computer, you're moving a switch into position to complete an electric circuit. A switch can have one or more contact points to allow multiple paths of current flow. In a car, for example, one ignition switch position lets you listen to the radio without wasting your gas, while another turn of the key lets you drive off. Typically, switches are designed so that you don't see the tiny poles (or "arms") that move to complete or break a circuit, but they're there. If you were to take a switch apart, you'd find them.

Switches are illustrated and named according to how many poles they have and whether the poles move separately or in unison. A single-pole single-throw switch is a basic on/off type of switch; its pole makes a connection with one of two contacts. On a schematic diagram, switches of all types are identified by the letter *S.* In cases of multiple switches, the *S* will be next to a number showing its listing in the circuit.

Relays

A *relay* is a special type of switch that's operated electrically or electronically instead of manually. It's like several automatic switches rolled into one. In a schematic diagram, a relay is identified by the letter *K,* and its contacts are usually numbered. The contacts are also identified as *normally open,* shown as *NO* or *normally closed,* shown as *NC.* A normally open contact is open when no electric power is applied. A normally closed contact is closed when no power is applied. A solenoid is a type of relay that uses a magnetic field to move a plunger or arm.

Appendix C shows common schematic drawings for various electronic components.

5

Tools

In addition to the hand and power tools commonly found in hardware stores, electronic security technicians work with many special tools. Part 1 of this chapter tells what tools you'll need to install electronic security systems and gives tips on how to get the most for your money when buying tools. Part 2 tells how to use some of them.

Part 1: Tools for Installing Security Systems

When buying tools for work, always get the best quality you can afford. Tools that easily break or don't work properly will give you many headaches. Be sure to have a wide variety of common hand tools such as chisels, screwdrivers, and striking and prying tools. Although you may be able to finish a job using a hand tool that's the wrong size, you'll work faster and do a more professional job with tools that are the right size and weight. Appendix B includes a list of suppliers of the tools. Some have online catalogs or let you request a printed catalog from their website.

Electric Drill

An electric, or *ac-powered,* drill is an alarm installer's most often used power tool. (See Figure 5.1.) A high-quality drill can cost several times more than a low-quality model, but it's worth the extra money. A good drill will give you many years of heavy-duty service and will save you time and sweat.

There are three basic drill sizes: ¼, ⅜, and ½ inch. Drill size is based on the largest-diameter drill bit shank the drill's chuck can hold without using an adapter. For example, a drill whose chuck can hold a drill bit shank up to ½ inch in diameter is a ½-inch drill.

A drill's power is a combination of chuck speed and torque. Chuck speed is measured in *revolutions per minute* (rpm) when spinning freely in the air.

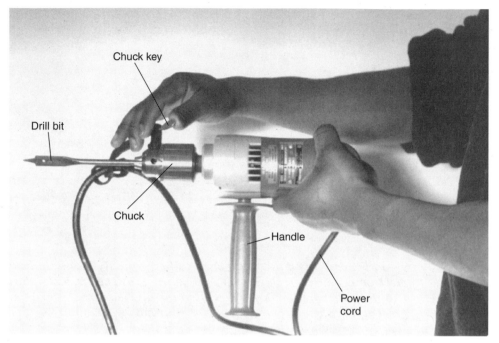

Figure 5.1 A chuck key is used for tightening or loosening a chuck's jaws, which hold the drill bit.

Torque refers to the twisting force at the chuck when the drill is being used to make a hole. The rpm alone is not a good measure of a drill's power, because a drill slows down when doing work. More important than its free-spinning speed is the speed of a drill's chuck while it's drilling a hole.

Reduction gears

The type of reduction gears on a drill largely determines the chuck speed and torque. Reduction gears work somewhat like car gears. One gear, for example, lets the car move quickly on flat roads; another gives the car more power to climb steep hills.

A drill with a single-stage reduction gear set has a chuck that spins very fast in the air (high rpm) but slows down considerably when drilling a hole. A drill with a three-stage reduction gear set has lower rpm but more torque. Generally speaking, the higher the reduction gear set, the slower and more powerful the drill.

Most ¼-inch drills have a single-stage reduction gear set, which can let a chuck spin at up to 4000 rpm. Such drills are lightweight and are used mainly for drilling plastic, thin softwood, and sheet metal. Drilling hardwood or steel with a drill that has a single-stage gear reduction set would be time-consuming and could damage the drill.

A ⅜-inch drill is generally faster than ½-inch models, and provides more torque than ¼-inch drills. The chuck of a ⅜-inch drill usually spins at about 1000 rpm. The drill can be useful for drilling metals up to ⅜ inch thick and wood up to ¾ inch thick.

A ½-inch drill usually has either a two-stage or a three-stage reduction gear set, and its chuck spins at up to about 600 rpm. The wide jaws of a ½-inch drill let it hold auger bits, boring bits, and a wide variety of shanks.

Quality

Not all drills of the same size are alike, however. They often differ greatly in quality and price. Some manufacturers label their drills as *heavy-duty, professional,* or *commercial.* Such labels have no standard meaning. When you are looking for a high-quality drill, it's best to ignore such labels and look for specific features. Important features include two- or three-stage reduction gear sets, rotation speed of at least 600 rpm, variable-speed reversible (VSR) control switch, double insulation, and all needle or ball bearings. For more specific selection guidelines, see Table 5.1.

Drills come with one or two speeds or variable speeds. Variable-speed drills are the most flexible. They have a switch that lets you use any speed from 0 rpm up to the drill's highest speed. This lets you drill different materials at different speeds.

Many drills also have a switch that reverses the direction of the chuck. This is useful for backing out screws or a stuck drill bit. Drills that have both variable-speed control and a reversible drive switch are called *variable-speed reversible,* or *VSR.*

Some drills feature double insulation. The drill is housed in nonconductive material such as plastic, and nonconductive material is used to isolate the motor from other metal parts of the drill. Double insulation is a safety feature that protects the user against being shocked. Most high-quality drills are double-insulated, so don't mistake plastic or rubberlike housing as a sign of low quality.

TABLE 5.1   Drill Buying Guidelines: Features to Look for

	RPM	Amps	Watts	Volts	Torque	Special*
Electric, ½-inch	0–600 or higher	4.8 or higher	525	115	373 in lb	B, D, T, V
Electric, ⅜-inch	0–1000 or higher	3.3 or higher	525	115	279 in lb	B, D, T, V
Cordless, ½-inch	0–1200		275	14.4 or higher	334 in lb, or higher	B, D, T, V, 2
Cordless, ⅜-inch	0–1200		280	14.1 or higher	220 in lb, or higher	B, D, T, V, 2

*Note: 2 = two-speed gear ranges; B = all ball, roller, or needle bearings; D = double-insulated; T = trigger-speed control; V = variable-speed reversing

Antifriction bearings help a drill run smoothly and last longer. Low-quality drills use all plain sleeve bearings. A few high-quality drills use a well-planned mixture of both types of bearings.

The amperage (measured in amperes) rating of an electric drill is a good indicator of its power. Usually the higher the rating, the more powerful it is. All other things being equal, get the model with the higher amperage. For cordless drills, voltage is a good indicator of power. The higher the voltage, the greater the torque.

In addition to the features mentioned in Table 5.1, other considerations for choosing a drill should be personal preferences such as look, weight, and feel.

The big names for manufacturers of professional-quality drills include Bosch, Dewalt, Hitachi, Milwaukee, Makita, and Porter-Cable. That isn't an exhaustive list of all high-quality drill brands, but they're among the most popular among alarm system installers.

Tool list

Ammeter

Armored-cable tool

Bits and hole saws, assortment

Cable tester, pocket

Combination tool

Conduit bender

Conduit reamer

Continuity tester

Drill, cordless hammer

Drill, electric ½-inch

Drill, electric hammer ½-inch

Drywall knife

Fish tape

Glue gun, cordless hot-melt

Hacksaw

Hammers

Keyhole saw

Level, 3-foot

Level, pocket

Multimeter

Pliers, needle-nose

Pliers, lineman

Pocketknife

Reciprocating saw, cordless

Right-angle drill attachment

Saber saw

Scoping (or *telescopic*) wire retriever with hooked end

Screwdrivers, assorted insulated

Screwdriver, cordless

Soldering gun

Steel fish wires

Stud sensor (see Figure 5.2)

Tape rule

Tin snips

Tool bag

Undercarpet tape

Voltage detector

Wire bits

Wire strippers (see Figure 5.3)

Wiring tackers (or *staple guns*)

Wood chisels, assortment

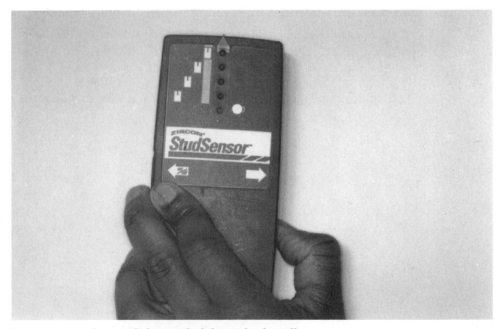

Figure 5.2 A stud sensor helps you find the studs of a wall.

Figure 5.3   Wire strippers are used for removing insulation from wire.

Questions for Review

1. What are three important considerations in choosing a drill?
2. What are two drill sizes?
3. What does a drill's chuck do?
4. What do antifriction bearings do?
5. Besides a drill, name three tools that are useful to electronic security technicians.

Part 2: Using the Tools

Using a Voltage Detector

To check for voltage with a voltage detector, place the tip of the device near a wire, outlet, or extension cord (see Figure 5.4). If the wire, outlet, or cord is *live,* the voltage detector will give an audible or visual signal. Some voltage detectors have leads that you touch across the circuit or wires at the point where you want to detect voltage. If you were checking a household plug-in, for instance, you would touch one of the probes (or *test leads*) to one terminal screw of the plug-in, and the other probe to its corresponding terminal screw. Voltage detectors are rated to detect voltage within a certain range, such as 100 to 600 volts ac. Never use a voltage detector on a circuit that has the same voltage as or a higher voltage than the detector's rating. Because ac ratings aren't precise, give yourself room for error.

Using a Voltmeter

In addition to checking if voltage is present, a voltmeter lets you measure how much voltage is present. That can be useful for troubleshooting circuits. Low voltage is a big problem with electronic systems, but sometimes the problem has nothing to do with the installer. You can save yourself a lot of time and trouble by finding that out quickly. If you use your voltmeter to take a reading at the service entrance and find that the reading is much lower than what it should be (usually between 230 and 240 volts for a 120/240 single-phase, three-wire service), then the power company will need to fix the problem.

If the voltage reads between 230 and 240 volts, then keep the voltmeter connected and remove loads from the circuit one at a time, while keeping an eye on the voltmeter. If the problem goes away after disconnecting some loads, then you may need to keep them off, replace them with smaller loads, or increase the wire size.

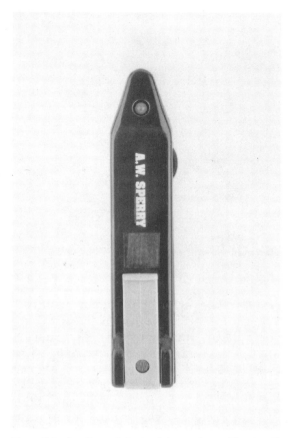

Figure 5.4 A voltage detector lets you know if a circuit is live. (*Courtesy of A.W. Sperry Instruments Inc.*)

Multimeters

A *multimeter* (or *volt-ohm-meter* or *VOM*) combines the functions of a volt detector, a voltmeter, an ammeter, and an ohmmeter. It can detect and measure voltage, current, and resistance. Usually, you can choose which to measure just by turning a selection knob on the multimeter. There are two basic types of multimeters, *analog* and *digital* (*DMM*). The analog is the least expensive. Figures 5.5 and 5.6 show the two basic types of multimeter.

Insulation, cable sheath, and walls can cover wires so you can't see a break. But because a break causes increased resistance, you can use a multimeter to discover breaks. Before using the multimeter to test for resistance, you must make sure the unit's probe wires are showing as little resistance as possible. First, set your meter's setting to the lowest resistance range (some auto-ranging DMMs have nothing to set). Then touch the two probes to each other. The meter should read 0 ohms. On an analog VOM, the needle will swing all the way to the right, and there will be an adjustment (usually marked Zero or Ohms Adjustment) that you can turn to make the meter read 0 ohms. That's called *zeroing out* the meter, and it should be done regularly before measuring resistance. You don't need to zero out DMMs.

After zeroing out the VOM, you can use it to check for continuity in a wire (or whether the wire is broken somewhere within its insulation). You do that by disconnecting the wire and touching one probe to one end of the wire and the other probe to the other end of the

Technical Tip

For an accurate meter reading, make sure the surrounding temperature is within the unit's recommended range, such as between about 65 and 83°F (or 18 and 28°C). If you're working in an environment that's too hot or too cold, your reading may be inaccurate.

wire. By reading the wire from end to end this way, you'll be able to notice if there's a break anywhere along it. If there's no break in the wire, you'll get a reading of 0 ohms. If you have measurable resistance, however, then there's a problem. The wire is probably broken or damaged somewhere.

Before you measure the resistance of a conductor that's connected to a circuit, make sure the power is off. To measure the resistance of a component in

Figure 5.5 An analog multimeter. (*Courtesy of A.W. Sperry Instruments Inc.*)

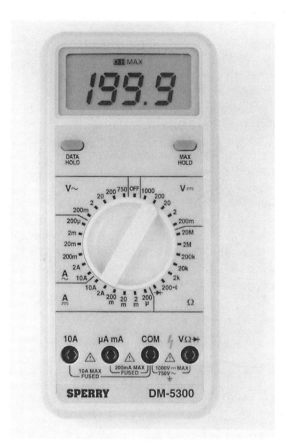

Figure 5.6 A digital multimeter. (*Courtesy of A.W. Sperry Instruments Inc.*)

a circuit, disconnect one side of the component from the circuit. That will keep other circuits from interfering with the reading.

To measure direct voltage, set the meter way beyond the voltage, such as to 1000 volts dc. Then connect the probes to the circuit, and turn the setting dial down until you reach the setting that gives a good reading.

Measuring ac voltage is a similar process. After setting the meter to its ACV position, turn the dial way above the voltage. For instance, if you're measuring house voltage that should be about 230 volts, set the meter to 1000 or higher ACV. Then connect the leads, and turn the selector down until you get a good reading. To measure high voltage, don't position both probes at once. Instead, use an alligator clip attachment to connect one to the circuit's neutral or ground, and then use the other lead to probe for voltage.

To measure dc current, set the multimeter to its DCA mode. Then break the circuit that you want to measure, and connect the meter's black probe to the negative side of the break and the red probe to the positive side. While it's in the DCA mode, never connect probes to a source of voltage.

Wiring

Part 1 of this chapter gives some basic information about types of wire and how to run wire. Part 2 goes into greater detail about coaxial and fiber-optic cable.

Part 1: Types of Wiring

Insulated wire is commonly used to carry electricity throughout a building. The wires come in many different materials, types, and sizes. Your choice of wire will have a lot to do with how your installed devices will run. To avoid short-circuiting the system, it's important to use wire with good insulation. Also the wire needs to be of the right amperage rating, and of a size that keeps voltage drop to a minimum. You can't prevent all voltage drop; but the bigger the drop, the greater the wasted electricity. Ohm's law, which is explained in Chapter 4, can be used to calculate voltage drop. The formula is $E = IR$, or voltage drop equals amperes times ohms.

The American Wire Gauge (AWG) standard is used in the United States for describing wire size. Residential wire can range from No. 60, which is very thin, to No. 0000 (also called 4/0), which is about $1/2$ inch thick. The thicker the wire, the smaller the number and the more current (amperage) it can safely carry. Most low-voltage wiring, such as for doorbells and alarm systems, uses No. 22.

Two or more wires wrapped together within insulation are called a *cable*. Nonmetallic (NM) sheathed cable has two or three insulated wires and a bare copper wire, all wrapped in paper, which is encased in a plastic sheathing. NM cable is most commonly used for residential wiring.

Armored (or BX) cable has insulated wires running through a flexible metal case. Usually the case itself acts as the ground, but sometimes BX cable has a green insulated ground wire. Older-style BX cable uses a steel case and is harder to use than the newer aluminum case.

Conduit is a thin metal or plastic piping that is used for running wire through. It is often used in commercial and residential applications.

To help avoid installation problems, make sure all your wire connections are secure. Before splicing wire or connecting it to a terminal screw, you may need to remove some insulation from the connection end of the wire. The easiest way to do that is to use a wire stripper (see Figure 6.1). Place the cutting edges of its jaws at a 60° angle where you want to begin removing the insulation. Cut into the insulation a bit, but not so much that you cut into the wire. Turn the wire around, and make a similar cut so that you'll have cut all the way around the insulation. Then use the strippers to slide off the insulation. More expensive strippers have wire gauges marked on them, with holes for you to insert the wire. One is shown in Figure 6.2b.

To join wire together, you tightly twist them to each other. Needle-nose pliers can be helpful for doing that. (See Figure 6.3.) To keep the wires secure, and to prevent them from shorting out the circuit, tightly wrap the joined wires with electrical tape, or twist a wire nut over their ends (see Figure 6.4). Wire nuts have metal threads that grip the ends of the wires, to press them close together and keep a good connection. When they are properly fitted, no bare wire should be showing. Wire nuts are typically used when the wires will be placed in an electrical box (or box, for short), which is a plastic or metal container for holding spliced wire. Examples of covered and uncovered boxes are shown, respectively, in Figures 6.5 and 6.6. Boxes need to be easily accessible, and they shouldn't be covered with woodwork or drywall. Make sure the box

Figure 6.1 Strip wire at an angle.

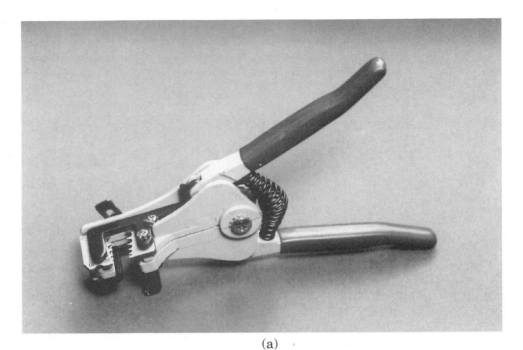

(a)

(b)

Figure 6.2   (*a*) Some wire strippers are preset for cutting certain wire gauges. (*b*) Close-up of multi-gauge wire stripper jaws in closed position.

that you use is large enough to hold all the wires without cramping. Electrical codes dictate the number and sizes of wire that may go into various sizes of box. Metal boxes are used if the system's grounding depends on armored cable or conduit. When NM cable is used with a ground wire, plastic boxes are usually employed.

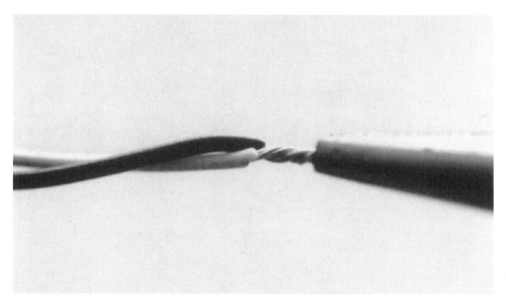

Figure 6.3   Pliers are helpful for twisting two wires tightly together.

Figure 6.4   A wire nut can be used to protect the bare ends of wires that are twisted together.

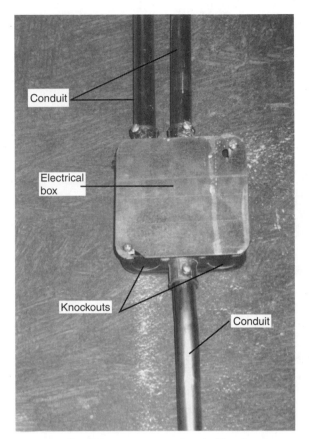

Figure 6.5 Conduit can enter an electrical box from various knockout holes.

Another way to join wires is by soldering them together. You don't use wire nuts on soldered wires. Soldered wires need to be insulated with electrical tape.

Questions for review

1. What should be a consideration in choosing wire?
2. What tool is used for removing insulation from wire?
3. Which gauge of wire is commonly used for low-voltage work?
4. Why is insulation needed on wire?
5. What formula can be used to determine the voltage drop?

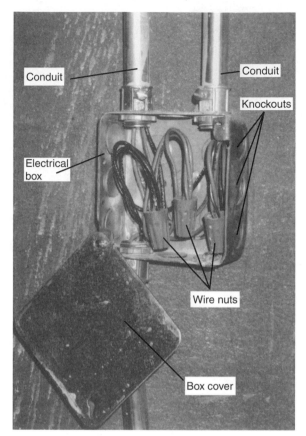

Figure 6.6   An electrical box should be large enough to secure all the wire without cramping.

Part 2: Coaxial and Fiber-Optic Cable

This part goes into greater detail about the uses of coaxial cable and fiber-optic cable and is comprised of contributed articles by experts in the field.

Coaxial Cable
by Al Colombo

Coaxial cables consist of a center conductor with an outer metallic shield. In most cases, the shield consists of a metallic web of conductors, with or without an additional metal-foil wrapping surrounding the center conductor. The entire assembly is then wrapped with a plastic covering, called a *sheath*.

In most cases, the shield is connected to an equipment ground, which is accomplished by connecting one end of the shield to the chassis of the equipment that it's connected to. The chassis, in turn, is connected to earth ground by the neutral connection of the power cord and receptacle.

In most cases, the shield on a coaxial cable is connected to only one ground, to eliminate ground loops. Ground loops occur when there is more than one ground along the path of a video signal. It occurs because there's a sizable potential difference (voltage) between the two grounding points.

This potential difference causes electrons to flow between the two ground points—this is a current that is not associated with the video signal. As the ground current combines with the current on the common side of the video signal, it causes the flow of electrons (current) to vary according to the electrical interference present in the ground current.

Because the most common electric current flowing through ground is 60-cycle power from the power line bus, a 60-hertz (60-Hz) component is added (modulated) to the video signal. This, in turn, effectively corrupts the otherwise nearly perfect video signal, causing any one of several effects. By eliminating one of the grounds, the ground loop current is essentially stopped.

Coaxial cable quality

The single most frequent cause of problems in closed-circuit television (CCTV) systems is low-quality coaxial cables. That's why it's important for installers to use a quality coaxial cable. Although coaxial cable is probably the least expensive part of a CCTV system, it is by no means the least important. Good coaxial cable, for example, has a low direct-current (dc) resistance because its center conductor is large enough to effectively carry the signal.

A good-quality coaxial cable also has a shield that's rated higher in its shielding capability than that of less expensive coaxial cables. This rating is commonly expressed as a percentage, reflecting the degree of shielding that's provided by a particular cable. It's not uncommon, for example, to see coaxial cables with shielding efficiencies of 80 to 95 percent.

A good coaxial shield is crucial to the proper, uninterrupted, and uncorrupted operation of a CCTV system. The shield around the center conductor of a good coaxial cable, for example, will stop stray electromagnetic radiation (EMR) that occurs in the environment from entering the cable and interfering with the video signal. Sources of stray EMR, for example, are common in homes and commercial buildings as well as along the street. Examples of EMR sources are electric power lines, motors, power transformers, and radio broadcast transmitters [that is, television and commercial radio transmitters as well as citizens band (CB) and amateur ham radio transmitters in the neighborhood].

The type of center conductor inside the coaxial cable that an installer uses is also important. Experts say that using anything less than a 100 percent copper center conductor will eventually result in the replacement of the cable, especially in outdoor applications where the cable is constantly exposed to EMR sources of all types.

The issue of whether to use a solid or stranded center conductor must also be considered. Cable with a solid center conductor is less expensive than stranded cable, but this type of cable should never be used on a camera that's mounted to a pan and tilt mechanism. Instead, stranded cable should be used in pan and tilt applications, as well as any other situation where the camera must move from time to time. Use of a cable with a solid core usually results in a broken center conductor at some point in the future.

The type of cable sheath used is also important to the longevity of a video installation. Installers should not use indoor-type coaxial cable in outside applications. When they do, ultraviolet radiation from sunlight can cause cracks to develop in the cable sheath. Cracks allow moisture and contaminants to penetrate the sheath, changing the impedance of the cable. The net effect will be disruption of the video signal that flows along the center conductor.

Choosing the right coaxial cable

Installers must select the right coaxial cable for each application that they encounter. The first consideration is cable *impedance*. Coaxial cable is available in several impedances. This is so because the coaxial cable must match the output impedance of a video device to the input of another. An impedance match makes possible the optimum exchange of energy between the two devices.

It's the dielectric insulator between the center conductor and braided shield (ground) of a coaxial cable that ultimately determines impedance. There are a number of dielectric materials available for this purpose. The type of dielectric material and its thickness determine the impedance of a particular coaxial cable. Like the Closed Circuit Television Manufacturers Association (CCTMA) industry, the video industry uses an impedance of 75 ohms. Thus, installers must be certain to use a 75-ohm coaxial cable when installing CCTV systems. Otherwise, the quality of the video signals carried by the coaxial cable that they do use will likely be less than desirable. The reason is that the attenuation of the video signal will vary with the instantaneous frequency of the signal. In other words, the quality of the output video signal will vary from one moment to the next because the coaxial cable will transport some portions of the signal with greater ease than other portions. This can cause ghosting, snow, and a generally poor video picture.

In addition, the type of coaxial cable selected will determine the distance that video signals will travel. Coaxial cables, for example, are categorized according to size and distance-carrying capabilities. For example, the most common coaxial cable used today is RG59/U. This coaxial cable will carry signals for distances of up to 1000 feet. The next most popular coaxial is RG6/U, which is capable of carrying video signals up to 1500 feet. Likewise RG11/U cable will carry video signals for up to 3000 feet without any appreciable degradation of the signal.

Fiber-Optic Cable
by Al Colombo

Although coaxial cable is probably the most widely used and most accepted form of video transmission today, it is slowly losing ground to its fiber-optic counterpart. One very good reason for this is the wider bandwidth realized by fiber-optic cable.

Although fiber-optic cable is not new, it's use in the CCTV market is relatively recent. Fiber-optic cable is now being used to transport both video and audio signals for short and long distances. This is made possible by modulating the video/audio signal(s) onto a beam of coherent light, which is generated by a solid-state laser. The modulated light is then passed through a single, minutely small strand of nearly pure glass fiber. Because this method uses light to carry the intelligence, data can be carried up to 3 miles or even farther without utilizing a repeater of any kind.

In many ways, a fiber-optic cable looks like a smaller version of a coaxial cable, until you closely examine the connectors and what's inside. For example, inside the center of a fiber-optic cable is a nearly pure glass fiber. This center glass fiber (core) is protected by several layers of material.

The first layer nearest the core is called the *cladding*. Cladding is comprised of a less-than-pure film of glass. Although the core carries the major portion of the modulated light, and thus the intelligence, the cladding aids in the return of light that's commonly lost through refraction.

The final layer is usually referred to as the *jacket,* or *buffer.* The buffer is designed to absorb some of the physical shock encountered by the fiber-optic cable in its environment. This layer has no optical properties, but its sole purpose is actually to aid in the protection of the inner glass fiber layers.

Installers are using more fiber-optic cable than ever before. One reason is that there are more channels of communication over which to transmit video images, audio, and other data. This means more images on a single cable than is possible with metallic coaxial cable. Longer signal transmission distances are also possible with less signal attenuation by using fiber-optic cable.

Fiber-optic cable is also unaffected by electromagnetic interference (EMI), like its metallic coaxial counterparts. It's also generally smaller in diameter than metallic coaxial cable when it comes to the number of communication channels available. Signal transmissions are more secure using fiber-optic cable, because the signals traveling on a fiber-optic cable do not emit electromagnetic radiation that someone can pick up with a EM-sensitive device and use. This makes it more difficult to tap with the intent of eavesdropping. To do so in an unauthorized manner will also introduce extreme signal loss or even total signal disruption.

Fiber-optic cable has a wider signal frequency bandwidth than its metallic coaxial counterpart. This means more channels of communication are available. For example, metallic coaxial cable has an effective bandwidth of 10 megahertz (MHz). By comparison, fiber-optic cable has an effective bandwidth of 44.6 MHz/km. This means an effective potential of more than 670 simultaneous telephone conversations over one glass fiber.

Fiber-optic cable can also carry light-modulated signals for longer distances than metallic coaxial cables can because there's less signal attenuation. Metallic coaxial cable experiences a higher degree of signal attenuation because of the inductive and capacitive properties of the wire that carries the video signal. The very nature of a metallic coaxial cable causes a higher degree of attenuation than fiber-optic cable does. Fiber-optic cable, however, experiences far less attenuation because glass fibers offer little resistance to the passage of light. In fiber-optic cable, it's more a matter of glass fiber purity that determines the degree of attenuation.

How to choose the right fiber-optic cable

To gauge the quality of a fiber-optic cable, engineers use a mathematical property called the *refractive index.* The refractive index of a fiber-optic cable is expressed as a ratio. It is determined by measuring the difference between the speed of light in a vacuum and the speed of light through a particular medium, such as a fiber-optic cable.

To prove the validity of this principle, one has only to pass white light through a prism. The result is the refraction of all the colors. The light that escapes through the other end is then separated into the basic colors of the rainbow: red, orange, yellow, green, blue, and violet. Because the wavelength of each color is different, these colors are viewed separately as they exit the prism. The wavelength of red is shorter than that of orange, for example, so the angle of refraction is also less.

Internal reflection is another factor that helps determine the quality of a fiber-optic cable. This property greatly minimizes the loss of light when the angle of refraction is equal to or greater than the critical angle. Thus, in better fiber-optic cables, nearly all the light transmitted is reflected back to the center of the fiber-optic cable. The glass cladding around the center glass core also helps to reflect some of the refracted light back toward the center of the fiber-optic cable.

Some types of fiber-optic cable have the ability to transport more than one beam of light, or *mode*. A mode is simply the path that a beam of light takes as it travels inside a fiber-optic cable. There are several types of fiber-optic cables on the market today that can transport from one to more than 1000 beams of light over multiple paths, or modes.

The number of modes over which a fiber-optic cable can transport is determined by the size of the glass fiber and other factors that determine its capacity and quality.

Fiber Optics and Your Facility: A New Era
by Jerry L. Jacobson, Ph.D.

It was not very long ago that fiber optics in security applications were an exotic, even bewildering technology. "Just how *does* that signal get down a glass fiber?" For many people with substantial experience in the security industry, fiber optics used to mean the bundle of colored light fibers attached to a little flashlight that you'd buy for your kids at the amusement park. Those toys still make good teaching aids, in fact.

But the reality is different now. Today, designing the fiber backbone of a new facility takes place right up front in the initial planning stages. Now there is a good probability that fiber will constitute the main communications backbone of a facility. In the last 10 to 12 years we've seen fiber go from being an exotic, misunderstood, and pricey alternative to copper to being the prime choice for all types of signal transmission in many facilities. At the same time, its price has gone down and performance has improved. People are no longer incredulous when someone shows them that it actually costs less to transmit video, for instance, over fiber than over copper coaxial cable.

Where we are today

Let's take a look at a modern, moderate-size facility. It will have multiple electronic systems, including fire and burglar alarms; access control; CCTV; audio systems (usually intercoms); lighting system controls; heating, ventilation, and air conditioning (HVAC) systems; and, of course, telephones. The facility is also likely to have a good number of other remotely controlled devices, such as door and gate locks. And it will have computers—some integrated into the systems just mentioned, but others as part of the basic business conducted in the facility, whether manufacturing, education, or trading stocks.

In short, a modern facility will have electronic information flying all over the place. To get a vivid picture of what this means in terms of cabling, just push up one of your ceiling tiles and look at the rat's nest of all kinds of cable running every which way in the ceiling. Fiber can replace most of that and can provide greater versatility and better signal quality at a lower cost. Today, a typical fiber link transmits from some signal source, such as a CCTV camera, to some receiving device, such as a video monitor. A small black box is located somewhere in the vicinity of the camera, and another one is located somewhere around the monitor. Or there can be multiple sources, such as several cameras, feeding into the black box and multiple outputs at the other end. Or different signals can be added, such as audio and data and control. Today's technology allows a wide range of signal combinations to be combined (multiplexed) onto a single fiber, and it also can permit two-way (duplex) transmission of multiple signals.

The benefits to date

By now, most people in the security and building management systems business have a good grasp of the benefits of glass fiber over copper, but it would not hurt to review the main issues.

Signal integrity.   Remember the rat's nest in the drop ceiling? Those copper cables are not the only electrical things up there. You'll also find plenty of fluorescent light fixtures and a smattering of electric motors. The lights, motors, and the cables themselves radiate electromagnetic interference, which can degrade signals carried over the copper cables that run near them. Signals carried on glass fiber are completely immune to EMI, no matter what the environment. If you want the signal to get to its destination and to be clear and usable, you must use fiber.

Lower installation cost.   If you're in the business, you know what it's like—and what it costs—to pull a bundle of eight RG59/U cables from a group of cameras back to the monitors. The bundle will be about an inch in diameter and as stiff as a solid rod. The alternative—a single fiber in this case—is very small and about as flexible as a piece of string. Multiple-fiber cables also are common, but the constant factor here is that, for any collection of transmitted signals, running the fiber will be easier and will require less labor time than running the equivalent collection of copper cables. Also, reductions in the cost of fiber in the last few years have contributed significantly to shifting the economic balance in favor of fiber-optic transmission.

Versatility. This issue isn't discussed much, but it ranks as one of the more important benefits of fiber. You may have noticed when you were looking above the drop ceiling that every different type of signal—video, audio, data, telephones, you name it—requires its own kind of copper cable. You can have dozens of specialized cables in a typical facility, and few of them are interchangeable. But it only takes two types of optical cable to cover all possible signals: multimode and single-mode cable. Currently, the most widely used of each of these in the United States are 62.5-m cable for multimode applications and 8.3-m cable for single mode uses. One constant factor in facility systems today is incessant expansion. You planned for every possible communication contingency when you put your building together 6 months ago, and now here you are, pulling more cable of various kinds to accommodate a host of expanded requirements, and possibly pulling your hair out, too. Or you have to accommodate some new technology that did not exist back then, but which needs its own dedicated copper cabling. It certainly is not practical or economical to try to guess future requirements by running extra copper cables, specialized for all your different systems, and just letting them lie there until needed. And often, if you end up adding more gadgets to your building systems, the gadgets are likely to end up going someplace where you had not run the extra cable.

But, as mentioned, there are only two types of fiber, and they can carry all signals; if you have an extra fiber or two up there in your cable troughs, you can send any kind of signal down it. And it's economical to leave a few extra fibers when you're installing the fiber backbone. Multifiber cables make this especially attractive. Or, if you have an emergency or a temporary requirement, you can disconnect something from an existing fiber and reconnect it to the new gadget, without having to snake specialized cable.

What's new and what's on the horizon

Like all other high-technology products, fiber-optic links are benefiting from advances in electronics and manufacturing methods. Surface-mounted device (SMD) technology, better integrated circuits, and advances in digital design are producing links that perform better than ever before. New connector designs are making high-quality installation easier, faster, and less expensive. One of the biggest developments in fiber optics right now is the digital broadband multiplexer, which is capable of transmitting up to 32 real-time videos over a single fiber, with drop-and-insert capability. It also has extensive audio, data, and control transmission capability, and adding a second fiber provides duplex operation. Basically, this new unit provides more signals over one fiber than has been possible for fiber-optic equipment in this industry, and the drop-and-insert architecture allows this new system to be a complete communications backbone where it is installed.

Instead of having a large number of individual point-to-point fiber links in a facility, the digital broadband multiplexer allows the signal transmission requirements of many devices to be integrated on a single communications backbone over only two fibers. This device will open the door to true system integration, which has been an elusive goal in building management systems for some years.

Summary

Fiber optics have established themselves solidly as a major resource for signal transmission in facilities of all kinds. The first generation of fiber-optic technology, which brought us to this point, is rapidly being replaced by new models that take advantage of the latest developments in electronic design and manufacturing, providing higher levels of performance and convenience. For instance, where you used to have to specify a different model for each type of data you wanted to transmit, soon it will be possible to specify one model which is compatible with all major data formats. Finally, the beauty of fiber optics as the signal transmission medium for a facility is that it utterly eliminates a host of problems associated with copper-based transmission.

Installing and Troubleshooting Alarm Systems

Part 1 of this chapter tells how to install wireless and hardwired alarm systems. Part 2 shows how to troubleshoot them. (If you're not familiar with the components of alarm systems, review Chapter 2.)

Part 1: Installing Wireless and Hardwired Systems

One of the first considerations in choosing components for an alarm system is cost. You have to decide how to provide adequate protection while making a good profit. Generally, that does not include using a system of redundant state-of-the-art perimeter sensors at every entry point, backed up by overlapping high-technology interior sensors that saturate the premises. Using the best of everything is usually overkill and more than customers will pay for. Under no circumstance, however, should you install a system that you know provides inadequate protection. Regardless of what you charge, you should always give a reasonable minimum standard of quality. If customers can't afford that, then let them go elsewhere. Otherwise, you're likely to face lawsuits and will get a bad reputation in your community. (For more information about good business practices, see Chapter 16.)

To plan an effective alarm system, you'll need to become familiar with the layout of the premises or areas to be protected as well as with the needs and limitations of the people who will be using the system. Talk with members of the household or business where the system is being installed. Don't make the mistake of doing cookie-cutter, one-size-fits-all types of installations. To compete with the giants in the alarm industry, you can't copy them. You have to offer superior personalized service.

Find out what your customers expect from a system. Ask about their concerns, and find out who will be using the system. Some people may have special needs, such as young children and persons with a disability. The more you learn about their thoughts, the greater chance you'll have to educate them. An educated customer is a good customer. When customers keep causing false alarms or get frustrated while trying to figure out how to use the system, they won't blame themselves. They will blame you.

Once you understand what the customer wants and will likely be able to work with, you need to either make a copy of a blueprint of the premises or draw a sketch of the area to be protected. The sketch should show all doors, windows, and other openings, along with all rooms and closets. Indicate at each door, window, and area to be protected which components and sensors you're planning to use. (For details on how to install the various components, see Chapter 2.) Also decide how many zones you want, and which components will be in which zones. When making the drawing, keep in mind how you'll run any wire that may be needed. The better you plan, the easier your installation will be.

Installing a Wireless Alarm

Be sure to read and understand the manufacturer's instructions before you start to install a system. If you don't understand something, you can usually call a technical support line or get technical information from the manufacturer's website. The tips in this chapter are general guidelines and aren't meant to take the place of the manufacturer's instructions.

Many wireless alarms combine the control panel with the keypad for easy wall mounting or placement on a table or desk. If it is wall-mounted, make sure it's at a comfortable height for your customers (usually about the height of a thermostat). The control panel should be installed inside a building near an electrical outlet and close to the most often used entrance. It shouldn't be visible from outside through a window or door.

The term *wireless* is a misnomer, because some wire is involved—but not much. There may be wire from the control panel to its plug-in transformer. In that case, you'll need to hide the transformer wire. You may be able to do that by drilling a small hole behind the control panel, and another hole just below the electrical outlet. Then you can fish the wire through the wall to keep it out of sight. If the system will be monitored (as it almost always should be), you'll need to also run two-pair 24-gauge telephone wire from the control panel to the box where the phone lines enter the home or business.

Install the interior bell or siren in an inconspicuous place where it can be heard throughout the home or throughout much of the building. Don't place it where the sound will be muffled by drapery or furniture. An X-10 compatible siren plugs into an electrical outlet and communicates with the other components over the building's wiring. Don't plug it into an outlet controlled by a switch. Then you use a small screwdriver to turn the dials to choose a "house code," to which you program all the other X-10 compatible components.

Next, program the control panel. Some systems use a synthesized voice to talk you through the programming steps. Then install all the sensors and test the system. Have members of the household or business work with the system, and make sure they know how to use it.

Hardwired systems

To install a hardwired system, you need to run wire from the control panel to various components—this is why they're far less popular among do-it-yourselfers. Although professional installers debate the matter, I believe a hardwired system is more reliable and easier to troubleshoot than a wire system.

What type and size of wire to use and how to run it are determined by the requirements of the National Electrical Code (NEC), the component manufacturers, your local codes, the importance of aesthetics, the amount your customer is willing to pay, and the structure of the building. The wiring for most hardwired systems is from 18 to 22 gauge (for more about wiring, see Chapter 6). Wire needs to be run from one floor to others, and within a room. You want to get the wire to places while exposing as little wire as possible. That's for aesthetic value as well as for the security of the system.

Wiring can be run open or concealed (or a combination of both). In open wiring, the wire is run where it's in plain view and easily accessible, such as on the surface of walls, columns, or ceilings. That kind of wiring doesn't look very neat, but lets you easily make changes to the wiring configuration. In concealed wiring, the wire is within walls, behind baseboards, over drop ceilings, inside of columns, and otherwise out of view. It's the more popular type of wiring for homes and other places where appearance is important. When you are running wire behind moldings or casings, consider cutting a cavity beneath them where the wire can be run. If the moldings or baseboard is painted, before prying it loose, use a utility knife to cut between the wall and molding or baseboard. That will help keep the paint from peeling. Then use a flat pry bar to carefully work it off. If the nails in the molding or baseboard aren't too bent, leave them in place so you can align them with their original holes later. That will make replacement easier.

Try not to run wire across finished walls through studs, because it requires a lot of cutting and patching. When you are considering where to run wire, look for existing holes and spaces. Most buildings have a lot you can use. Good places to run wire include an unfinished attic, crawlspace, or basement and over drop ceilings. You may be able to run wire along the plumbing stack from the attic to the basement, by lowering a fishing weight attached to a thin chain or string. When it reaches the basement, have a helper attach a cable to the chain or string. Pull the cable back up past the stack, and you'll then have a cable from the basement to the attic. You may need to install a new electrical box (if you're not familiar with electrical boxes, see Chapter 6).

If you have to drill holes, look for inconspicuous places, such as a closet that's directly above another closet. Other options include stapling wire along the edges of carpet and hiding it behind baseboards, window casings, and moldings. See Figure 7.1 for places to hide wire.

When you can't hide wire, you may need to use a *raceway,* which is a channel made of metal or insulating material that's used for holding wire and

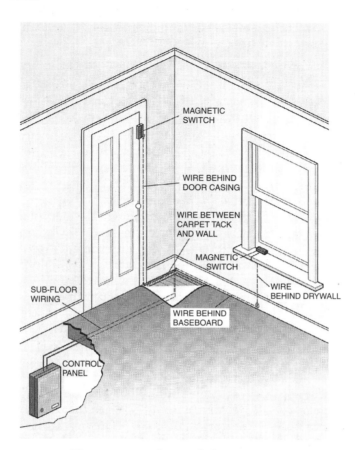

Figure 7.1   There are many places to hide wire.

cable. Some raceways include electrical metal tubing (EMT), rigid metal con-duit, rigid nonmetallic conduit, intermediate metal conduit (IMC), and flexible metal conduit.

Corrosion-resistant metal conduit and fittings are used when corrosion is likely to be a problem. Plastic-coated steel, aluminum, and silicon bronze alloy are corrosion-resistant. If the location where the conduit is being installed is wet, space the conduit at least ¼ inch away from the mounting surface.

Lengths of conduit are installed with a threaded coupling at one end. To cut conduit to size, you can use a hacksaw, power band saw, or conduit cutter. After cutting, you'll need to ream the conduit to remove any burrs and sharp edges. Then lubricate the conduit with cutting oil and run a cutting die up the conduit until you have a full thread.

Questions for review

1. What is a wireless alarm?

2. Why do you need to talk with members of a household before installing an alarm?

3. What size wiring is typically used for alarm systems?

4. What are three good places to hide wire in a hardwired installation?

5. What do you need to do to compete with the giants in the alarm industry?

Part 2: Troubleshooting Alarm Systems

Most alarm installers can eventually figure out what's wrong with a system if they spend enough time fiddling with it. But if you're working to make money, instead of as a hobby, you don't want to waste a lot of time. You want to go in, quickly fix the problem, and leave. To do that, you need to be thoughtful about your troubleshooting approach. A good troubleshooter thinks logically and creatively, is a good interviewer, and knows how to properly use troubleshooting equipment.

Many problems you'll face will be common to the types and models of the devices you're using. Become familiar with the manufacturer's installation and service guides. The troubleshooting tips in those guides will make your job much easier.

The first step in fixing a problem is to try to pin down what the problem is, usually by talking with your customer. Listen closely, but don't assume that customers are giving you accurate information. Customers are likely to be vague and unintentionally misleading, because they don't know much about alarms. If the customers think they may have done something wrong, they may be intentionally deceptive. Ask simple and direct questions such as these that may give you more information:

- To the best of your recollection, when was the last time the system worked properly?

- Is the problem continuous, or does it occur intermittently?

- What were you doing immediately before you noticed the problem?

- What was the weather condition immediately before you noticed the problem?

Don't ask questions in a way that sounds as if you're blaming the customers, even if you suspect they did something wrong.

Then do a walk-through and look at the system components to see if there are any obvious problems, such as a loose terminal wire or unplugged component.

Next, go to the control panel to determine if the trouble lies in the protective loop—the circuit that includes the detection devices—or elsewhere. Disconnect the protective loop wires, and jump the protective loop terminals. That's a way of bypassing the protective circuit, temporarily taking all the detection devices out of the picture so you can see if the trouble is elsewhere. If the alarm system sets up properly in this configuration, remove the jumper to break a closed loop, or short an open-loop terminal. If you don't get an alarm condition, there's a problem with your control panel. But if you do get an alarm condition, the problem is in the protective loop. Most problems involve the protective loop.

Different types of protective loops are jumped in different ways. For an open loop, you don't use jumpers. You just disconnect both loop wires, and try to activate the alarm by shorting the terminals.

To test a single closed loop, disconnect both loop wires and place a jumper wire across the two terminals. Arm the system, and then try to activate the system by removing the jumper.

For an open and closed loop, disconnect the three or four wires and connect a jumper wire from the normally closed (NC) terminal to the common. Arm the system. You should then be able to activate the system by removing the jumper or shorting the normally open (NO) to the common.

For an end-of-the-line (EOL) resistor with one side grounded, you disconnect the ungrounded side only and insert a substitute resistor of the right value across the terminal loops. You should be able to activate the alarm by lifting one end of the resistor.

If the EOL resistor is ungrounded, disconnect both sides before substituting a resistor of the correct value across the loop terminals. You should be able to activate the alarm by lifting one end of the resistor.

After deciding that the problem is in the protective loop, you'll need to use a multimeter to figure out if it's the result of a short, open, or ground. Before you use a multimeter, make sure there's loop voltage in the control panel, because voltage is needed to operate the meter. Some panels have continuous loop voltage, even when the system is off; others have no voltage when the system is off. For information on using a multimeter, see Chapter 5.

Security Lighting

Part 1 of this chapter gives a basic overview of the nature of light. Part 2 goes into the practical uses of light sources and lighting controls within a security system.

Part 1: The Nature of Light

Light is a form of radiant energy that travels at specific wavelengths. A wavelength is the distance between one energy wave peak and the next. Many people describe light as *on, off, dim,* and *bright.* As an electronic security professional, you need to be much more specific than that. You need to be aware that all light is made up of many colors. Even daylight is made up of many visible (mostly red and blue) and invisible (ultraviolet and infrared) colors. If you take color photographs in different lighting, you'll get different color prints—unless you use color-correcting film or filters. A photograph taken indoors using standard household bulbs (tungsten), for instance, will have an orange tint. One taken indoors under fluorescent lighting will have a yellow-green tint.

Measuring Light

There are some useful rules for measuring light. To appreciate them, you need to understand three terms: luminous intensity, luminous flux, and illuminance. *Luminous intensity,* symbolized by I, is the illuminating power of a light source in a given direction. A unit of luminous intensity is the *candela* (abbreviated as cd). The *luminous flux,* symbolized by F, is the rate of light flow from a light source. A unit of luminous flux is the *lumen* (abbreviated as lm), which is the flux emitted in one steradian (1 sr) (solid angle) from a point source of 1 cd. *Illuminance,* symbolized by E, is the intensity of light falling on a surface and is measured in lumens per square meter. A unit of illuminance is the *lux* (abbreviated as lx).

One guide for measuring light is the *inverse square law*. Because light travels in straight lines, there is a fixed relationship between source intensity and distance between the source and the illuminated surface. It can be stated mathematically as $E = I/d^2$ (where E is measured in lux, I in candelas, and d is distance between source and surface to be illuminated).

Lamp efficiency, or *efficacy,* is another important lighting factor. It's measured in lumens per watt (abbreviated as lm/W) and varies among lamp sources.

Some lumen output is lost by lamp fittings, which may block light or direct it to walls or ceilings that will further absorb the light. Light output is also lost by the shape, thickness, and color of lamp fittings, as well as any dirt or dust on the fittings. Only a portion of the light being emitted reaches the working surface. That portion is called the *utilization factor.* The lower the utilization factor, the more power the light source needs to provide the desired illuminance.

Using a lightmeter

A lightmeter (or *photometer*) can help you quickly make light-related calculations. It gives a direct reading of illuminance in lux, within its rating scale range. Scales range from 0 to 0.25 to 0 to 10,000 lx. Some models will also tell you the type of light source (such as tungsten). You use the meter by placing it parallel to the surface to be illuminated.

Light Sources

The most common light source is the sun, which is often an important consideration in choosing and positioning alarm system components. At night, and sometimes indoors during the day, artificial light sources need to be used. Important differences among artificial light sources include color, softness, brightness, energy efficiency, and initial cost.

Light sources you might consider include standard incandescent, halogen, fluorescent, and high-density discharge (HID) light. The HID family of lighting includes low-pressure sodium, high-pressure sodium, mercury vapor, and metal halide.

An *incandescent* light source relies on heat to produce light. The standard bulbs used in most homes are incandescent (lighting designers call them *A-lamps*). They have a metal filament that's heated by electricity. Standard incandescent bulbs are inexpensive, readily available, and suitable for most home fixtures. They light up almost immediately at the flip of a light switch. Using heat to produce light isn't energy-efficient, however. In the long run, incandescent lighting can be more costly than other sources that require special fixtures.

Halogen, a special type of incandescent source, is slightly more energy-efficient than standard incandescent lighting. A halogen bulb uses a tungsten filament and is filled with a halogen gas.

Fluorescent lighting uses electric current to make a specially shaped (usually tubular) bulb glow. The bulbs come in various lengths, from 5 inches to about 96 inches, and they require special fixtures. Ultraviolet radiation is present in fluorescent lighting, because the tubes of such lights are coated with a powder that makes ultraviolet waves visible. You might not want to use fluorescent lighting with certain types of electronic security systems, because it can interfere with radio reception. Nor would you ordinarily use fluorescent lighting outdoors in cold climates. It's very temperature-sensitive.

For outdoor lighting, you might use high-intensity discharge sources, which are energy-efficient and cost little to run for long periods of time. Like fluorescent lighting, HID sources require special fixtures and can be expensive initially. Another potential problem with HID sources is that they can take a long time to produce light after you've turn them on. You can often get around that problem by using a light controller to automatically begin the start-up so the lights will come on when needed.

Light Controllers

Timers are among the most popular types of controllers for indoor and outdoor lighting. Some models can do more than just turn lights on and off at preset times. Programmable 24-hour wall switch timers, for example, will randomly turn lights on and off throughout the night and early morning. That feature can be useful for making a home appear lived in while occupants are on vacation. Lights coming on and off in different rooms of a house can give a more realistic appearance of people being home, than all lights simultaneously going off and coming back on at a preset time.

Another feature of some timers is built-in protection against memory loss. After a power failure, they "remember" how they had been programmed. Some models adjust themselves automatically to take into account daylight savings time changes.

Another way to control lights is with sound or motion sensors. You can connect one to, say, a living room table lamp, so that when someone walks into the living room, the light will come on automatically. That can be a useful safety feature.

Some floodlights come with a built-in motion sensor. If you install them outside at strategic places, they will warn of nighttime visitors. You might install one facing the driveway, for instance, so it will light up the area when a car pulls in.

Questions for review

1. What's the most common source of light?

2. What are two artificial light sources?

3. What type of radiation is present in a fluorescent tube?

4. What are two members of the high-density discharge family?

5. What is luminous flux?

Part 2: Practical Uses of Light

Planning Security Lighting

When you plan for security lighting, it's usually a good idea to also take safety lighting into consideration. Many times less light is needed for a security application than may be needed to avoid accidents. When the two needs differ, make sure there's enough light to meet safety needs. Otherwise you'll put your customer (and yourself) at risk of being sued if someone gets hurt because there wasn't enough light to see a hazard.

Residential Lighting

A dark home is an invitation to crime and creates a high risk for accidents. When people come home late at night, they need to be able to walk from the car to the entrance without tripping over something, or someone, in their path (see Figure 8.1). Once inside, they need to be able to move from room to room safely. A house or apartment should be well lighted on the inside, in the areas directly outside the doors, and throughout the yard. *Well-lighted* doesn't necessarily mean a lot of light; it means having the right light sources and controls in the right places.

To prevent accidents, at nighttime occupants of a home need to be able to see potential hazards. Good interior lighting also helps them more quickly exit in an emergency, and it acts as a deterrent to intruders. When walking down a flight of stairs, occupants need to be able to see whether any objects are in the way. In many homes, people have to stumble through dark areas, groping for a light switch or a series of light switches, before reaching the bathroom or kitchen.

In those cases, motion-activated sensors may be useful. But you might need to use a lot of them to cover every pathway from each bedroom to the kitchen and bathroom. Simpler and more convenient options are available.

Figure 8.1 Good outdoor residential lighting provides a path of light from the car to the building entrance.

One option is to use three-way switches. They let someone turn a light on and off at more than one location, such as at the top and bottom of a flight of stairs. The most convenient way to control lighting indoors is to tie all or most of the switches into an easily accessible master control panel. An occupant could then turn on a specific group of lights by just pushing a button. One button could turn on a pathway of lights from, say, a bedroom to the kitchen. Some of or all the outdoor lights could also be tied into the master control system. (To learn more about how lighting can be integrated into the security system, see Chapter 10 on home automation.)

Tech tip

When installing low-voltage lighting outdoors, make sure your lights work before digging any holes or burying cables.

Installing outdoor low-voltage lighting

First, draw a lighting plan that includes a wiring layout and shows where you plan to place the transformer. Mount the transformer bracket and transformer where they can't easily be seen, such as at the back of the building, at least 12 inches above the ground and within 6 feet of a grounded electrical outlet. Attach the low-voltage cable to the transformer, turn it on, and stretch the cable to its full length.

Next, install the fixtures. If the ground is soft, you can just push the fixtures—ground stake first—into place. Otherwise, you may need to dig small holes for them. Don't try to hammer a fixture into place. After you insert a fixture, place soil or gravel around it. Then starting from the transformer, run the cable from fixture to fixture, leaving a little slack at each fixture.

With low-voltage cable, you have the flexibility of running it under bushes and along foundations, or burying it under wood chips or along the edges of walks or fences without using conduit. As a rule, however, it's best to use polyvinyl chloride (PVC) piping and bury it in a 6-inch trench. That helps prevent a lawn mower from damaging the wire.

To bury cable across a lawn, cut into the soil at a 45° angle. After you remove the soil, drop the cable into place and pack the soil on top of it. If concrete for a driveway or sidewalk hasn't been poured (new construction), lay a ¾-inch conduit across the walkway for the lighting cable. If you need to run cable under a walk or driveway, dig two parallel holes, one on each side of the width of the pavement. Dig the holes several inches deeper than the thickness of the pavement. Then use a pipe-to-hose attachment to attach a short length of pipe to a water hose. Push the pipe into a hole and turn the water on to make a tunnel under the pavement that connects the two holes. Attach the cable to the free end of the pipe and pull the cable through.

Connecting the cable is usually just a matter of sliding and snapping connectors into place. Typically, no splicing, soldering, or special tools are needed. Because the power is on, you can easily test the fixture connections as you go.

120-Volt lighting

A 120-volt lighting system will provide brighter light than a low-voltage system. The brighter light may be especially useful outside if you need to illuminate a large area. Installing a 120-volt system is more involved, and the materials are more expensive than those used in a low-voltage system.

Before you begin the installation, familiarize yourself with your local electrical code and get any required permits. You may have to draw up a plan and have it reviewed by your local building inspector before you're allowed to install 120-volt lighting.

You'll need to decide what materials to use—receptacles, cables, switches, boxes, conduit, conduit fittings, wire connectors, and so on. Your local code may have already made some of those decisions for you. You may have to use rigid metal conduit rather than PVC conduit, for instance; or you may be restricted to using only certain types of wire.

The easiest way to install new lighting is to tap into an existing fixture or receptacle or junction box that's part of the 120-volt circuit. Make sure it isn't part of a 240-volt circuit. (For information on testing circuits, see Chapter 4.) Look for an outlet that has two cables entering it, a hot supply wire uninterrupted by a switch. (A junction box may have only switch-controlled wires.)

Before you tap into an existing power supply, turn off the power at the service panel or fuse box. Remove a knockout from the electrical box, and install a new cable connector. Insert a new cable into the box. Use wire connectors to connect the new cable's black wire to another black wire, white wire to another white wire, and bare copper ground wire to another bare copper ground wire (or to the green wires). Then run the wire to the place where you plan to install the fixture.

Industrial Security Lighting

Designing a good lighting scheme is partly a science and partly an art. If you were to never visit a place and only use computer software to create the lighting, it wouldn't be as good as it could be with a human eye surveying the scene. When you make a personal judgment of lighting needs, you can also consider any objects that may affect the lighting and the special needs of the people who will be using the light. Here are some sound general principles to follow for designing effective security lighting:

As with residential lighting, good industrial security lighting doesn't always mean a lot of light. In some cases, you may want a flood of extremely bright light to come on, such as in response to an alarm system being triggered. That kind of light can be helpful in stunning an intruder for a moment while guards get to him or her.

Outdoor (or exterior) lighting at night is important for security. Some people believe the myth that such lighting makes a home or business less secure by attracting thieves. The belief is that the security measure will make thieves think that the home or business must have a lot of valuables. But that's nonsense, because burglars don't pick targets in that way. Studies have shown that burglars prefer easy targets to hard ones.

Of course, lighting alone doesn't stop intruders. It's just one factor. As a rule, however, intruders would rather attempt a break-in without being seen than attempt one where they're likely to be seen.

Although motion-activated lighting, or *trigger lighting,* can be great for residential use, it's less helpful for outdoor industrial use. Intruders can exploit the lighting to figure out how to defeat the security system. They can keep purposely triggering it, to study how the guards or police respond. For businesses, exterior lighting should be on continuously from dusk to dawn.

Another reason for continuous lighting is that triggered lighting has to come on quickly, which limits the choice of lamps to tungsten or fluorescent, rather than the more economical HID lamps (which take longer to come on).

Closed-Circuit Television Systems

Due to improved technology in recent years, next to biometrics, closed-circuit television (CCTV) is the fastest-growing segment in the electronic security industry. Part 1 of this chapter is an overview of the CCTV market and the components of a system. Part 2 delves into the past, present, and future of digital cameras, video transmission options, and pan and tilts.

Part 1: Overview of CCTV Market

CCTV Basics

CCTV systems can allow several areas, such as elevators, entrances, exits, parking lots, lobbies, and cash handling areas, to be monitored constantly. The systems can also be used by businesses to keep watch on multiple areas at once. With enough cameras, the business can simultaneously watch for intruders, shoplifters, and dishonest employees throughout the premises (see Figure 9.1).

Figure 9.1   Using a monitor station, a business can watch for many potential problems at once. (*Courtesy of Winsted Corp.*)

When combined with intruder alarm system components, a CCTV can deter and detect crime as well as keep a company's security costs to a minimum.

In its *2001 Report on the CCTV/Video Surveillance Market,* J. P. Freeman Company studied technology trends, dealer and systems integrator forecasts, and video market share and growth rate through 2005. Users that dealers expect to increase between 2001 and 2005 include proprietor video systems, which received 4.1 points based on a 5-point scale. Installing video cameras for retailers to monitor shoppers also ranked high on the list at 3.6. Systems integrators saw the sales and service potential of CCTVs differently. While they still rank CCTV at the top of their list of importance with a 4.6 rating, asset tracking is a rapidly growing area with a 3.5 rating. More and more these days, cameras are being used to monitor assets, instead of just people. Video conferencing is a slower potential growth market among systems integrators, with a rating of 3.5.

To begin selling and installing CCTV systems, you don't need to be an electrical engineer. Although few alarm technicians can handle the large multiplex systems used in airports and banks, most CCTV systems used in small offices, stores, and apartments are easy to install. Many CCTV systems come preassembled as a complete package.

It's still important for you, the security professional, to have a basic understanding of each of the components you'll be working with. That lets you be more helpful to your customers—which can mean greater profits for you. The most basic CCTV system consists of one video camera connected by a cable to a video monitor (or television). A sophisticated system can incorporate a wide variety of controllers, cameras, lenses, housings, and recording devices, and can be tied into an alarm system.

Cameras

There are two main types of CCTV cameras: vacuum tube (or *tube*) and solid-state charge-coupled device (CCD), or *chip.* (See Figure 9.2.) Tube cameras are inexpensive, but have a short life span. CCD cameras not only last longer, but also provide better resolution and adapt better to varying light conditions. As a rule, CCD cameras are a much better value than their tube counterparts.

Cameras come in color and in black and white (or *monochrome*). Black-and-white models are less expensive and are better for outdoor and low-light applications. Less light is needed to see a scene through a black-and-white camera. Color cameras have the advantage of showing more natural-looking scenes. They're necessary when making color distinctions is critical.

One critical consideration in choosing a CCTV camera is the camera's ability to produce usable images in low-light conditions. A minimum of 1.5 to 2 lux (lx) is normal for color cameras and 0.01 lx for black-and-white models. Another important consideration is *resolution,* which is the ability of the camera to reproduce images with as many details as possible. Resolution is expressed in TV lines (abbreviated as TVL): 330 to 460 TVL for color and 380 to 580 TVL for monochrome are normal.

Figure 9.2 A ⅓-inch c/s-mount lens CCD camera. (*Courtesy of Ultrak, Inc.*)

Another consideration in camera selection is the *signal-to-noise ratio (s/n)*, which is stated in decibels (abbreviated as dB). A camera with a 52-dB *s/n* specification will produce a better picture than one with a 40-dB *s/n* specification. An *s/n* ratio of 47 to 50 dB for color and 50 dB for monochrome is normal. This specification becomes more apparent under low-light conditions where "noise" or "snow" may enter the picture due to a lack of scene illumination.

Cameras can be overt or covert. Overt models are designed to let people know that perhaps they are being watched. Some are styled to attractively blend into a home or business environment. Covert models are designed to go unnoticed. Some covert models have been built into common items such as working wall clocks, radios, smoke detectors, and exit signs. Various covert cameras are shown in Figure 9.3.

Lenses

A CCTV camera needs a lens that focuses light from the scene being watched onto the camera imager, to convert the image to an electric video signal. Lenses are configured with different "speeds," or the amount of light that is allowed to enter through the lens. Speeds are given in *f-stop* numbers, which indicate the ability of the lens to transmit light from the scene. The smaller the *f*-stop number, the "faster" the lens and the more light that's allowed to pass through. Fast lenses can operate at lower light levels than slow lenses. For a fixed lens *f*-1.2 to *f*-1.4 is normal; for an adjustable or *zoom* lens *f*-1.4 to *f*-1.8 is normal.

> **Legal Tip**
>
> Generally it's legal to covertly videotape areas where there is no reasonable expectation of privacy, but audio recordings often require consent of one or more of the parties.

Figure 9.3 Covert cameras can be installed in many different items. (*Courtesy of Ultrak, Inc.*)

The focal length of a lens determines its viewing angle. Focal lengths are measured in millimeters (abbreviated as mm). The lower the focal length number, the wider and higher the field of view, and vice versa. Lenses are configured as *fixed focal length* (fixed lens) or as adjustable focal length (zoom lenses).

The required focal length (or magnification) of a lens to produce the desired field of view is determined by calculating (in feet) the width and height of the required viewing area as well as the distance from the mounting position of the camera to the viewing area. Because lenses are manufactured for different camera imager sizes, the formula for calculating the lens focal length for each imager size will vary. Many lens manufacturers have "field of view" calculators available.

Pan/Tilt/Zoom units

Cameras can be mounted on remotely movable platforms called *pan/tilt units* so that the camera can be used to view many different areas. These cameras are usually equipped with a zoom lens as well. Figures 9.4 and 9.5 show pan/tilt units. (More details on pan/tilt units are given in part two of this chapter.)

Housing

Special housings are available to protect cameras from such things as vandalism, weather, dust, and dirt. The housings can make the camera installation look nicer and help make the camera less noticeable. Figure 9.6 shows some housings. Accessories incorporated into housings include heaters, hoods, and

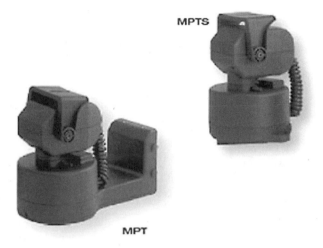

Figure 9.4   Indoor pan and tilts. (*Courtesy of Ultrak, Inc.*)

Figure 9.5   An outdoor pan and tilt unit. (*Courtesy of Ultrak, Inc.*)

lens-cover wipers. Housings are generally made of metal or high-impact plastic. The National Electrical Manufacturers Association (NEMA) rates camera housings on their ability to withstand environmental conditions.

Figure 9.6   Housings protect cameras from weather and vandalism. (*Courtesy of Ultrak, Inc.*)

Speed domes

A recent development for the pan/tilt/zoom (PTZ) camera is the integrated *speed dome*. It combines a color or color/monochrome/frame integrating camera, a zoom lens, and a high-speed pan/tilt unit into an attractive indoor or exterior dome case. A dome case (or *dome*) is a dark-colored Plexiglas housing. Someone looking up at it can't tell where the camera is pointed. As a cost-saving measure, domes can be augmented with *drones,* which look like domes but have no equipment inside. The mixture of domes and drones can be a cost-effective way of giving the appearance of more coverage. Figure 9.7 shows a dome.

The PTZ camera is a high-resolution (usually better than 470 TVL) color camera that changes to black and white when the light level drops below that needed for good-quality color; then it goes into a frame integration where up to seven frames are combined to make one image. It is similar to a time exposure on a conventional film camera. Infrared illumination can be used with these cameras in the monochrome mode.

Monitors

Like cameras, monitors are available in color and in black and white. If you don't use a color camera, there's no need to use a color monitor. (See Figure 9.8.) To view a scene in color, both the monitor and the camera have to be color models. Some monitors include a built-in switcher, which lets you automatically or manually view scenes from multiple cameras. As with televisions, monitor size is based on the diagonal measurement of the tube. Typical monitor sizes are 9, 12, 14, 17, 19, and 21 inches. Except for special situations, it's best not to use a screen smaller than 9 inches because the screen will be hard to see.

(a)

(b)

Figure 9.7 Domes are attractive ways to house cameras. (*Courtesy of Ademco.*)

In some installations a television is used as a monitor. That's often the case in small installations. Also some apartment complexes have their cameras set up to let tenants turn to a certain television channel from their apartments to see certain monitored points of the building (such as entry points). That's cheaper than giving every tenant a monitor. (Chapter 11 describes an access control system that uses tenant televisions as monitors.)

Although a television can be used as a monitor, the picture quality isn't as good as that of a CCTV monitor. The CCTV monitor has higher lines of resolution and accepts only video signals (no radio-frequency or antenna signals) for better picture quality. The higher the resolution, the better the picture. A typical television in the United States has 525 lines of resolution. (In Europe, where the programmable array logic (PAL) format is used, typical televisions have 625 lines of resolution.) A closed-circuit television may have more than 1000 lines.

Figure 9.8   A monitor generally shows better resolution than televisions. (*Courtesy of Ultrak, Inc.*)

Video recorders

A CCTV system has limited value if it can't record select events. Two basic types of video recorders are videotape and digital videotape.

Switchers

A video switcher lets the images from different cameras be switched to different monitors for viewing and recording. In a small system, a manual switcher lets users choose the camera they want to see by pressing a button.

A sequential switcher, which is the most popular type, has circuitry that switches from one camera scene to another automatically. The operator can set the *dwell time,* which is the length of time that a scene remains on the monitor, before moving automatically to the next camera's scene. This lets operators keep tabs on multiple cameras with one monitor. The downside is that it also creates *switcher dilemma.*

Imagine a system with, say, 10 cameras, each set to switch after dwelling on a camera's scene for 5 seconds. There will be a big gap between the time when the first image appears on the monitor and the time when the tenth image is displayed. If the dwell time is shortened, operators may not be able to get much from each image before the camera switches to another image. The problem is compounded when you are recording the scenes. When you play the scenes back, you may see a door closing on camera 1, then see another scene of a person's back on camera 2, followed by short scenes from all the other cameras. When the videotape gets back to the first scene, the door may have closed without your ever having seen who came in.

Digital quad

A digital quad lets you view and record up to four cameras on one screen at one time. Playback of recorded tape is in four-quadrant format.

Multiplexer

Unlike conventional recording systems, a video multiplexer (or *mux,* for short) quickly sequences full-screen images through each camera for recording purposes and allows single- or multiple-camera formats for viewing. (See Figure 9.9.) Operators have the option of replaying sequentially from any one camera or from multiple cameras.

Multiplexers also can record all cameras in the system onto a single videotape. The cameras are recorded sequentially at a high rate of speed. As mentioned earlier, a standard video signal is comprised of 30 separate frames each second. In a video system containing 15 cameras, the multiplexer selects two frames from each camera and records them to a single videotape. The result is an effective frame rate of 2 frames per second, instead of the standard 30.

Most multiplexers today contain a motion detection feature that enables the system to record more frames of video from cameras showing motion than from those not showing any motion. The multiplexer does this by reallocating frames from one camera to another as needed. The net result is higher-quality recordings of scenes that are more likely to be important to security personnel.

Figure 9.9 A multiplexer organizes the recording order. (*Courtesy of Ultrak, Inc.*)

Video Transmission

There are several ways to transmit the camera video scene output to a monitoring or control center. Coaxial cable, fiber-optic cable, microwave, wireless or radio-frequency (RF) transmission, and more recently, your existing office local-area network (LAN) are a few of the most common.

Another option is transmission over standard telephone lines. Telephone line transmission, however, will cause a delay in scene video reproduction at the monitoring end and is often referred to as *slow scan.* When using this type of transmission, you run the danger of not seeing or recording a critical moment of an alarm event as well as causing operator fatigue from viewing jerky-appearing scenes similar to those in movies of the 1920s.

Coaxial cable, the most common form of video transmission, consists of two conductors: a solid inner conductor and a woven outer copper braid. Both conductors are used for video transmission. The woven braid also acts as a shield against unwanted signals that might adversely affect the video signal. The more wire strands in the braid, the better.

For CCTV applications, copper conductors are needed. Cable using aluminum foil braid or foil wrap may distort the video signal, especially over long cable runs, and is not recommended for use with CCTV systems.

Questions for review

1. What format is shown through recorded playback of digital quad?

2. What is a multiplexer?

3. What does a video switcher do?

4. Why is the picture shown through a television not as sharp as one shown through the same size of monitor?

5. What are three common uses for closed-circuit television systems?

Part 2: Digital Cameras, Pans and Tilts, and Video Transmission Options

Digital Cameras—Yesterday, Today, and Tomorrow
by Charlie Pierce

Digital camera technology opens up new worlds of visual interaction, but buyer beware. Are you old enough to remember the hype surrounding digital effects when they were first introduced in the movies? I am! I specifically remember wondering just what *digital effects* meant. The same thing has been happening to the video camera. Over the past 10 years, it has gone from the basic tube technology that started the digital motor running, to the charged-coupled device, which slammed it into third gear. Digital technology is nothing new; it is actually more than 30 years old. The effect it is having on the development and application of the video camera, however, is just beginning. Since the move to the CCD, digital interfacing has been taken to new heights, opening up new worlds of visual interaction.

First came the CCD

The first and most obvious effect of the digital revolution on cameras came when the tube walked out the door, and the CCD ran in. Although the original CCD cameras were a great innovation, they left a lot to be desired, including two of the singularly important features of security video cameras—resolution and sensitivity. Also, because the rules and wording of the CCTV game had changed, many people spent thousands of dollars on the new cameras without understanding the language that described them. Consequently, many of these pioneering users felt cheated. Buyer beware of new technology. If you don't understand the language used or the general differences between what you have and what you are getting, learn early, fast, and before you spend your money.

One of the original digital options was the ability to control the "electronic" shutter speed of the CCD. Shutter speed normally refers to how fast a mechanical shutter will open and close, exposing standard film to a given amount of light. In video cameras, however, electronic shutter speed refers to the amount of time that the CCD is left turned on. It is a form of electronic light control, and it was the first step toward developing a camera that required no auto-iris under adverse lighting conditions. This control started out as a manual adjustment and was adapted to automatic application very quickly.

Then came digital zoom

As the world turned, however, electronic shuttering was replaced with supplemental, after-the-fact electronic signal enhancement techniques. Digital zoom, another attempt to replace the lens, came down the video enhancement path right at the beginning. Digital zoom takes an existing image and explodes a portion of it. Imagine laying an invisible grid over a 12-inch by 9-inch image, creating grid squares of 1 inch by 1 inch. Pick any area within the grid that is eight squares wide and three squares tall. Explode this grid area, and fill the screen. You have now digitally zoomed in on the image.

The downside of digital zoom, however, was an extreme loss of resolution. It is one thing to come closer to an image; it is another to blow up a bunch of squares. What good was making an image larger, if you couldn't tell what it was after a given amount of expansion? Early digital zoom efforts were clumsy and ineffective for the security industry. The good news is that, after years of experimentation and a whole lot of creative technology, digital zoom enhancements are now available with incredible accuracy and resolution. We still work from the same grid theory, but now built-in computers average and smooth the gaps between grid squares, creating very sharp close-ups of far-away images without an expensive lens. Buyer beware: Test all zoom claims personally before investing, to ensure you are not purchasing the older, clumsy technology. As for worries about whether such images hold up in a courtroom (because they are digitally enhanced), have no fear. Since the enhancements are automatic and take place at the image's point of origin, there is no room for personal or secondary alterations. Therefore, the image is considered original and unmodified.

Video motion detection

Video motion detection is another great option that suddenly became available, built into the camera. No longer did we need a black box interface to determine whether there was motion within an image, creating an alarm. Now we had cameras that could be pointed and programmed to detect motion within their scope of view. Motion detection could be activated or deactivated at the camera, at the controller (on an individual basis), or on a timer, depending on the camera and interactive controlling system. This greatly improved the integration of video systems with security. Not only do such cameras detect motion, but also some highlight the area that is moving with an overlaid white square or rectangle. In this way, the person viewing the alarm-causing image can see the point of alarm quickly and efficiently.

Video motion detection works on the basis of contrast change. Again, lay an imaginary grid over your image. You have only to look for a change in the brightness of any square, and you have contrast change. The sensitivity of motion detection depends on the total number of grid squares that must change and on how much difference from the original brightness of the grid square is detected before an alarm is activated. Buyer beware: These cameras are best used in fixed, indoor environments. Even in the newer, more sophisticated cameras, built-in video motion detection is still very simple. This form of video motion detection is not desirable for use outside or in areas that can have drastic and sudden light changes. There are too many potential false alarms outside. If you are looking for sophisticated motion detection, you still need to use a separate digital video motion detection unit that interfaces with your camera system.

Menu-driven programmability

Another digital enhancement to cameras that came onto the scene early was menu-driven programmability. With the push of a button, a whole menu of programmable options shows up on the screen, such as indoor, outdoor, and fluorescent lighting setup for color cameras; the ability to turn on the automatic light control circuit to enhance dark shadows; and auto-iris override, giving the operator the ability to open or close the iris manually from the camera or the controller. Buyer beware: In many cases, some of the options available for manual override or programming are not something you want your operators to be able to do during their shift. There are still some things better left alone and for automated decisions.

Seeing into light and dark simultaneously

Seeing into light and dark simultaneously was another task that was left for the human eye alone. Cameras could not handle this function until recently, primarily because the art of light control was left to the iris on the lens. If the iris closed down to compensate for a bright area, the shadows in the scene became deeper. If the lens opened to compensate for a darker area, the bright spots became unbearable and washed out. We had been up against the proverbial wall for 30 years when it came to seeing someone standing in front of a glass door or window. It just couldn't be done—until digital cameras. Watec was the first to develop a camera with near-human eye quality sight into bright and dark areas simultaneously. It did so by concentrating on the video signal after it was created by the CCD. Toning down the bright areas and amplifying the dark points of the scene, Watec developed the *electronic iris*. The problem? This technology is only available on a few select cameras. Panasonic recently took the lead by developing a completely different approach to this age-old problem. By using electronic shuttering techniques, two pictures are taken simultaneously. One image is taken at ¹⁄₆₀ second to see into the dark areas of a scene; the other image is taken at ¹⁄₁₀,₀₀₀ second to see into the bright areas of a scene. The two images are then digitally combined, and the result is a very clear, sharp image of human eye equivalence. Panasonic calls the design *superdynamic*—a fitting enough name. Buyer beware: Since there are no standards for terminology in the CCTV industry, carefully investigate exactly what you are buying. Every vendor has its own labels for its technology. What one vendor calls electronic iris another may call electronic shuttering. Consequently, you must know the manufacturer and the details underlying its terminology. In the end, a complete test or demonstration of different manufacturers is advisable prior to making a big-bucks investment. The rule of thumb is: If it gives you the image you need under the circumstances you have, use it.

Today and tomorrow

Just how far are we from the perfect, completely digital camera that will do it all? We are on the road, but we have a long way to go. For today's small systems, the sophistication of digitally enhanced cameras is such that they offer many functions and features which, in the past, either were restricted to big controlling interfaces or were too cost-prohibitive. Today's large systems now offer operators greater control over individual and group functions and features from a single point of operation. As for the future, I believe that soon we will see a completely digital camera that requires no lens, no setup, nothing. Just mount it on a wall, point, and walk away. You want it to pan across an area? Set the digital screen for the exact area that you want panned, and there you go. You want to zoom in or out? Push a button and digitally take care of the job. You need to see into a shadow? Push a button, and suddenly the shadow is gone. But buyer beware: Not all digital technology is fully proven before it is thrown onto the market. Don't feel foolish for requesting an in-field demonstration. Remember to verify warranty conditions, and ask about serviceability. It will not do you much good to purchase 100 wonder cameras only to find that if one fails, it will have to go to Japan to be repaired. It is equally bad if the unit you buy today will be discontinued a month or two after it is delivered. Choose your digital enhancements and applications carefully, and you will enjoy the results for years to come.

Pan and Tilt Technology
by Jerry L. Jacobson, Ph.D.

The current capabilities of pan/tilt devices must be well understood by the system designer and end user in order for the system to perform as expected. Everyone knows how sophisticated the front end of a security system can be, with the multitude of functions and the clever on-screen controls operated by mouse or touch screen. At the far end of the system things are changing, too, including the old standby of CCTV systems—the pan and tilt drive.

The basic function of a pan and tilt is simple: It swivels horizontally (panning) and vertically (tilting) in order to bring the camera to bear on a subject within its viewing area. In its simplest form, control of these actions is carried out by an operator pressing buttons or moving a joystick that routes power to the pan and tilt motors. In its earliest incarnations, this was its limit.

The current capabilities of these devices must be well understood by the system designer and end user so that the system, once installed, performs as expected. Some early pan and tilt uses have become obsolete, but the thinking associated with them still influences users' expectations and, to some extent, limits the overall effectiveness of their CCTV systems.

No matter how many extras are added to a pan and tilt, pointing the camera remains its basic function. Most models move at a fixed, relatively slow speed that allows the scene to remain in reasonably good focus while the camera moves. These speeds ensure more accurate final positioning with fewer readjustments, but a faster-moving subject might get away from a camera mounted on such a pan and tilt.

Variable-speed drives address this requirement by providing a range of operating speeds, allowing the operator to follow a fast-moving subject or to move slowly when needed. Currently, variable-speed drives range from less than 1° per second to more than 100° per second. Drives with fixed high speeds have less value since the images deteriorate. Speeds above about 20° per second produce an unintelligible image, so they are most useful for fast preset-position acquisition. The effect of fast speeds can be demonstrated dramatically by recording an image from a camera on a fast panning drive and then playing the image back on still frame.

Variable speed is achieved with alternating-current (ac) motors, dc motors, or stepping motors, and the three types have some important differences. The dc units require less expensive controls; basically, the speed is proportional to the load and to the input voltage level. Lowering the input voltage slows the speed, and vice versa. However, dc motors generate radio-frequency noise that can affect the video signal quality. Variable-speed ac motors do not have the RF noise problem, but they require an electric control interface that adds considerably to the cost. The dc motors have an additional problem: The contact brushes that provide current to the rotating armature of the motor wear out and have to be replaced. Today, most constant-speed pan and tilt drives use ac motors to avoid the problems associated with dc motors.

A stepping motor has begun to appear in pan and tilt drives. It can provide variable-speed operation with less expensive control circuits than those required by variable-speed ac motors, and it does not have the RF noise problem or the brush replacement problem of dc motors.

Range of pan motion

There really is only one significant distinction in pan and tilt drives regarding range of motion: units with or without slip rings. The vast majority of drives can pan over a range of 350° to 355°, which meets most system requirements. These units have a permanent pan limit stop that prevents movement beyond this range. This limited rotation is imposed by the wiring that brings electric power to the tilt motors in the upper mobile part of the drive. It is usually achieved by a coil cord, which looks exactly like a coiled telephone handset cord. A coil cord can be flexed many times over a limited range without breaking; but it can't be turned continuously in one direction, or it will soon knot up and tear loose.

This mechanical arrangement has a drawback in some applications. If a subject moves through the dead zone created by the permanent pan limit stop, the drive has to be reversed through almost a full circle to pick up the subject again. During this time, the subject will be out of view for a considerable time. This problem can be eliminated by a drive which can pan continuously in either direction.

Such pan and tilt drives are available and use a device called a *slip ring assembly* to achieve continuous rotation. To visualize a slip ring, place your right forefinger on a ring on your left hand. Your forefinger is a spring-loaded contact that slides on the ring. If your finger could rotate continuously, the electrical connection between the ring and the contact would remain unbroken, no matter how many revolutions were made.

The slip ring assembly can transfer motor power, camera power, lens control signals, preset feedback, and video between the moving head and the fixed base of the drive; and this may require more than 20 contact rings in the slip ring assembly. Slip ring assemblies are expensive, so continuous-rotation pan and tilts cost significantly more than the limited-rotation versions.

Range of tilt motion

The range of tilt motion is a simpler issue. Many units offer a tilt range of $\pm90°$, from straight up to straight down. Drives with the heaviest load capacity often are limited to $\pm60°$ or a similar figure, and a few specialized units may offer less.

The range of tilt motion is a simple issue, but it has one unique additional consideration—the torque effect of gravity on the pan and tilt's load. (The force of gravity is exerted uniformly in the pan function and doesn't require special attention.) If the load on a pan and tilt is well balanced, gravity pulls evenly on the load and there is no unbalanced torque as long as the tilt head is level. When the load is tilted up or down, it pulls unevenly to one side and the torque effect of the load is magnified. The unbalanced torque is a minimum at zero tilt and a maximum at $\pm90°$.

Well-designed medium- and heavy-duty drives include either springs or counterweights or both to reduce the torque effects of tilting. Light-duty or less expensive medium- or heavy-duty units may not have these features. All other things being equal, it is reasonable to expect a longer service lifetime from pan and tilts with these features because the forces on the tilt drive are more balanced.

Autopanning

Autopanning occurs when the head of the pan and tilt (or scanner) pans continuously back and forth over an angle selected by the system owner. Generally, the autopan range is set by positioning two movable pan limit stops, although in more sophisticated units the limits may be set electronically. Autopanning is something of a dinosaur. In the earlier days of CCTV, the camera and lens assembly was a very expensive part of the system, and one camera had to cover as much area as possible to be economically effective—thus the need for autopanning. Even then, however, there were some factors that reduced the effectiveness of surveillance using autopanning.

If the camera is in motion, then, to the operator, the scene or background is in motion. An object moving against a moving background is much less likely to be noticed, especially if the object is moving slowly. If this is combined with the dulling of the operator's senses that develops as the duty period wears on, there is a high likelihood that some important security breach may go unnoticed. Also, if a person or object moves at the same rate as the camera, an illusion of non-movement is created, regardless of the fact that the background is moving. You can demonstrate this for yourself with a camera in the autopan mode, a VCR, and a monitor. Just walk at a speed that matches the pan speed of the camera, then look at the tape.

With camera prices having dropped drastically, it makes more sense to put two or three cameras on fixed mounts to oversee the same area that formerly would have been covered by a single autopanning camera. The overall effectiveness of the surveillance will be greatly increased.

Random panning has one obvious feature in common with autopanning: The motion of the drive unit is automatic. The similarity ends there. In random panning, the drive unit moves a random distance in one direction, stops, and moves again. For the person watching, the problems are similar to those for autopanning. The main advantage of random panning is at the other end, in front of the camera. The random movement of the camera is supposed to be interpreted by an intruder as indicating that the camera is under the active control of a security person. If this ruse works, the intruder may be dissuaded.

Preset-position operation

Today, greater use is being made of *preset-position operation,* which is the ability of a pan and tilt drive to return automatically to a specific scene within its overall field of view. To achieve this, the drive unit must be united with a control device, usually digital, which "remembers" a programmed combination of pan angle and tilt angle. The position information may be provided either electrically by potentiometers (specialized variable resistors) or optically. Whichever method is used, the pan and tilt angles of each programmed scene are retained in memory.

The quality of the pan and tilt drive becomes a significant issue with preset operation. For accurate acquisition of a preset scene, the drivetrain of the pan and tilt must have precise gearing with a minimum of play or backlash. A sloppier unit may be adequate for manual operation; but if a given preset recall repeatedly displays a slightly different scene, the preset function loses effectiveness.

Since a camera on a pan and tilt drive almost always has a motorized zoom lens, it follows that a lens on a pan and tilt with preset capability also will have preset capability. The lens will have potentiometers or optical encoders for the zoom and focus settings, which allows the exact angle of view of the scene to be programmed as well as the focus settings for the specific subject of interest. The iris mechanism usually is controlled independently by an auto-iris circuit or by a combination manual and auto-iris arrangement.

A preset position may be recalled manually by an operator or automatically. In the manual mode, the operator decides to view some scene and presses one or two buttons, and the camera automatically moves to the scene. Although this is manual recall, the process is more precise and probably faster than if the operator had panned and tilted and zoomed and focused manually to the same scene. But the full advantages of preset operation are obtained in conjunction with alarm operation and in camera touring.

Let's say that within the viewing area of a pan and tilt are two alarmed doors, two alarmed windows, and a driveway exit. Each has been programmed into the control central processing unit (CPU) as a preset position for the drive unit and for the zoom and focus settings of the lens. The alarm device on each subject is connected to the CPU via an alarm interface or a host computer. The CPU is programmed to associate each alarm device with a specific preset, so that when an alarm goes active, the camera is automatically directed to view that scene. At the same time, a VCR will start recording the scene, probably in the real-time, 2-hour mode. With the latest technology, the CPU can be programmed to display on the monitor screen a title specific to the selected preset, in addition to the usual camera identification.

If the installation is very sophisticated, combining alarms, presets, and a variable-speed drive, the drive will move at high speed to acquire the preset scene and then will slow down for the last few degrees of movement before it locks on its target. At the same time that the pan and tilt is solving the preset, various auxiliary equipment, such as lighting and locks, can be programmed to go active. The most advanced control systems also provide an acknowledge preset, which is a preset position to which the camera returns after the alarm is acknowledged. Such controllers allow auxiliary functions to be programmed to activate or deactivate on acknowledgment.

Preset-position operation also is required for guard tour operation of a CCTV security system. A CCTV guard tour simulates its namesake by displaying on a monitor a succession of scenes that represent the locations that a walking guard might visit on rounds. CCTV touring takes two forms; one is merely a new term for an old function, and the other makes good use of the capabilities of modern CPU-based controllers and pan and tilt drives. Some companies offer a form of guard tour that is, in fact, merely a variety of sequential switching. This is called *video touring,* and it consists of the display of different scenes from different cameras on the monitor.

The other type of CCTV touring is *camera touring,* and it requires cameras on pan and tilt drives with preset positioning and motorized zoom lenses with presets, combined with a CPU. A fully programmed camera tour can include a variety of different preset scenes from one or more cameras interspersed with each other with variable dwell time (duration of the scene on the monitor) and individual preset scene titling. The sequence of the tour has complete flexibility in programming in regard to scene viewed, duration, and frequency of repetition in the overall tour plan.

The basic pan and tilt drive has not changed much over the years, but there have been some changes in materials and in what one might call style. Recent pan and tilt designs are taking greater advantage of modern polymers. The tendency to associate plastic with the adjectives *cheap* and *inadequate* can mislead us into making judgments about modern products using today's polymers. It is not unusual for these materials to outlast metal equivalents, and they do not corrode.

On the other hand, we are seeing the introduction of pan and tilts with new shapes and configurations. There is a certain amount of freshness to these designs since the basic functions remain unchanged. Some of the newest units have a classy molded exterior with nothing exceptional inside. The overriding factors in choosing a pan and tilt must remain the functional considerations: Will it do what I want it to, and will it last?

One new type of pan and tilt for which there is a growing market is the teleconferencing pan and tilt drive. Because these are used in environments where audio also is being transmitted or recorded, noise must be kept to a minimum. In addition, extreme smoothness of motion and very precise gearing with the smallest possible backlash are necessary for teleconferencing. Finally, many teleconferencing drives are designed to have a very low profile. These units typically are used with a preset-position controller with a large preset capacity.

The major changes in pan and tilt drives in recent years have been more in the area of control systems than in the drives themselves. The basic function, which is to point a camera in a certain direction, has not changed; but modern controllers have made this pointing function a much more versatile part of modern surveillance systems. New materials, including polymers and stepping motors, probably can be expected to improve performance and longevity. The pan and tilt drive will have a secure place in CCTV for a long time to come.

Fiber-Optic Cable
by Al Colombo

Although coaxial cable is probably the most widely used and most accepted form of video transmission today, it is slowly losing ground to its fiber-optic counterpart. One very good reason for this is the wider bandwidth realized by fiber-optic cable.

Although fiber-optic cable is not new, its use in the CCTV market is relatively recent. Fiber-optic cable is now being used to transport both video and audio signals for short and long distances. This is made possible by modulating the video/audio signal(s) onto a beam of coherent light, which is generated by a solid-state laser. The modulated light is then passed through a single, minutely small strand of nearly pure glass fiber. Because this method uses light to carry the intelligence, data can be carried up to 3 miles or even more without utilizing a repeater of any kind.

In many ways, a fiber-optic cable looks like a smaller version of a coaxial cable, until you closely examine the connectors and what's inside. For example, inside the center of a fiber-optic cable is a nearly pure glass fiber. This center glass fiber (core) is protected by several layers of material.

The first layer nearest the core is called the cladding. Cladding is comprised of a less-than-pure film of glass. Although the core carries the major portion of the modulated light, and thus the intelligence, the cladding aids in the return of light that's commonly lost through refraction.

The final layer is usually referred to as the *jacket,* or *buffer.* The buffer is designed to absorb some of the physical shock encountered by the fiber-optic cable in its environment. This layer has no optical properties, but its sole purpose is actually to aid in the protection of the inner glass fiber layers.

Installers are using more fiber-optic cable than ever before. One reason is that there are more channels of communication over which to transmit video images, audio, and other data. This means more images on a single cable than is possible with metallic coaxial cable. Longer signal transmission distances are also possible with less signal attenuation using fiber-optic cable.

Fiber-optic cable is also unaffected by electromagnetic interference (EMI), like its metallic coaxial cable counterparts. It's also generally smaller in diameter than metallic coaxial cable, when it comes to the number of communication channels available. Signal transmission is also more secure using fiber-optic cable. This is because the signals traveling on a fiber-optic cable do not emit electromagnetic radiation that someone can pick up with a EM-sensitive device and use. This makes it more difficult to tap with the intent of eavesdropping. To do so in an unauthorized manner will also introduce extreme signal loss or even total signal disruption.

Fiber-optic cable has a wider signal frequency bandwidth than its metallic coaxial cable counterpart. This means more available channels of communication. For example, metallic coaxial cable has an effective bandwidth of 10 MHz. By comparison, fiber-optic cable has an effective bandwidth of 44.6 MHz/km. This means an effective potential of more than 670 simultaneous telephone conversations over one glass fiber.

Fiber-optic cable can also carry light-modulated signals for longer distances than metallic coaxial cable because there's less signal attenuation. Metallic coaxial cable experiences a higher degree of signal attenuation because of the inductive and capacitive properties of the wire that carries the video signal. The very nature of a metallic coaxial cable causes a higher degree of attenuation than fiber-optic cable. Fiber-optic cable, however, experiences far less attenuation because glass fibers offer little resistance to the passage of light. In fiber-optic cable, it's more a matter of glass fiber purity that determines the degree of attenuation.

How to choose the right fiber-optic cable

To gauge the quality of a fiber-optic cable, engineers use a mathematical property called the *refractive index*. The refractive index of a fiber-optic cable is expressed as a ratio. It is determined by measuring the difference between the speed of light in a vacuum and the speed of light through a particular medium, such as a fiber-optic cable.

To prove the validity of this principle, one has only to pass white light through a prism. The result is the refraction of all the colors. The light that escapes through the other end is then separated into the basic colors of the rainbow: red, orange, yellow, green, blue, and violet. Because the wavelength of each color is different, these colors are viewed separately as they exit the prism. The wavelength of red is shorter than that of orange, for example, so the angle of refraction is also less.

Internal reflection is another factor that helps determine the quality of a fiber-optic cable. This property greatly minimizes the loss of light when the angle of refraction is equal to or greater than the critical angle. Thus, in better fiber-optic cables, nearly all the light transmitted is reflected back to the center of the fiber-optic cable. The glass cladding around the center glass core also helps to reflect some of the refracted light back toward the center of the fiber-optic cable.

Some types of fiber-optic cable also have the ability to transport more than one beam of light, or *mode*. A mode is simply the path that a beam of light takes as it travels inside a fiber-optic cable. There are several types of fiber-optic cables on the market today that can transport one to more than 1000 beams of light over multiple paths, or modes.

The number of modes that a fiber-optic cable can transport is determined by the size of the glass fiber and other factors that determine its capacity and quality.

Advancing Lens Technology and CCTV
by Robert A. Wimmer

A great deal of information has been presented on the advancements made by the surveillance camera industry. The introduction of digital signal processing (DSP) cameras, advancing camera features such as backlight compensation, automatic gain control (AGC), aperture correction, electronic sensitivity, and the like, has made great strides in enhancing the image quality of the surveillance market. But we cannot forget the other main part of any surveillance system, which plays a very important role in producing a quality image—and that is the lens. As you already know, the main purpose of any lens assembly is to focus the desired image on the faceplate of the charge-coupled device (CCD) sensor. However, enhancements of lens designs and features especially in the angles of lenses (measured in millimeters) drive assemblies of the auto-iris (video or dc), and the speed or *f*-stop rating of the lenses has also entered into the security market.

Enhancements in lens angles

Selecting the proper lens angle of view for many different applications can be challenging, to say the least. It always seems that once the camera system is installed, the customer is not satisfied with the camera viewing angles and/or wants to make changes to the system design. This is usually a cause for many headaches for both the installing technicians and the customer. Research shows that about 65 percent of all indoor camera applications usually incorporate a lens which is listed as either normal or wide-angle viewing. To help enhance, or in other words reduce frustration, the industry has developed what is known as a *varifocal* lens assembly. This lens group combines both a normal and a wide viewing angle into a single lens assembly. The same characteristics discussed for fixed-focal-length lenses are true for the varifocal lens. This lens helps to reduce inventory by allowing the installer more flexibility when trying to accurately set the desired angle of view for each customer. The normal viewing angle for varifocal length lenses is usually 30° with the widest angle being 60°.

Iris drive assemblies

Auto-iris lenses are required for all outdoor applications, and their basic function is to automatically control the opening and closing of the iris, allowing the proper amount of light to reach the camera's sensor. The earliest type was called the *video-controlled* auto-iris lens. In a video-controlled auto-iris lens, the lens requires two inputs. The first input is a positive dc voltage that operates the electronics and the iris motor. The second input is a video signal. This video input along with the internal electronic circuits of the lens controls the opening and closing of the iris. This internal control board made the lens assembly rather expensive. To enhance CCTV camera applications, the industry developed a lens known as the *dc-controlled* auto-iris lens. The difference between the two lies in how they accomplish this iris control. The dc-controlled auto-iris lenses do not have any internal electronic circuitry to control the iris opening, and therefore they must rely on the camera to supply this information. Since it is much less expensive to insert the components into the camera body than the lens, the price of the lens assembly can be reduced as much as 30 percent. This saving has greatly enhanced the overall cost of today's surveillance systems. As a final note, not all cameras have the auto-iris feature built in, so you must be careful when selecting any camera/lens combination.

Aspherical lenses

I believe that the latest and most challenging enhancement in today's lens selection is that of the aspherical lens. This form of lens is becoming very popular, especially as more and more customers turn to color cameras for nighttime surveillance. To fully understand the difference between spherical and aspherical lenses, we must start with what is called the *f*-stop rating of a lens assembly.

The *f*-stop

This section deals with the iris of a lens and how the lens can pass light. As the light becomes brighter, the iris of your eyes closes to allow only the proper amount of light to react in your retina to produce a quality image. It is the same with the lenses used in CCTV. However, a growing concern in lens selection is the minimum *f*-stop rating of the lens, or its light-gathering ability at low light levels. With the increased use of color for CCTV applications, this concern has become a very real issue. Even with advancing technology, color cameras require more light to produce the same quality picture as that of a black-and-white surveillance camera. It in this area that aspherical lenses has greatly enhance CCTV surveillance. But what is an aspherical lens, and how does it differ from the standard spherical lens which most of us are familiar with? To start, the *f*-stop rating of any lens is the ratio of the focal length to the lens diameter or the actual diameter of the iris opening.

$$f\text{-stop rating} = \frac{F \text{ (focal length, mm)}}{D \text{ (iris opening, mm)}}$$

The lower the *f*-stop rating of the lens, the "faster" the lens or the greater the light-gathering capability of the lens. The normal minimum *f*-stop rating of a spherical lens is between *f*-1.2 and *f*-1.8.

Lens manufacturers were able to produce faster spherical lenses (*f*-1.0) to meet the low-light requirement for color cameras; however, they had problems maintaining the optical performance at the widest opening of the lens, especially where illumination was dim. To overcome this, manufacturers have produced a lens whose curved surface does not conform to the shape of a sphere, thus it is known as aspherical.

Because an aspherical lens has less severe image aberrations and distortion than a normal spherical lens, the aspherical lens can be manufactured to offer higher light transmission factors. This new design also offers increased advantages over the older spherical lenses. (1) It offers higher definition of large-aperture lenses. (2) It corrects the distorted image associated with wide-angle lenses (commonly referred to as the fish-eye effect). (3) It offers more compact and higher-quality zoom lenses. As the cost and manufacturing methods keep improving, this design is starting to be incorporated into more and more of the elements found in today's zoom lenses.

All of the aforementioned enhancements found in today's lens industry have made a finite impact on the performance of any CCTV surveillance system. However, anyone working on applications involving low lighting levels should consider the use of low-*f* rated lenses. They do cost more than conventional lenses; however, the benefit of adding more light is well worth it, especially for nighttime color surveillance systems.

Smart Homes and Home Automation Systems

Although locks, light, sound, and other elements play a part in home security and safety, each must be controlled separately in most homes. By using a home automation system, occupants can make several of or all the systems and devices in a home work automatically to provide greater security, safety, and convenience. If the right attachments are used, all home automation systems can perform many of the same functions. However, there are important differences among the standards that affect system cost, reliability, and expansion options. Part 1 of this chapter gives an overview of the most common standards used for home automation systems: X-10, CEBus, LonWorks, and Smart House. Part 2 deals with Open Systems Architecture.

Part 1: Common Standards for Home Automation systems

X-10 Compatible Systems

The simplest and least expensive home automation systems use the X-10 standard, named after the company that developed it. The X-10 compatible modules need only to be plugged into any standard well outlet and programmed to match the code of the other X-10 compatible devices in the home. Each module is designed to control a specific appliance. One module may let you turn a light on and off from a remote location; another may automatically start your coffee pot at a certain time.

Because the modules are sold separately, you can use them to custom-design a home automation plan. The X-10 standard is so popular that hundreds of manufacturers of security and safety products advertise their products as being X-10 compatible.

One weakness of an X-10 system is that the components don't share memory. In effect, each component works independently of all the others. However, you can design a system that coordinates the functions of several X-10 components to give them the appearance of sharing memory. Another common problem with X-10 systems is that they're sensitive to home wiring line noise.

CEBus

The CEBus (Consumer Electronics Bus) standard (EIA-600) is a standard developed by the Electronic Industries Association (EIA) for connecting and operating consumer products in a home. The standard is media-independent; it can send signals over power lines, coaxial cable, and unshielded twisted pair (UTP) cable. It's also proprietary, meaning other manufacturers have to pay license fees to use the standard to make compatible devices. That tends to make devices more expensive than their open-architecture counterparts.

LonWorks

Based on a standard called *Echelon,* LonWorks is a media-independent system. The heart of the LonWorks system is a computer chip. The original one, called the *Neuron,* was developed by Toshiba and Motorola. But Echelon began allowing other chips to be used in the system's home and commercial control network.

Smart House Integrated System

One of the newest and most sophisticated home automation systems is the Smart House. Although the term *Smart House* is sometimes used to refer to many types of home automation systems, it's a brand name for a type of system. The Smart House integrates a unique wiring system and computer chip language to let all of a home's televisions, telephones, heating systems, security systems, and appliances communicate with one another and work together.

If your refrigerator has been left ajar, for instance, Smart House could signal your television set to show a picture of a refrigerator in the corner of the screen until you close the door. A smoke detector in the Smart House could signal your heating system to shut down during a fire. Its communication ability is one of the most important differences between Smart House and other home automation systems. The basic installation cost of a Smart House system is about the same as that of a power-line system, but with a Smart House system you have to buy special Smart House–compatible devices to use the system.

How the Smart House works

Smart House technology was the result of a joint effort of many appliance manufacturers, security system manufacturers, and home builders and electronics trade associations. All agreed on standards that allow special appliances to work in any Smart House.

A Smart House uses a system controller instead of a fuse panel and *Smart blocks* instead of standard electrical outlets. Appliances that are designed to work in a Smart House are called *Smart appliances*; all of them can be plugged into any Smart block. The same Smart block that you plug a television into can be used to plug in a telephone or coffeepot and other Smart appliances.

A big difference between standard electrical outlets and Smart blocks is that electricity is always present in the outlets. If you were to stick a metal pin into one of your standard electrical outlets, you would get a shock. If you were to stick a pin into a Smart block, you wouldn't get shocked because no electricity would be present. Only a device that has a special computer chip code can signal the Smart House system to release electricity to a particular Smart block—unless you override the signal.

With a Smart House you have the option of programming any of or all the Smart blocks to override their need for a code. That option lets you use standard appliances in your Smart blocks in much the same way as you use your electrical outlets now. Standard appliances can't communicate with one another or with other Smart appliances. Because the Smart House technology isn't widely used, few Smart appliances are available.

The Bill Gates Automated Home

Computer mogul Bill Gates calls his 5-acre home on the shore of Lake Washington, near Seattle, a "home of the future." It took over four years to build and cost an estimated $100 million.

The automated (and personnel-monitored) security/entertainment system is redundant. There are over 52 miles of communication cable, mostly fiber, on the property. Hidden cameras have been placed throughout the premises. Sensors in the floor can track a person to within 6 inches. The system is monitored at the Microsoft campus. Some interior doors weigh over 800 pounds and are balanced to make them easy to use. There are interior stone walls. The entry gate senses when a car approaches and, if it's authorized to enter, it opens fully by the time it arrives.

When you enter the home, you're given an electronic pin to clip to your clothes, reminiscent of the kind of pin worn on Star Trek. The pin keeps track of your location and can prompt changes in various rooms to suit your needs and tastes. When you walk into a room the music, art (digitized paintings), temperature, and other things will change to suit your taste. As you move around at night, lights behind you fade and lights in front of you brighten to provide a constant path. Unoccupied rooms remain dark until you enter. When you leave the room, lights automatically turn off.

Touchpads are conspicuously placed to let you manually change the art, music, temperature, lighting, and other features. The touchpads also let you create a personal profile, so that the next time you visit, the system will know what you like. Fiber communications cables run throughout the premises along with computers packed with Microsoft software.

Home automation controllers

With a Smart House or power-line system, you need only one controller to make the system do what you want. For convenience, however, people often prefer to have controllers installed at several locations. In addition to keypads, you can use telephones, computers, and touch screens for remote control of a system.

A touch screen looks like a large television that's mounted into a wall. It displays a menu of options, such as lighting, security, audio, video, and temperature controls, and you can make selections just by touching the screen. If you were to touch *security,* for instance, a blowup of the home's floor plan would appear on the screen so that you could see whether any windows or doors were left open, whether the alarm system is turned on or off, and other conditions related to security. You would also be able to secure various areas of the home just by touching the screen.

Questions for review

1. What is a touch screen?
2. What is one difference between a standard electrical outlet and a Smart block?
3. What standard is LonWorks based on?
4. What is a weakness, or shortcoming, of the X-10 system compared to the Smart House system?
5. What is a weakness or shortcoming of the Smart House system compared to the X-10 system?

Part 2: Open Systems Architecture: A New Paradigm for the Security Industry*

There is an increasingly active debate in the electronic security industry over the use of open versus closed systems architecture. While industry publishers, editors, consultants, and vendors continue to discuss the pros and cons of open systems, end users are demanding such systems. Although the computer and software industries unequivocally resolved this debate years ago in favor of open systems, the security industry still hasn't come to terms with it. There are two key reasons for this:

- Electronic security offerings are traditionally years behind the technological curve.
- Many system vendors like having proprietary systems with closed architecture. It allows them to control customers, keep their prices high, and avoid competition.

It is primarily for the second reason that most of the systems installed today are proprietary in nature. Specifically, this means they have proprietary networking architectures and communications protocols, databases and file formats, proprietary flavors of operating systems, custom graphical-user interfaces, and custom device drivers and interfaces between the application and various field devices. As a result, if a system is unreliable, does not perform according to specifications, or is lagging technologically, the user cannot easily replace it with a more advanced system. Simply put, end users are at the mercy of system manufacturers. This has produced a tremendous amount of dissatisfaction among end

*Part 2 has been contributed by Rudy Prokupets.

users and a high level of distrust between end users and vendors. What a sorry state for the electronic security industry to be in!

Who Needs Open Systems and Why

Traditionally, electronic security systems were selected by a committee consisting of people from security and facilities departments. The principal criteria used to select a system to handle security management functions, such as access control, were that (1) the system must be reliable and (2) the system must support a user-specified feature set. Because most users lack the ability to fully test a system, they had to rely on vendors' marketing claims and on customer references that were selected and supplied by those vendors. As a result, any system that appears to satisfy those two criteria can potentially be chosen, even if the system is proprietary and has closed architecture.

In recent years, as technology has evolved at an incredible speed and as security management systems have grown in complexity, information technology (IT) departments have become actively involved in the security system selection process.

They have added a new dimension to that process. Out of their involvement have emerged these completely new and very important selection criteria: (1) The system must adhere to real or de facto standards, and (2) the system must fit into the existing corporate IT infrastructure, which includes any external applications, corporate databases, and networks. Therefore, to fit into the IT infrastructure, a security management system must be able to exchange data with these applications in real time, be compatible with many different databases, and be able to seamlessly plug into corporate networks.

These new requirements are having an enormous impact on the security industry, forcing established system manufacturers to find a way to adapt their legacy systems to the new IT world. At the same time, new and technologically advanced vendors have a unique opportunity to satisfy these criteria by offering systems with open architecture.

Open Systems Architecture: What Does It Mean?

For a system to have a truly open architecture, it must satisfy two criteria:

1. It must be designed in accordance with accepted standards in use in the computer industry.

2. It must be able to easily integrate with other applications and devices.

An open system must be designed according to de facto computer industry standards. Typically, enterprises, corporations, and organizations may support many different databases on a corporate, regional, or departmental level. To be truly open, therefore, a security system must support, at a minimum, several widely used de facto standard databases, including Oracle and SQL Server. To achieve this level of support, the system must use the Open DataBase Connectivity (ODBC) standard, which offers data base independence.

Although ODBC is the de facto database management standard, many security system vendors who claim to support ODBC have misled customers with the implications of that statement. In fact, their products use an ODBC-compliant database with an available ODBC driver. But database-level ODBC compliance is not enough. There also must be application-level ODBC compliance. In other words, the actual security system applications must work with different databases. The vendors do not certify that their applications can be used with a variety of different database standards. For each database type, database certification tests must be performed and verified for each released version of the application. To support their claims, vendors also must have a proven installed base of customer systems that are working with different standard databases.

An open system must employ recognized networking standards. TCP/IP is the primary de facto networking standard in use today, and it is truly a unifying standard. However, an open security application must be able to support a mixed environment, including other networking standards such as NetBios, IPX, and HTTP. Every server, workstation, system device, and field hardware component used by the system must be TCP/IP compliant. The phrase *application compliance* should imply that every component down to the field device level is also compliant.

The user interface of an open system must adhere to recognized standards as well. Clearly, the de facto standard for this is Windows, because Microsoft owns 95 percent of the desktop market share. Therefore, any application that resides on the desktop must fully support Windows, be Internet-compatible, and support standard browser interfaces, including Netscape Navigator and Internet Explorer.

A truly open system also must be able to support myriad peripheral devices, including ID printers, video equipment, and digital cameras. In practical terms, the system must support all Windows-compatible devices, using standard Win32 device drivers. Users should be able to choose any devices that meet their needs, from the many options available to them today.

Another open system requirement is that the system must be thoughtfully designed for ease of integration with other systems and components. There are two ways a system can communicate with the external world: through devices and through applications. Therefore, only a system that is both device- and data-exchange-independent can be considered truly open.

Users want an all-encompassing, secure environment that integrates and manages functions which have historically existed in separate and distinct systems. There are two ways to accomplish this. One way is to write a custom driver for each external application and device to be integrated into the security management environment. This is a costly, time-consuming, and inefficient way to manage the problem, especially since the eternal applications and devices are upgraded and changed. A second, better approach is to develop a standardized method by which a security system can interface with third-party devices and applications. Such an approach eliminates the cost and time required to customize the security application to accommodate external software applications and devices. Manufacturers of third-party products then can easily plug their applications and devices into the security system, which benefits both end users and vendors alike. By employing a Standard Device Interface, third-party electronic hardware and devices—including access controllers, fire controllers, burglar controllers, building management controllers, CCTV, digital video recorders, nurse call systems, intercom systems, asset management controllers, and many more—can be integrated into the security system.

Similarly, a Standard Application Interface can be used to interface third-party software applications with the security system. Such an interface could be used for time and attendance systems, payroll, digital video management systems, human resources, building automation systems, contractor management systems, enterprise resource planning systems, and any other customer applications.

Benefits to end users of open systems architecture

- By using a Standard Device Interface to create a device-independent architecture, the end users' significant investment in installed field hardware is preserved. They will not need to invest in expensive proprietary devices.

- System installation and expansion is straightforward and uses simple plug-and-play technology.

- System support is simplified because the software and hardware are not proprietary in nature.

- End users are not limited in the third-party products they can use. Their security system can integrate with any external system or application that uses the Standard Application Interface. This leaves end users free to choose whatever products best meet their needs and wants.

- By using a Standard Device Interface and a Standard Application Interface, a standardized method is established for developing integrated, total security solutions that serve the best interests of end users.

- This level of integration makes vital information more readily available. End users can download information from external applications directly to their field hardware.

- End users enjoy a substantially reduced total cost of ownership.

How can one select a truly open system?

Using the definition of Open Systems Architecture given above, end users working in collaboration with their IT departments should be able to easily select the right system. There are several essential features the user should look for in an open system. Vendor claims should be verified by visiting specific installations that support these features, or by requesting documentation and benchmark test results. Key system characteristics are as follows:

- The system must use as its networking operating system the de facto industry standard Windows NT Server. Furthermore, if the user's needs or desires dictate it, the exact same system must be able to support Unix database servers.

- The system must run on several de facto industry standard databases, including Oracle, SQL Server, and others.

- All components of the system (including servers, clients, controllers, etc.) must be able to be plugged into the user's existing TCP/IP network with no more than a negligible effect on its bandwidth.

- The system must provide a well-documented, standard application interface to enable other user applications to exchange data with the security system.

- The system must provide a well-documented, standard device interface so that other manufacturers' field devices can be easily integrated with it.

- The system specifically must provide a real-time bidirectional interface to corporate human resources databases.

- The system must have the flexibility to interface field devices to any client workstation, if so required.

Summary

Today's users and their IT departments increasingly demand open systems. Some vendors have argued that the use of Open Systems Architecture diminishes security by exposing the system to external attack. This is false and misleading. In fact, both open and proprietary security management systems, if improperly designed, are vulnerable in two areas: the database, where sensitive data are stored, and the communication links, when data are transferred across the wire.

The use of robust access authentication and data encryption methods can successfully prevent access to sensitive data and eliminate these vulnerabilities. Powerful authentication and encryption technologies are available off the shelf today, and they are widely used in financial and e-commerce transactions to secure intellectual property and billions of dollars in transactions. All those millions of e-commerce transactions employ industry standards and open protocols that are defined by the Internet Engineering Task Force.

The reality is that proprietary, closed architecture systems are a thing of the past. One need only look at two examples from the past decade to see this trend. Compare Apple Computer's proprietary architecture with IBM's open PC architecture, and Apollo's proprietary architecture with Sun Microsystem's open architecture. Where is each company today? The bottom line is this: Arguing against the adoption of open systems is as futile as trying to stop progress itself!

Corporations and end users all over the world are rapidly adopting information systems that employ new technologies in integrated, open architecture environments. The time has come to bring the security industry up to those standards.

Access Control Systems

Part 1 of this chapter describes various types of access control systems and components. Part 2 shows how to install and service electromagnetic locks, which are commonly used in access control systems.

Part 1: Access Control Systems and Components

As the name implies, an access control system controls the flow of pedestrian or vehicular traffic through entrances and exits of a protected area or premises. Basically it's an electronic way of controlling who can go where and when. Typically such a system uses coded cards, biometric readers, or magnetic keys.

Card systems are often used at hotels for entering the rooms. The coded information on the key card works only to the extent that the person controlling the access control systems wants it to. He or she can make the card invalid anytime, which is useful if a guest doesn't pay the bill on time.

Biometric systems control access by comparing some physical aspect of a person to information on file. Hand and finger scanning technologies are popular among biometric systems. A hand reader is shown in Figure 11.1. For a comparison of biometric technology sales, see Figure 11.2.

A popular type of magnetic key is the Corby data chip. It's a dime-shaped, sealed steel canister that contains sophisticated electronics to store a personal identification number. That lets it be easily attached to any smooth surface, including photo ID cards, badges, and keychains. The design also protects the electronic circuits inside the canister from dirt, moisture, corrosion, and static discharge.

Touching a data chip to the reader instantly transfers a 46-bit stream of digital data that gives the user access to a secured area. Unlike keys or other security cards, the data chip is user-forgiving—it doesn't need to be precisely aligned to transfer its digital data.

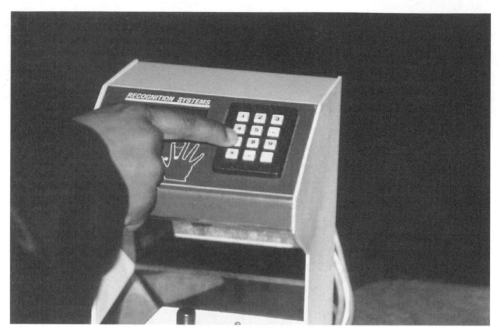

Figure 11.1   A hand reader is a popular biometric device.

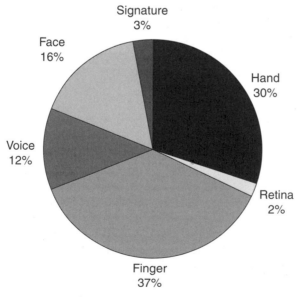

Figure 11.2   Hand and finger scanning are among the most popular biometric technologies.

Along with the chip reader, you'll need a lock of some type. Usually it's an electric strike or magnetic lock. Often an intercom or telephone system is part of the system, too.

An Access Control Configuration for an Apartment Complex

Access control systems can be designed in many different ways, depending on your creativity and the needs of your customer.

Here's one configuration used for an apartment building. When someone comes to one of the main doors during the daytime, the person can enter the building by pushing a push pad (or just by pulling the door open), because the door is unlocked. A push pad is shown in Figure 11.3. That gives a visitor access to the manager's office, but not to the apartments. There's a separate door to the apartments, and it's locked 24 hours per day. At night the main door is also locked, and only people with keys may enter (see Figure 11.4), such as tenants and people to whom tenants gave keys. After entering the lobby, a guest uses the in-house phone to call a tenant and ask to be buzzed in, as shown in Figure 11.5. Because a video camera watches the lobby 24 hours per day, the tenant can turn to a certain television channel to see the person who's calling (see Figures 11.6 and 11.7). The tenant who doesn't want to let in the caller can deny entry and call for help.

Figure 11.3 A push plate makes it easy to open an unlocked door.

Figure 11.4   In the Corby system, doors are unlocked by placing a dime-shaped key over the reader.

Figure 11.5   Some access control systems require guests to call someone to be buzzed into the living (or other protected) areas.

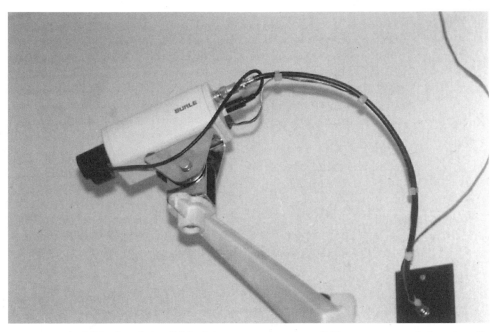

Figure 11.6 A visible closed-circuit television camera is very useful in an access control system; it lets unauthorized persons know they're being watched.

Figure 11.7 A television can be used as a monitor.

Strikes

To allow someone to "buzz open" a door, you need an electric strike. There are many models made by many manufacturers, but all electric strikes do the same thing. What makes one different from another are things such as voltage, current, size, back depth or backset, durability, lock compatibility, and price. Avoid any very cheap model that's less expensive than everyone else's. It's probably made of inferior material and isn't likely to hold up well over time.

Questions for review

1. What is the purpose of an access control system?
2. What is a data chip?
3. What is a biometric system?
4. In what ways do electric strikes differ from one another?
5. What is the purpose of an electric strike?

Part 2: Electromagnetic Locks

Because they're safe, strong, and practically maintenance-free, electromagnetic locks are often a part of an access control system. They have no moving parts to wear out or to jam. And unlike deadbolts and other mechanical locks, these electrically controlled locks can be wired into fire alarms, smoke alarms, and sprinkler systems so they'll unlock automatically in an emergency. See Figure 11.8.

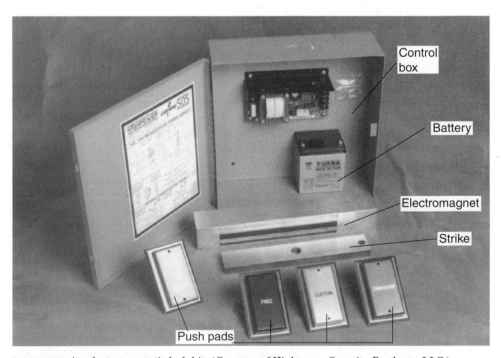

Figure 11.8 An electromagnetic lock kit. (*Courtesy of Highpower Security Products, LLC.*)

How They Work

Although they can be actuated with a key, electromagnetic locks operate on a different principle from mechanical locks. Instead of using a bolt or latch to secure a door, an electromagnetic lock relies on magnetism. A typical model consists of two basic parts: a rectangular electromagnet and a matching metal strike plate, as shown in Figure 11.9. The magnet, about the size of a brick, is installed on a door's header. The strike plate is installed on the door in alignment with the magnet.

When the door is closed and the magnet is powered (usually by using a key or pushbutton code), the strike slaps against the magnet and the door is held secure. Electromagnetic force is all that is needed to hold the door locked. Electromagnetic locks can provide more than 3 times the strength of deadbolts—up to 3000 pounds of holding force. In most cases, the door will give way before the lock does.

The lock's position at the top of the door is important. In a typical deadbolt installation, on the side of the door, the lock absorbs direct pressure during an attempted kick-in. An electromagnetic lock at the top of a door, however, receives little pressure when someone kicks near the center of the door. The door just flexes a little and absorbs most of the force.

Electromagnetic locks usually require 12 or 24 volts (dc) of power at 3 to 8 watts. Some offer optional ac/dc operations at 12 or 24 volts. The low-power requirements let you install enough standby battery power to all for continued operation during a power failure.

When no power (including standby power) is flowing to the electromagnet, the door will not be locked. When power is restored after a failure, the door will automatically lock again, unless you've set up the lock to remain unlocked.

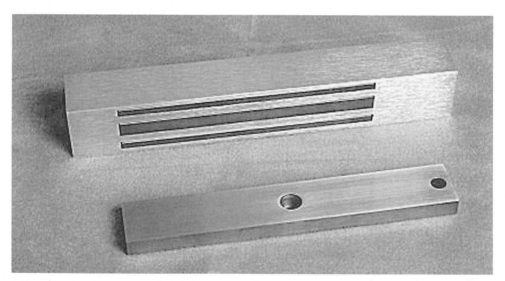

Figure 11.9 An electromagnetic lock has a rectangular electromagnet and strike. (*Courtesy of Highpower Security Products, LLC.*)

Many electromagnetic locks are designed for surface mounting. Installation consists of drilling holes, driving a few screws, and connecting color-coded wires. Electromagnetic locks can be used alone or with a mechanical lock for added strength and convenience.

Problems

Three common shortcomings of electromagnetic locks are their appearance, possible health effects of the electromagnetic field, and cost.

Some people consider a typical electromagnetic lock—about $2^{3}/_{4}$ inches high, 11 inches long, and $1^{1}/_{2}$ inches deep—to be unsightly. But if you don't need as much holding force, you can use a smaller, less viable model. Some people worry about the potential health effects of the lock's magnetic field. But the magnetic field's strength is at the surface of the lock. Perhaps problems would occur if someone with a pacemaker were to strip down to bare skin, climb up to the lock, and press his or her chest against an activated lock for a while. Beyond about 6 inches there is no detectable magnetic field. Normally healthy people have nothing to fear from ordinary usage of electromagnetic locks. Price is another matter. Electromagnetic locks costs more than mechanical locks. There isn't much that can be done about that. But to paraphrase a common saying, you don't get what you don't pay for. If you need the benefits of an electromagnetic lock, then a mechanical lock really isn't an option.

Installation on Doors

Electromagnetic locks can be used on any kind of door. Lock installation methods depend on the door and frame. Manufacturers provide templates and detailed instructions for their products, but some general rules apply.

First, the lock needs to be mounted on a strong, flat surface. Second, the wiring should be protected from damage by intruders. Usually, wiring can be run through the door frame to avoid exposure.

For an out-swinging door, the lock is mounted horizontally under the door frame header, in the corner farthest from the hinges. But when the horizontal header isn't as strong as the vertical extrusion (such as on many aluminum-frame glass doors), vertical mounting might be better.

The strike should be mounted to mate with the magnet on the upper corner of the door. Securing the strike to the door is crucial; it is the only point of attack for an intruder from the outside. Use hardened steel sex bolts. Avoid brass or aluminum bolts, which can be defeated with a chisel.

Make sure the strike flexes freely around the washer stack when you mount it. This flexing lets the lock pull the strike into alignment for maximum holding force even if the door warps or moves due to settling. The most common error made in installing an electromagnetic lock is to make the strike too rigid.

There are three conditions that should be met when mounting the magnet: The frame header must provide a flat surface for the magnet; the frame area you choose must be structurally strong enough for a secure installation; and the magnet must make solid contact with the strike but still let the door close properly.

If the frame isn't flat and wide enough for the magnet, get filler plates and header brackets from the lock maker. If the header is weak, reinforce it with a steel plate. In cases where the lock must be mounted on the in-swinging side of a door, mount the lock body flush on the wall above the door frame and affix a Z bracket to the door.

With a wood frame, use 3-inch-long screws to mount the lock. If the frame isn't solid enough to secure the lock, use a wood-frame bracket. The lock mounts to the bracket using machine screws, and the bracket lets wood screws penetrate more deeply into the header. Drill and tap screw holes in steel frames where necessary.

Installation on Gates

A popular application for electromagnetic locks is on gates. Since gates tend not to be precisely fitted, electromechanical locks on them suffer from alignment failures. Electromagnetic locks, however, are designed to tolerate misalignment. They're also sealed and unaffected by wet environments.

Because of the many gates available, custom installation is required and brackets usually must be made up on the site. Mount the magnet on a fixed post and the strike plate to the swinging or sliding part of the gate.

Installing the HighPower Thunderbolt 1250

The Thunderbolt 1250 is a 2-inch narrow-profile electromagnetic lock for outswinging doors. Providing 1500 pounds of holding force, the unit features a dual-voltage epoxyless coil design that operates at 12 and 24 volts. Units can be equipped to operate with ac or dc power and feature a standard surge/spike suppression circuit. For easy serviceability, the Thunderbolt 1250 features a user-replaceable magnetic coil assembly, integrated-circuit options board, and a patented modular cover design.

Make sure that you have the proper ac or dc equipped model for your power supply. Highpower recommends the Highpower Lightning 505 1-ampere regulated dc supply (P/N 2000505) for optimal holding performance. This lock is intended for use in a controlled environment and shouldn't be used for external applications. Damage caused by water and other external elements may create unsafe operating conditions and will void the warranty.

Mounting instructions

For the purposes of these instructions, the *front* of the door is the side on which the armature is mounted. The mounting template should be used as a reference to hole numbers and mounting features. *Note:* Templates included in this book are not drawn to scale; for installations, get templates from the manufacturer.

1. *Set the mounting plate.* Fold the mounting template shown in Figure 11.10 along the dotted fold line. Place the folded template against both the front of the closed door and the above header. Use tape to secure the template. If the template hangs off the header, you will need to purchase a filler plate, which is used to take up space between the header and the Thunderbolt's base. Filler plates are commonly needed with metal door frames and come in three different thicknesses including $3/8$ inch (#1070000), $1/2$ inch (#1070020), and $5/8$ inch (#1070040).

2. *Mark the door and header with the template and an awl.* To mark a hole, place the point of the awl at the intersection of the circle crosses and punch with a hammer lightly. The door has three holes that must be marked. Mark the two guide pin holes (#1 and #3) and the armature hole (#2). The header has at least five holes that must be marked. Use the awl to mark the four mounting holes (#4, #5, #6, and #7), and choose the wire hole(s) to use for wire routing.

3. *Remove the template.* Now that the holes are marked, remove the template so that it is out of the way during drilling, and use the template as a guide.

4. *Drill the guide pin holes (#3 and #4) in the door.* There are two $1/4$-inch-diameter holes that have to be drilled into the door for the guide pins. Set the drill bit to drill to a depth of $9/16$ inch deep and drill both holes.

5. *Drill the sex nut support hole (#2).*

- *Metal door.* In the case of a metal door, use the armature hole mark to drill a 21/64 (0.328-inch) diameter hole through the front metal layer of the door. Then switch drills and drill a $1/2$-inch-diameter hole through the back of the metal door. Make sure not to drill completely through, leaving the smaller-diameter hole in the front layer of the door after drilling.

- *Wood door.* Using the armature mark on the door, drill an accurate $1/2$-inch-diameter hole through the door.

6. *Set the armature.* See the Thunderbolt 1250 armature assembly diagram in Figure 11.11. First, place the two supplied roll pins into the small holes in

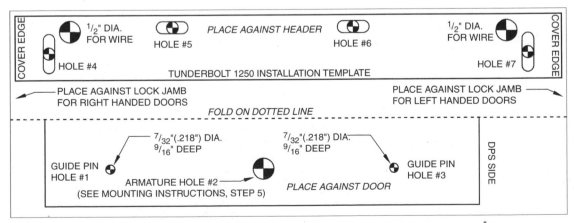

Figure 11.10 Thunderbolt 1250 mounting template (not drawn to scale). (*Courtesy of Highpower Security Products, LLC.*)

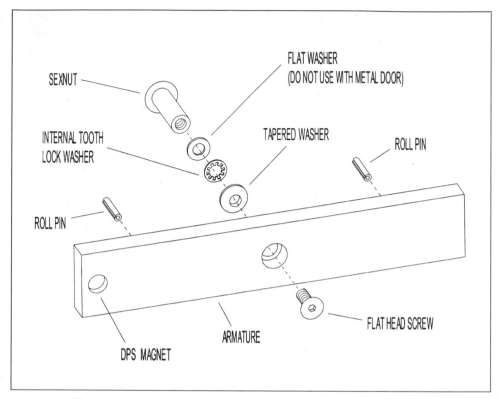

Figure 11.11   Thunderbolt 1250 armature assembly (not drawn to scale). (*Courtesy of Highpower Security Products, LLC.*)

the back of the armature. Place the armature on a clean, flat surface and, using a hammer, lightly tap two roll pins into the holes. Next, place the sex nut through the door and assemble the Thunderbolt 1250 armature assembly according to the diagram. Please note that the pin holes are *not* symmetric. This ensures that the armature is placed on the door with the correct orientation. Some armatures may have a door position switch (DPS) magnet in the face. Correct orientation ensures that this magnet is aligned with the DPS sensor for proper DPS operation. When you mount the armature on a metal door, leave the flat washer out of the assembly, as the sex nut supports the inner layer of the door.

Finish installing the armature by using an Allen wrench to firmly tighten the allen screw to the sex nut, compressing the lock washer. Make sure that the armature "floats" and allows limited movement.

7. *Are you using a filler plate?* If not, go to step 8. When you are using a filler plate, the filler plate must be mounted before you drill any mounting holes. Place the filler plate on the header, and align one end of the filler plate with the "cover edge" mark that was made in step 2. Use the filler plate as a template. Mark the three hole positions in the plate with an awl. In a metal door,

remove the filler plate, drill the three hole locations with a no. 7 drill (0.201 inch), and tap each with a $\frac{1}{4}$-inch-20 tap. After drilling, replace the filler plate and secure with the three supplied 1/4-20 flathead screws. Use tapping screws for wood or other frame materials.

8. *Drill holes #4 and #7 on header.* Drill the appropriate type of mounting hole, based on the type of door frame you are working with:

- 1 $\frac{1}{8}$-inch thick aluminum frame. Drill the three mounting holes with a no. 7 (0.205-inch-diameter) drill. Tap all three holes with a $\frac{1}{4}$-inch-20 tap.
- Hollow metal frame. Drill the mounting holes for threaded inserts.
- Wood-frame. Drill the mounting holes with an 11/64 (0.172-inch) drill. (Use supplied #14 pan-head tapping screws.)
- Frame with filler plate. When utilizing a filler plate, use the supplied $\frac{1}{4}$-inch-20 pan-head metal screws for mounting holes that are over the filler plate. For mounting holes that are over the door frame material, use the appropriate screws as described above.

9. *Verify mounting hole locations for proper operation.* Using the two drilled side mounting holes (#4 and #7), temporarily mount the Thunderbolt, using only the two screws. Close the door, and make sure that the armature does not "slap" the magnet face when the door is closed. The armature should mate with the magnet, but should not forcefully hit the magnet due to tolerance in the floating armature. Look at the rear mounting slots (holes #5 and #6), and verify that the drilling marks align with the rear mounting slots. If not, (1) ensure that the marks were made correctly and (2) verify that the armature was installed correctly. If everything checks out but the marks are still off, remark the rear mounting holes and wire holes(s) to ensure correct operation. Remove the magnet to perform the next step.

10. *Complete the mounting installation.* Drill the back mounting holes (#5 and #6), using the same methods as for the side mounting holes, as described in step 8. Then drill maximum $\frac{1}{2}$-inch-diameter wire hole(s) for wire routing. Place the magnet, and apply the four mounting screws. After you tighten the mounting screws, verify that the armature does not forcefully hit the magnet when the door is closed.

11. *Cover installation.* Place the cover over the magnet base assembly. For Thunderbolts that are equipped with the cover tamper switch (CTS), make sure not to damage the small microswitch that protrudes from the circuit board when you apply the cover. After placing the cover over the base assembly, slide the cover back. There are two small holes at the upper corners of the face of the Thunderbolt 1250. Secure the cover by placing the provided Allen wrench into these holes, and turn the setscrews clockwise until snug.

12

Systems Integration

There's a lot of money to be made for companies that can provide businesses with a total integrated security package—CCTV, access control, intruder alarms, etc. Part 1 gives an overview of the market and shows why some systems are more adaptable to integration than others. Part 2 of this chapter focuses on the integration of information technology.

Part 1: Overview of the Market

In 2001 the leading sellers of integrated security systems included ADT Security Services, CompuDyne Corp., Diebold Inc., Mosler Inc., Pinkerton Systems Integration, and Security Technologies Group. According to a survey by *Security* magazine, the top 100 earned more than $1.6 billion in revenues.

Security's New Golden Rule: Automation,
Integration, and Consolidation
by Robert Pearson, PE

Cost-effectiveness and rapid information exchange are at the heart of all successful businesses today. With the corporate world going to the global marketplace, security must evaluate its role in reducing costs, exchanging critical data, and measuring its performance. Outsourcing, the "do more with less" mentality, cost pressures, and management's desire to centralize or decentralize control exacerbate this challenge. The security department managers of today's companies face major challenges. This section will address the topics of automation, integration, and consolidation as the electronic solutions to these challenges as well as some of the issues associated with the technology needed to incorporate consolidation.

One basic issue of philosophy must be addressed before we proceed: centralized versus decentralized management control. The differences in these two philosophies will have an impact on the direction and means of reaching the goal of automation, integration, and consolidation. The existing company philosophy will drive the ease of gathering data and standardizing processes. The desired goal can be accomplished using either philosophy, but the level of effort needed to gather the required information to reach the goal would be substantially more difficult with the decentralized approach. There are advantages and disadvantages to both approaches.

Centralization

- It ensures standards are in place.
- It tends to utilize vertical organizations.
- It tends to develop experts in different areas as a resource.
- It tends to make decisions slowly.
- It allows career opportunities and personnel development via specialized expertise.

Decentralization

- Multiple facilities set their own rules and policies.
- Employees tend to be more generalist, because they handle many different responsibilities.
- Facilities in the same company tend to reinvent the wheel.
- Decisions tend to be made quickly.
- Decentralization allows career opportunities and personal development via a broad knowledge base.

Each of these items can have both a positive and a negative aspect. To some extent, the impacts of the positive or negative aspects are influenced by personal bias. For example, in a centralized organization typically many standards exist from a security prospective. This usually means multiple facilities operate by the same guidelines and use the same equipment. This also means there is a cost saving by utilizing the same equipment, and employees traveling between facilities are able to use their badges to operate any facility. The negative is that the centralized philosophy does not allow for individual facility issues that can at times be cumbersome. The best solution is to mix these two philosophies and maximize the strengths of both. The mixed organizational philosophy will allow ease of data gathering and standard formulation, which in turn provides the most cost-effective security program.

Mixed centralization and decentralization

- It ensures minimal standards while allowing individuality.
- It incorporates both vertical and horizontal organizations.
- The decision-making processes are rapid.

■ It develops experts and rewards multitalented employees.

■ It minimizes turf issues via teams.

For the purposes of this section, it is assumed that no matter which philosophy a company has chosen, the desired goal and direction of the security department are to automate, integrate, and consolidate. The structure of a given company will provide the network that the security manager must work within. Obviously a centralized or mixed philosophy is the most conducive for gathering the needed data to reach these goals. The goal is actually a three-step process. Reaching one of these areas does not necessarily ensure success. The three steps are in a specific order and must be approached as a three-stage process. Skipping any step or starting with any step other than automation will provide much less success.

Automation

Definition. Automation means to automatically control operation of a process or system by electronic devices that take the place of human organs of observation, effort, and decision.

Benefits
■ It reduces operator and guard workloads.
■ It minimizes head count.

Negatives
■ It requires time.
■ It entails a cost.

Approach
■ Evaluate each task.
■ Search to find a better way to do all processes.
■ Look for electronic solutions versus people-intensive solutions.
■ Decide whether the task is a security task or can be shifted to another department.
■ Develop a task force to eliminate all false alarms.
■ Utilize the task force to minimize all nuisance alarms.

The automation of the different security processes should include every single aspect of the tasks performed. There will be many opportunities to eliminate time-consuming tasks. A careful study must be initiated that will review a process with the goal of accomplishing the task with the aid of electronics. Following are some tasks that can be automated:

Data entry

■ System backups
■ Camera call-up/intercom call-up

- Logging reports
- Guard tours
- Fire extinguisher inspections
- Recording (video, audio, phones, radios, etc.)
- Uses of multiple keyboards, monitors, and display screens

Integration

Definition. Integration is the process of forming a whole, uniting with something else, or incorporating into a larger unit.

Benefits
- It minimizes operator fatigue.
- It improves operator effectiveness.
- It provides faster and more accurate response.

Negatives
- It requires time.
- It entails a cost.
- Higher-skilled operators and repair technicians are needed.

Approach
- The operator should have equipment placed within the control center in such a way as to enhance its use and ease of use.
- Equipment must operate together whether interconnected, integrated, or via an interface.
- The control center must be reviewed as a holistic ergonomic project.

The goal of integration is to reduce the control center operators' discomfort and fatigue, allowing them to operate efficiently even during emergencies. The integration of systems is for the operator's benefit. Therefore it includes every possible electronic approach to be utilized in order for the functions within the control center to be integrated. In reality, whether one uses interconnectivity, communication ports, or actual integration does not matter. Integration is seen from the operator's viewpoint, not the engineer's.

Following are some functions that can be integrated:

- Security alarms
- Fire alarms
- Badge readers
- Closed-circuit television
- Guard tour
- Peopletraps
- Intercoms

- Human resources database
- Energy management
- Telephones
- Radios and pagers
- Video and audio recording
- Video switchers
- Elevator controls

Consolidation

Definition. Consolidation is the merger of two or more control centers.

Benefits
- It eliminates the upgrading cost for multiple control centers.
- It reduces the cost of personnel and equipment at multiple control centers.
- It provides a higher level, more consistent security operation.

Negatives
- It requires time.
- It entails a cost.
- Higher-skilled operators and repair technicians are needed.
- It requires considerable facility-related study to address individual facility, management, and employee-related issues.

Approach
- Evaluate every technical and practical problem of connecting a facility to a consolidated control center prior to proceeding.
- Develop a *proof of concept.*
- Involve the facility management team.
- Evaluate facility-specific security issues.
- Review with the facility management team the cost tradeoffs and proposed schedules.
- Communicate with the facility's employees.

The goal of this step is to connect multiple control centers into a single control center. This is a very complicated step because it requires extensive effort to address the technical and personnel/management issues at each facility impacted. There will be a tremendous amount of resistance at remote facilities. To be successful, particularly with the first control center that is consolidated, there must be a detailed assessment of the existing security systems. Upgrades may be necessary prior to consolidation to ensure compatibility with the consolidated control center systems. Procedures must be standardized prior to consolidation to allow the operators in the consolidated control center to be effective. The technical issues of consolidating the control centers and the amount of data that will be sent to the consolidated control center must be determined.

As part of the consolidation step, the technical system to be used to transmit the data must be determined. To a large extent the selection will be driven by the amount of data that must be transmitted. For example, if a control center is left operational during business hours, then the alarm monitoring is switched to the consolidated control center after hours, and the bandwidth needed to send these data is minimal. If video, audio, fire alarms, security alarms, etc., are all sent to the consolidated control center on a 24-hour 7-day basis, then much larger bandwidth is needed. Video will be the largest bandwidth requirement. Typically one or two video channels are provided from each facility to the consolidated control center. The consolidated control center must be able to switch any camera at a remote facility and receive the new video selection over the video data channel. Video recording is usually left at the remote facility to allow all cameras to be recorded. This reduces the need for many video data channels and provides recording of all remote cameras.

As far as the availability of transmission media for data, there are several options. Each option has its benefits and negatives. As mentioned, the data required in the consolidated control center would establish the bandwidth requirements. The media options are as follows:

Telephone dial-up lines
- 26 to 64 kbits/s
- Primarily for alarms and access control
- Dial-up connection
- Very inexpensive

ISDN lines
- 128 kbits/s
- Primarily for alarms, access control, and non-real-time video
- Dial-up connection
- Inexpensive

Internet
- Speed limited by connection
- Primarily for alarms, access control, and near real-time video
- Dial-up connection
- Inexpensive

T1 lines
- 1.5 Mbits/s
- Primarily for alarms, access control, and real-time video
- Continuous connection
- Fairly expensive; rates based upon distance

At first blush, the obvious answer to the selection of transmission media is the Internet. As with all media, there are benefits and negatives. In larger companies the information technology (IT) group usually controls access to the Internet via an intranet and firewall server. This can be a problem. The IT group wants the intranet to be operational at all times. It does not, however, take the position that the network is critical and therefore cannot be down at all. If an employee utilizes the intranet and sends e-mail to someone, it is not a problem if the e-mail is delayed for 5 minutes or more. This is a serious problem for fire alarms and most security alarms. If the alarm initiates from a government security area, the delay could be long enough to cause a loss of the government contract, because the required response time was not met. There are no guarantees in regard to delays on the Internet or intranet.

There are other issues with using the Internet for sending security data. One is the use of an address on the Internet or intranet. The address of a security field data-gathering panel is given a TCP/IP address. The address allows anyone with access to that address to attempt to attack the security system. In the case of a disgruntled employee who wants to cause problems, the security system on the company intranet is a easy target. The person may try to gain access to the security network. If the person cannot hack into a security field data-gathering panel, he or she can make a request to the TCP/IP address and will receive *denial of service.* If these requests are programmed into the PC and sent rapidly, the address can lock up the system.

A third area of concern relates to the authority levels required by the IT department for servers residing on the IT network. The IT requirements of system administrator levels cause two possible problems. First, the data on the system often are sensitive or classified, which requires safeguards. Second, if government contract areas are being monitored, then non-U.S. persons employed by the IT group could gain access. Both difficulties have to be considered if this approach is taken.

The other data transmutation options mentioned earlier also have benefits and negatives. It is important to know these media solutions' pros and cons before you proceed with consolidation. There is no perfect solution. Consolidation, just like the other steps, requires careful evaluation. There are no two companies exactly alike, and there are no "fix all" solutions. These steps require a strong understanding of the security processes and a grasp of technical approaches to solving problems. In the end the solution reached will reflect not a mathematical formula, but more of an art form. This is particularly true in the last two steps.

As corporations are pressed for efficiency improvements, to do more with less and to meet the ever-increasing customer demand requires that the golden rule of security be applied. Automating all processes possible, integrating the control center functions, and finally consolidating control centers are the way to be successful in the global corporate world. When these steps are taken, then gathering information for metrics is much easier. It also ensures that the data gathered are an accurate reflection from one facility to the next. Security processes are standardized, and taking measurements of these processes is much easier. Security must function as other groups must function within the global company. Other groups also must do more with less, and all groups are trying to gain access to tight funding. Therefore the security department must measure its performance against other security departments in other companies and develop metrics to measure its progress. The golden rule allows success as each step is correctly implemented. This is not a fast cure-all, but a methodical journey.

Questions for review

1. What is a difference between centralized and decentralized management?

2. What are two benefits of centralization?

3. What are two benefits of decentralization?

4. What is a benefit of automation?

5. What are two security functions that can be integrated?

Part 2: Computer Networks and the Internet: Integration of Information Technology*

Information technology experienced revolutionary changes in the early 1990s. The proliferation of the new paradigms for object-oriented software, PC-based client-server architecture, graphical-user interface (GUI), open architecture, and distributing networking, coupled with the Internet explosion, dramatically changed the landscape of corporate computing. The information technology groups responsible for building and maintaining the information infrastructure within corporate organizations were faced with the dilemma of trying to integrate proprietary application solutions with fast-paced technology trends and evolving systemic changes in the IT marketplace. The growing complexity of information infrastructures and the need for seamless integration of third-party solutions have forced IT groups to impose standards for acceptance of third-party solutions before they are brought into the corporate domain. Due to massive investments in new information technology within corporate entities, IT groups have become much more actively involved in evaluating, recommending, and even rejecting all software and technology solutions, including security management systems. IT managers have developed specific criteria for accepting third-party application solutions, and they are actively participating in product evaluation committees, bid specification requirements, and product demonstrations by vendors. The primary criteria used by IT managers when selecting products for corporate adaptation are as follows:

- Use of latest technology which extends the product life cycle and provides the best return on investment

- Open architecture to allow for easy integration with the existing infrastructure

- Scalability which allows for system growth without performance degradation

---

*Part 2 was contributed by Rudy Prokupets.

- Use of current de facto industry standards in database technology, networking, and operating systems for seamless integration with corporate infrastructure

Let's take a more detailed look at these requirements and how they specifically apply to security management systems.

Modern technology and architecture of security systems

Unfortunately, the security industry has traditionally fallen behind the technology curve. While the computer and software industries are moving at lightning speed, many vendors of security management systems still offer proprietary systems based on old technology. Characteristics such as limited networking capabilities, lack of robust client-server database architecture, lack of flash memory architecture, old 16-bit application and operating system software, and old 16-bit (or even 8-bit) controller architecture with proprietary interface protocol make it very difficult, if not impossible, to integrate such products within a corporate infrastructure. These systems are often called DOA (dead on arrival) from a technology point of view, and they are therefore less readily accepted in the marketplace. Even security managers and directors who are more conservative than IT managers have begun to realize that installing an archaic system is a bad investment in the long term.

Modern security systems may be comprised of access control, alarm monitoring, ID management, CCTV, and fire and burglar alarm subsystems, preferably integrated into a single solution. Traditionally these systems were driven by proprietary hardware solutions while the application software was a mere afterthought. Quite often the application software was given away or offered at a significant discount to ensure the system sale. While this strategy was acceptable a few years ago, the reverse is now true. With hardware quickly becoming a commodity (as in the PC industry overall) software has become critically important as the glue that makes it all work. Software and system architecture are what differentiate modern systems from older ones. The complexity and quality of software, its conformance to corporate standards, and its capability to grow with the system are the new factors that make the difference in corporate decision making.

The modern security application software must be written utilizing a 32-bit native API such as Win32 from Microsoft Corporation. This offers high performance, access to a very rich set of APIs, flexibility and compatibility with other applications such as Microsoft BackOffice.

Applications that are written utilizing 16-bit (DOS-based) code or that are "ported" (modified) from older code and other operating systems should be avoided. For example, even though there are tools available to port the application code from OS/2 or Unix to Windows NT, these tools are still immature and inflexible and result in a ported application that does not fully utilize the power of Win32. The best security applications are written "natively" from scratch. At the beginning of the 1990s, the software industry quietly underwent an object-oriented revolution. As a result, instead of writing an application as a single, monolithic program—which is difficult to develop, maintain, and enhance—the application is developed as a set of small self-contained components (objects), each of which performs a specific function. Very large and complex applications can be easily created by selecting the appropriate components from a library of well-tested, reusable objects and "gluing" them together. The major benefits to vendors and end users are evident:

- Application development is rapid through a plug-and-play component architecture.
- The reliability of applications is enhanced due to reusability of objects.
- Programs are smaller. Many lines of repetitive code are replaced with a single line.
- Product upgrades and the enhancement cycle are shortened. New features and capabilities are delivered faster to end users.
- Cost of development is less, resulting in more aggressive prices to end users.

It is essential that modern security applications be designed and developed as object-oriented applications utilizing such tools as Microsoft Visual C++ and COM, DCOM (distributed component object model), and COM+ platform technologies. COM technology is the single most important platform technology currently being used in application development at Microsoft. Windows NT 5.0 (the next generation of Enterprise Operating System), MTS (Microsoft Transaction Server), and many other important emerging technologies are architecturally built around COM. COM technology is a 100 percent commitment from Microsoft, and it will affect many third-party applications in the future. Security applications that do not utilize today's object-oriented architectural tools, such as Microsoft COM, will be more difficult to integrate with NT 5.0, MTS, OLE DB, and other technologies from Microsoft, as well as many applications from other vendors.

As part of a total security system, the field hardware must support the architecture and should be designed to have the same characteristics as the application software: It should be powerful, flexible, and easy to upgrade and interface. One of the most important field hardware components is the *intelligent system controller* (ISC), where local access decisions are made. For IT managers to accept these devices on a corporate network, the devices must meet the following minimum requirements:

- A 32-bit bus and CPU architecture
- TCP/IP protocol support
- Flash memory for firmware
- Support for a very large (minimum 250,000) local cardholder database
- Support for a large number of readers (up to 64) and I/O alarm panels

A 32-bit microprocessor, data bus, and address bus are mandatory for a system to be able to support the most demanding network applications with a large number of transactions (events) without suffering performance degradation.

Seamless support for TCP protocol and IP addressing is a must for these controllers to be part of the corporate local-area network (LAN) or wide-area network (WAN) infrastructure. Systems that lack these network capabilities will not be seriously considered for integration by IT groups.

One of the most critical features of modern security systems is the use of flash memory in the controllers to store the firmware. Because application software is rapidly changing with the technology, so must the capabilities and feature set of the firmware. Flash memory allows the new versions of firmware to be dynamically downloaded from the server or PC workstations to every controller in the system in minutes. Without these capabilities, controllers quickly become obsolete, and the only way to upgrade them is to physically replace their EPROMS. That is very impractical and very costly and would therefore be unthinkable to any IT manager.

Support for a very large cardholder database is very important for truly distributed network systems where the access decisions are made in the local (controller) database. The full-capacity database allows all cardholders in the corporation, including contractors, to be downloaded into the controller so that the controller can make access decisions in real time. In many systems the cardholder database in the controller is limited, and in order to make an access decision, the request is sent to the host (database) computer. During peak traffic hours or in a system having a large number of transactions (such as a major corporation or university), the people who are trying to gain access may have to wait an unreasonably long time for the system to open the door. This scenario can also arise in a smaller system when a large and demanding report is run against a full cardholder database that consumes most of the database bandwidth. Of course, if the host computer is down, no decision can be made in the entire system at that time! Decision making at the host should be avoided at all costs, as it is incompatible with the modern concept of distributed architecture, where decisions are always made locally and in real time.

Finally, modern controllers must support a large number of downstream devices such as a combination of readers and I/O alarm panels. That simplifies the installation of a security system, minimizes the cost of installation and maintenance, and most importantly allows some global functions to be performed on the controller level instead of always referring them to the host computer.

Open Systems Architecture

Open architecture is one of the most important criteria for IT groups in selecting the right system. Unfortunately, many vendors claim to have open systems without clearly understanding what the phrase means from an IT point of view. *Open system* implies that every major component of the system, every communication protocol, and every interface are designed according to industry standards which allow easy integration with other systems and components. Specifically with regard to security management systems, it should satisfy the following minimum requirements:

- The application software (front end) must be hardware-independent. It can seamlessly interface with multiple ISCs from different vendors within the same system.

- The application software must be database-independent. It can seamlessly interface with multiple relational database management systems (RDMSs) from major vendors including Microsoft, Oracle, Sybase, and Informix.

- The application software must be network-independent. It can seamlessly interface with all major network protocols including TCP/IP, IPX, and NetBios.

- The application software must be peripheral device–independent. It can seamlessly interface with digital/video cameras, badge printers, and scanners from different vendors.

In addition, the most advanced systems should provide the following capabilities:

Universal I/O. The application must have the ability to interface with any external system or device through a simple unidirectional ASCI string protocol (fire systems, building/time management systems, alarm systems, CCTV switches, paging, and e-mail systems).

Universal data import/export. This is the ability to move any data including multimedia (pictures, signature, fingerprints, voice, video) from/to an external file or database system with custom business rules applied to the data moved between systems.

Open interface protocol. This is the availability of a generic protocol to interface to ISC. This is the most controversial requirement. Most of the protocol information is regarded by vendors as proprietary and is not published. On the other hand, if an installed system is not performing well or is becoming obsolete, an end user should be able to replace the front end without incurring the major expense of replacing the complete system.

Scalability

Security system scalability is measured not by the number of doors or the number of cardholders it can support, but by the number of transactions (events) the system can consistently sustain without any visible degradation of performance. In practical terms, it means that the same system should perform equally well whether supporting two doors or several thousand doors. The number of transactions generated by the security system in the real world can range from several to dozens of transactions per minute for a small system, to several hundred per minute for a medium system, and to several thousand per minute for a large system. Security and IT managers must be very careful in selecting a security system with properly designed scalable architecture to make sure that no performance degradation will occur with system growth. Systems with a scalable architecture will perform the same way without any modification to the application code, whether they're supporting several transactions per minute or several thousand transactions per minute.

It is important to ensure that the security system vendor provides a seamless upgrade path as the security system grows beyond its initial installation. This should involve only a possible upgrade in database and operating system technologies or hardware platforms (faster and more powerful computers, more memory, etc.). The application software should remain the same. Either many vendors do not provide an upgrade path beyond the maximum configuration of the installed system, or they require the customer to purchase new application software capable of supporting the expanded growth. Furthermore, the new application software often has a different "look and feel" which requires complete retraining of system resellers and end users, a very expensive undertaking.

Properly designed architecture means that scalability is distributed across many system components rather than being concentrated in one place. Even though the database is the single most important component that affects system scalability, there are other important criteria to consider in designing a system with scalable architecture:

- Transaction-based application design
- Client-server database design
- Application support for symmetric multiprocessing
- Distributed network and application partitioning

Transaction-based application design. Security applications continually process transactions by accessing the database. A properly designed application breaks these database accesses into small atomic operations. The design rule should be: Make it small and make it fast. The application code dealing with transaction processing must be small, tight, and scalable. This design will guarantee minimum overhead during transaction processing and, consequently, the ability to process a large number of transactions.

Client-server database design. Robust client-server database architecture is essential for effective transaction processing. A database server and a powerful SQL engine are critical components of true client-server architecture. Many vendors use file server technology instead of a database server. In properly designed client-server architecture, the client workstation sends the query request to the database server. The server processes the request, and only the final result is sent back to the client workstation. This guarantees the database integrity up to the last transaction in the event of a database crash, and it significantly minimizes the network traffic. As a result, significantly more clients can be added to client-server database systems than to file-oriented database systems.

Application support for symmetric multiprocessing. The application should provide support without any modifications for a multiprocessor-based database server. A truly scalable system should demonstrate a substantial increase in performance when the number of processors increases.

Distributed network and application partitioning. Distributed networking is an integral part of scalable architecture. This means that every intelligent hardware component of the system is designed as a network plug-compatible module with its own processing and decision-making capabilities. The application is partitioned accordingly, so that only specific software components or processes are running within these modules. A dedicated database server contains SQL engine and MTS, while a nondedicated database server will also have running the access driver to support the attached ICSs. Client workstations can be configured to run alarm monitoring, system administration, image capture, image viewing, or badge printing software components only (see Figure 12.1).

In the event of transaction overload on the database server, an additional access server can be configured with only an access driver component running on it, as illustrated in Figure 12.1. This access server can be located anywhere on the network, and it provides transaction load balancing for the database

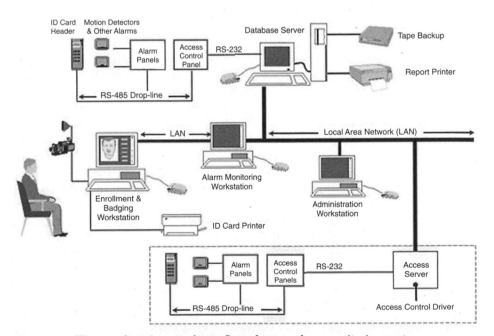

Figure 12.1 Client workstations can be configured to run alarm monitoring, system administration, image capture, image viewing, or badge printing software components.

server. And finally, the networked ISCs with their own local processing power, full cardholder database, and access decision making are an important part of the distributed network architecture.

Security database integration

Probably the most important issue for IT personnel involved in the evaluation and selection of a security system is its ability to seamlessly integrate the application with external corporate databases such as human resources, payroll, accounting, fixed asset management, inventory management, time management, building management, and many others. The security application and database design must comply with corporate standards and satisfy the following requirements:

- The application must be Open DataBase Connectivity (ODBC) compliant.
- The application must support a bidirectional interface with an external database.
- The application must download and distribute security-related data to every ISC in the system in real time.
- The application must guarantee the delivery of security data to each ISC in the system.

ODBC compliance.   Many security system vendors claim that they support the new ODBC database interface standard (are ODBC-compliant). Although their security database is ODBC-compliant, their application quite often is not. This difference is significant.

Database compliant means that the security database has an ODBC driver available and that other nonsecurity applications have access to information stored in the database. It also means that the security application can access only its own security database. But this is not as important to corporate security and IT personnel. In most cases various corporate applications have no need to access data from the security database. For the security application to access external corporate databases, vendors of such systems must write a custom application interface for each external database.

What's required is the ability of the security application to work with multiple external corporate databases (sometimes simultaneously). An ODBC-compliant application is one in which that security application can interface directly through ODBC driver(s) to any corporate database(s) and can exchange the data between the security database and external database(s) (see Figure 12.2).

Bidirectional interface with an external database.   The security application must support a bidirectional interface. That means when changes to the data are made in an external database, the modified data are moved to the security database and vice versa. For example, changes to personnel information in the

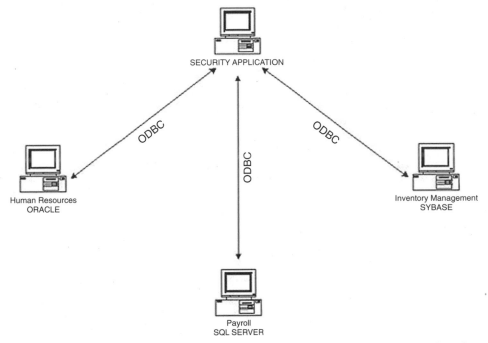

Figure 12.2 ODBC-compliant application means that security application can interface directly through ODBC driver(s) to any corporate database(s).

human resources database may apply to the security database, while changes in access level of the employee in the security database may apply to personnel information in the human resources database.

Real-time data download and distribution.   When changes occur in employee or badge status that might affect employee access, it is very critical to download such information from the human resources database to the security database in real time, rather than in batch mode, which is typically performed once a day. But this is only one-half of the solution. The data must also be distributed automatically in real time to every ISC in the system to modify the affected employee access levels in the local database, to prevent unauthorized access by those employees. Within minutes, changes in employee information that could compromise corporate security are communicated to the security database and automatically distributed across the entire security system.

Guaranteed data delivery.   While distributing security data across the system, the application must detect whether any communication paths are unavailable or whether transmission errors occur. The application must store the undelivered data and continuously monitor the communication lines for availability. As soon as a communication path is restored, the security data must be delivered to the target ISC(s). This design guarantees data integrity across the entire system.

Only by conforming to the above design criteria can a security application claim to achieve seamless integration with an external corporate infrastructure.

Network integration

In order for a security system to be seamlessly integrated within a corporate infrastructure, it must comply with corporate networking standards. In most environments, TCP/IP protocol support is sufficient to allow integration with Windows NT, Unix, and even Novell networks. Database servers, workstation clients, and ISCs must be easily configurable as network nodes with IP addresses assigned to them and must be flexible enough to be plugged into any segment on a corporate LAN or WAN. When deciding whether to integrate a security system into the corporate infrastructure, security and IT personnel face a dilemma: Should the security system be a stand-alone type with its own dedicated network, or should it be integrated into the existing corporate network? The solution requires positively answering the following questions:

- Does the corporate network have enough bandwidth available to support the security application?

  If many demanding mission critical applications are running on the network and the bandwidth utilization is approaching 50 percent, then the answer is no.

- Is the corporate network properly secured?

  Log-in, password, access privileges and network access control procedures, network segmentation, firewalls, virus protection, and encryption are some of the safeguards that must be properly implemented and constantly maintained by the network administrator to qualify the network as secure.

- Is the security application designed as a network intelligent application?

  The traditional security application polls the ISCs continuously (the poll rate can be measured in tenths of a millisecond) for events. With a large number of controllers and other polled devices on the network, this process can consume a substantial amount of corporate bandwidth and can affect the performance of other mission-critical applications. A properly designed network security application minimizes the effect of polling by making the polling interval user configurable in seconds rather than milliseconds. The ISC should be designed to be event-driven, meaning that events are transmitted when they arrive at the ISC, instead of relying on a polling mechanism. Network-aware security applications should consume only a fraction of the corporate bandwidth.

Enterprise security integration

As world markets become more open, many corporations are expanding globally. To meet the security needs of multinational enterprises that have many locations worldwide, security solution vendors must design and deploy a new type of enterprise security system. The integration of such Enterprise security management systems poses a unique challenge for corporate security and IT managers. Many local or regional security managers need to have direct control over hardware configuration, cardholder enrollment, and management of the cardholder privileges associated with the operations in their regions. These fiefdoms have developed over time. As a result, in a regional office, there are real service issues (such as special access requirement) that render the central corporate office an obstacle in delivering a quality service for a company's internal customers.

Because the typical enterprise consists of many geographically dispersed independent regions, the single database server solution may satisfy the need of individual regions but may not be suitable as an enterprisewide integrated security solution. What's required for the enterprise is a new multiserver database architecture with wide-area network integration and database synchronization. By using an innovative design and new technology, an enterprise configuration can be created to satisfy both IT standards and regional operation security needs (see Figure 12.3).

In this configuration each region consists of an independent, fully configured client-server access control and ID management system with its own LAN-based regional database server, client workstations, and field hardware. Corporate headquarters have a central enterprise database server interfacing with the corporate human resources database for the purpose of receiving updated cardholder, badge, and employee status information regularly. The enterprise and regional servers communicate with each other over a wide-area network to synchronize the information in their respective databases.

For example, any changes to cardholder information within the enterprise server or within a specific region are distributed through the enterprise server to all regional servers. Cardholder and badging information as well as cardholder access levels are distributed and synchronized across all database servers to allow any authorized employee access to any regional facilities using a single ID card. The enterprise server's main role is as a central database repository and regional distribution source for all corporate personnel and security-related information. Concurrently the security administrator at the enterprise site can execute any kind of systemwide reports, manage cardholder information for the whole corporation, and assign access levels to any cardholder at any region.

The enterprise security management system just described is a security solution that rises to the challenge of technological innovation in order to satisfy the demands of a new and changing security market. With this type of highly integrated enterprise solution, the security market is finally catching up with the technology innovation curve and is bound to satisfy the needs of both corporate security and IT personnel.

In order to be seamlessly integrated into the corporate IT infrastructure, the new integrated security system must satisfy the technical criteria of modern design as described above.

Enterprise Security Architecture

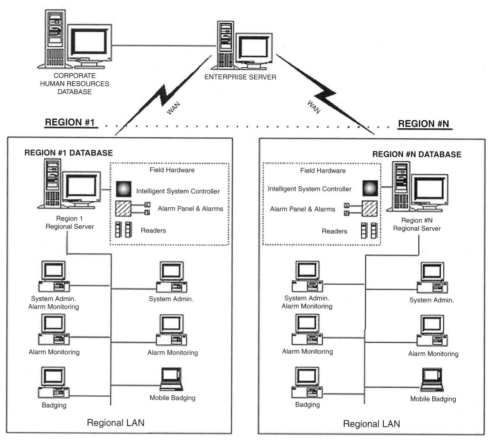

Figure 12.3 By using an innovative design and new technology, an Enterprise configuration can be created to satisfy both IT standards and regional operations security needs.

13

Vehicle Security

This first part of this chapter is an overview of vehicle security devices and systems. Part 2 tells how to install car alarms.

Part 1: Overview

In addition to a home, vehicles are among the biggest purchases most people make. One vehicle is stolen in the United Kingdom almost every minute. Throughout the United States a vehicle is stolen once every 27 seconds, resulting in an estimated $7 billion dollars in annual loss. Car theft prevention has pretty much been left up to car manufacturers and drivers. There are many high-technology electronic options that you need to know about. Some are aftermarket devices that you can sell and service.

There are three basic types of electronic vehicle antitheft systems: kill switches, retrieval systems, and alarms (see Figure 13.1). Patented kill switches are built into many Ford, General Motors, and BMW models. They all use a special key, but work differently. There are also many aftermarket kill switches. They shut off the starter or the fuel supply. Shutting off the starter is safer, because the vehicle doesn't move. With a fuel kill switch (or *cut off switch*), the thief can start the car and drive it a bit before it stops. Depending on where it stops, that could cause injury or death and could make the owner of the car (and perhaps the kill switch installer) vulnerable to a lawsuit.

General Motors Antitheft Systems

The General Motors Vehicle Anti-Theft System (VATS), later called the *Personalized Automotive Security System* (PASSKey), has been in use in select GM models since 1986. The system has proved useful in preventing automobile thefts.

Figure 13.1   Components of a car alarm. (*Courtesy of Black Widow Vehicle Security Systems.*)

VATS is an electromechanical system that consists of the following basic components: a computer module, keys that each have a resistor pellet embedded in them, an ignition cylinder, and a wire harness that connects the ignition cylinder to the computer module.

The turning of the ignition cylinder is a mechanical process that is independent of the system's electronics. When any properly cut General Motors key is inserted into the ignition cylinder, the cylinder will turn. If the key is embedded with the correct resistor pellet or has no resistor pellet, the computer module shuts down the vehicle's electric fuel pump, starter, and power train management system for about 4 minutes.

That happens because vehicles with VATS are designed to operate only when one of 15 levels of resistance is present. Although most electrical circuits have resistors in them, a VATS system simply has one of its needed resistors embedded in the key bow (rhymes with *toe*). Other than having a resistor pellet, the key is like any non-VATS General Motors key.

When a VATS key is inserted into a VATS ignition cylinder, contacts within the cylinder touch the resistor pellet in the key, and the resistor pellet's resistance value is transmitted to the VATS computer module by the wire harness connecting the cylinder to the computer module. Only if its resistance value is at the right level can the vehicle be started.

Stolen Vehicle Retrieval Systems

A stolen vehicle retrieval system entails having a small, unnoticeable transmitter installed on the car. The transmitter constantly receives a small amount of power from the car's battery, and it has a backup battery (in case the car's battery runs down or a thief disconnects it). With most systems, if your car is stolen, you need to report it to the system's monitoring station, which will begin tracking your car. The oldest and perhaps most popular stolen vehicle retrieval system, *LoJack,* is set up so that you call the police directly and the police track your car. Some systems let you go to your home computer and track the car yourself. Those are used in businesses to keep track of fleet vehicles. But it also might be useful for parents who want to check up on their children. (By the way, that's a key to a successful business these days; find new and creative uses for the products you already offer.)

Many stolen vehicle retrieval systems have additional convenience and security features, such as a kill switch, alarm, door locking/unlocking, and 24-hour monitored sensors. The Tracker System, for instance, has sensors that detect movement, and the company will call the owner anytime there appears to be unauthorized movement (which includes the movement a tow truck would make).

Questions for review

1. How does VATS work?

2. What are three types of electronic vehicle security systems?

3. What extra features do some stolen vehicle retrieval systems come with?

4. How does a stolen vehicle retrieval system work?

5. With respect to safety, what's the difference between a kill switch that cuts off fuel and one that shuts off the starter?

Part 2: How to Install a Car Alarm

There are two basic types of car alarms: *passive* and *active*. A passive alarm automatically arms itself—usually when the car is turned off and the last door is closed. An active alarm requires you to do something special, such as push buttons or flip a switch, to arm the car. Because it's easy to forget to arm a system, the passive systems provide more reliable security. Many alarms are basically passive, but allow you the option of active arming and disarming with a remote control unit.

Car alarm installation is basically a matter of choosing the best detection devices (or *sensors*) and choosing the best places within a car to mount the various system components. The fewer components an alarm has, the easier it is to install. The simplest type to install is a portable self-contained model that has a built-in current sensor, motion detector, and siren. It's usually installed by plugging a cord into the cigarette lighter, or by connecting a single wire to a fuse box.

Before you install any alarm that needs to be tied into the electrical system, disconnect the negative battery cable (see Figure 13.2) and make sure the disconnected cable doesn't touch any metal parts of the car or the other cable. The size and configuration of your vehicle will limit your choices of where to install the alarm components. But you need to be as creative as possible, so a thief can't easily and quickly disarm the system. You may want to run false wires and false switches, for instance. Because the control module should be both readily accessible and hidden from view, it's generally mounted under a seat, in a glove box, or under the dashboard. The siren is usually mounted under the car hood, pointing downward.

You may need to run wire from one component to another. If so, take that into consideration when you plan where to mount the components. Look for preexisting holes in your firewall that will allow you to easily wire the siren to the control module. Usually car alarm wires are attached to a harness, which means you need only snap the harness connections into place. All wires you run should be hidden from view.

Figure 13.2 For safety, disconnect the negative battery cable before working with a vehicle's electrical system.

Detection Devices

Most car alarms have current detection devices that sense the current drop that occurs when a car's courtesy light comes on. But that alone is seldom enough to protect a vehicle, because a thief can gain entry in ways that don't activate the courtesy light. Other types of detection devices respond to the sound of breaking glass, vibrations, or motion within a car. Generally, the more types of detection devices a system uses, the more effective it will be.

The simplest type of detection device is the pin switch. It senses the opening of a door or trunk. The thin spring-loaded switch is installed in a small hole in the metal frame around the door (or trunk), so that it is compressed when the door is closed. While it's compressed, the switch helps complete an electric circuit. But when the door is opened, the switch springs up, breaking the circuit. (Your refrigerator uses a pin switch to turn the light on and off.)

For maximum protection, a car alarm should include a motion detection device. Such a device can detect thieves who gain entry by using glass cutters or opening vent windows.

Special features

The biggest problem with most car alarms is that they depend on passersby to intervene. Car thieves know that if they disarm an alarm quickly, they will attract little or no attention from passersby. Not many people care enough about a stranger's car to risk offending someone who may or may not be a thief. Rather than rely on passersby, you can use a remote pager. You can carry it with you in your pocket, and it will warn you whenever your car alarm is activated. Some models allow you to remotely arm and disarm the alarm system.

Before you buy an alarm that allows remote control operation, make sure it has antiscanning circuitry. A handheld frequency scanner that can be made from parts found in any electronic hobby shop is being used by car thieves to rapidly transmit different codes until one is found that will disarm a car's alarm. Antiscanning circuitry detects the use of a scanner and allows the alarm to resist being controlled.

Another useful feature to look for in an alarm is a *cutoff function*. That cuts the engine off if a thief tries to drive off without properly disarming your alarm. Some cutoff functions disable the car's starter; others cut off fuel to the engine. All such functions work with a relay, which may be normally open or normally closed. The normally closed type is more common. But if a thief cuts the car's battery cable, or otherwise disables a system that uses a normally closed relay, the cutoff function won't work, and the thief will be able to drive off. A system that uses a normally open relay, on the other hand, will continue its cutoff function when the car's battery cable is cut or the system disabled.

The main problem with using a normally open relay is that if it's malfunctioning, you won't be able to start your car. To avoid that potential inconvenience, you could install a hidden bypass switch in your car. That switch would allow the car to operate as if you didn't have the cutoff function.

14

Certification and Licensing

In many cases, licensing is mandatory prior to installing electronic security systems. Sometimes a certification is a prerequisite to licensing. Even when they're not required, certifications can be helpful in promoting your business. Part 1 of this chapter is a general overview of licensing and certification. Part 2 is a sample general test for an alarm systems technician.

Part 1: Overview

A license differs from a certification in that a license is issued by a municipality, rather than by a school or an association. The license grants you permission to do business, but it may or may not require a demonstration of skill level. The criterion for a license varies from place to place. You may need to take a competency test, be fingerprinted and photographed, and pay an annual fee. Since 1998, when the licensure law was enacted, in Alabama an alarm company must carry at least $250,000 of general liability coverage, and all employees must undergo a criminal background check and have completed certification training. Colorado, on the other hand, leaves the regulation of alarm companies to local jurisdictions.

Certification is recognition of a certain level of competency or skill level. Certification can come from a school, association, or municipality.

Under the National Fire Alarm Code (NFC), published by the National Fire Protection Association (NFPA), those who install, test, and perform service on fire alarm systems must be qualified to do so. The five basic ways to meet those criteria are to be:

- Factory-trained and -certified
- Fire alarm–certified by the National Institute for Certification in Engineering Technologies

- Fire alarm–certified by the International Municipal Signal Association
- Certified by a state or local authority
- Trained and qualified by an employee of an organization listed by a national testing laboratory for the servicing of fire alarm systems

A certification signifies that you've demonstrated a level of knowledge or proficiency that meets a school's or association's standard for that certification. A certification test can help you become aware of shortcomings in your knowledge, and it can be a useful promotional tool. In some cases, you can earn the right to use initials after your name; that might impress some people. And you usually get a certificate to hang on your wall. Also, in your advertisements, you can say that you're certified, and you may be able to use special logos. The value of a certification depends in large part on the integrity of the organization issuing it. If it's too easy to earn (such as just by paying a fee), you'll be risking your reputation if you use it to promote yourself.

For select state license requirements, see Appendix D. For a list of certification training programs, see Appendix E.

Questions for review

1. How does a license differ from a certification?
2. In what way can a certification test be useful?
3. What are two NFPA requirements for fire alarm systems installers?
4. What organization publishes the National Fire Alarm Code?
5. What are three state requirements for intruder alarm installer licensing?

Part 2: Test Your Knowledge

The following general knowledge test can help you prepare for licensing and certification tests, by showing you which areas you need to study further. When you answer the questions, choose the best answer for each question. For more accurate results, when you are taking this test, don't search through the book for answers (it isn't designed as an open-book test).

1. To what wavelength of light are PIRs sensitive?
    a. 0.750 to 1 mm
    b. 1 to 5 mm
    c. 3 to 100 mm
    d. 1 to 20 mm
2. Which reader technology can have problems from dirt and moisture?
    a. Proximity
    b. Weigand
    c. Magnetic stripe
    d. None of the above
3. Non-power-limited fire alarm (NPLFA) systems use wire with a maximum insulation rating of 600 volts, with at least 22-gauge wiring.
    a. True
    b. False
4. Which is the bandwidth of a typical Cat 5 cable?
    a. 2 GHz
    b. 10 MHz
    c. 200 GHz
    d. 100 MHz

5. What is the flange back distance for a CS mount lens?
   a. 13.5
   b. 20.5
   c. 12.5
   d. 17.5
6. PTX cameras are mounted on a fixed bracket and cannot move.
   a. True
   b. False
7. What is the flange back distance for a C mount lens?
   a. 20.5
   b. 12.5
   c. 13.5
   d. 17.5
8. How many frames per second are accepted as *real time?*
   a. 5.5
   b. 5
   c. 10
   d. 30
9. No adapter is needed to use a CS mount lens on a C mount camera.
   a. True
   b. False
10. Ohm is a unit of measurement of what?
    a. Resistance
    b. Voltage
    c. Current
    d. None of the above
11. What can a multimeter be used to measure?
    a. Voltage
    b. Resistance
    c. Current
    d. All the above
12. A *frame grabber* is a computer expansion board that can digitize video signals.
    a. True
    b. False
13. What is the basic unit of measurement for electric power?
    a. Coulomb
    b. Watt
    c. Proton
    d. None of the above
14. If 15 volts is applied to a circuit that consumes 75 watts, what is the current flow?
    a. 112.5 amperes
    b. 11.25 watts

    c. 5 amperes

    d. 0.2 watt

15. The frequency range of ultrasonic detectors is 10 to 50 MHz.

    a. True

    b. False

16. The result of connecting battery cells in series is that it

    a. Increases voltage

    b. Decreases voltage

    c. Reverses polarity

    d. Decreases current

17. What are other names for *variable resistors?*

    a. Rheostats or potentiometers

    b. Sliding resistors or ohm modifiers

    c. Ohm extenders or ohm stretchers

    d. None of the above

18. Service panels installed in homes before 1965 typically use fuses and have 300-ampere or greater service with more than 40 circuits.

    a. True

    b. False

19. How is foil used in alarm installations?

    a. On glass windows and doors

    b. To connect two or more PIRs in series

    c. To connect two or more PIRs in parallel

    d. To hold the control panel closed

20. Which is an example of Ohm's law?

    a. $I = E/R$

    b. $E = I/R$

    c. $R = E/I$

    d. All the above

21. According to the NEC, it is always necessary to use plenum rated wire (FPLP or FPLR) when pulling power-limited wiring up from one floor to another.

    a. True

    b. False

22. Who was an inventor of the first electric intruder alarm?

    a. Thomas A. Edison

    b. Edwin Thomas Holmes

    c. Benjamin Franklin

    d. D. Thomas

23. What was the first central station?

    a. Pinkerton Fire Alarm

    b. New York Burglar Watcher

    c. Boston's fire alarm center

    d. Western Union Burglary Watcher

24. In a CCTV system, color generally produces a more natural, richer image than black and white, and color is easier to view in very low-light situations.
   a. True
   b. False

25. What is an advantage of auto-iris control in CCTV systems?
   a. It lets the operator manually change between color and black and white.
   b. It lets the camera move to view multiple scenes.
   c. It lets the camera's auto-iris lens open or close to adjust the amount of light passing through the lens.
   d. It lets the monitor show multiple scenes on the screen at one time.

26. What kind of wire is used for wiring non-power-limited fire alarm (NPLFA) systems?
   a. Wire with a minimum insulation rating of 240 volts, 26 AWG
   b. Wire with a maximum insulation rating of 300 volts, 26 AWG
   c. Wire with a minimum insulation rating of 600 volts, 18 AWG
   d. Wire with a maximum insulation rating of 600 volts, 18 AWG

27. A single-phase, listed electronic power supply whose output supplies a two-wire single-voltage circuit is an example of a non-power-limited electrical supply.
   a. True
   b. False

28. What type of mount does a fixed focal lens have?
   a. C mount
   b. FF mount
   c. B mount
   d. F mount

29. What is the name for a lens that shows two separate scenes on one monitor?
   a. A two-way lens
   b. A double-imaging system
   c. An image-splitting optical or bifocal lens
   d. A video dual-technology lens

30. Fiber-optic cable is immune to most RFI, EFI, and electromagnetic interference (EMI).
   a. True
   b. False

31. What are important considerations in determining the best wiring methods for a given installation?
   a. Requirements of the system manufacturer
   b. Location of other wiring in the building
   c. Requirements of the NEC
   d. All the above

32. What are common maintenance problems of resistors and rheostats?

a. They break or have loose or broken connections.
b. They lose power or burn out.
c. They heat up too much and melt down.
d. They lose their magnetism and disconnect from their subcomponents.

33. Service panels use fuses or circuit breakers to protect each circuit from overload.
    a. True
    b. False

34. What does *roughing in* mean with respect to building construction?
    a. Pushing conduit through walls
    b. Pushing conduit from one floor to another
    c. Retrofitting an electrical system
    d. The early stage of an electrical installation done before the finishing work

35. What is the frequency range used by microwave detectors?
    a. 10 to 20 GHz
    b. 10 to 50 MHz
    c. 20 to 100 KHz
    d. 20 to 100 Hz

36. A junction box (or electrical box) is usually made of plastic or metal and is used to hold wire and cable splices.
    a. True
    b. False

37. What are three elements of a simple circuit?
    a. Switch, diodes, and a power source
    b. Power source, conductors, and a load
    c. Power source, conduit, and resistors
    d. Switch, a capacitor, and a power source

38. What is the *f* stop of a lens?
    a. The relationship between the lens aperture and focal length
    b. A device to control movement of a fixed lens
    c. A frequency filter
    d. An attachment that filters out UV light

39. A quad PIR design filters out disturbances that affect only three channels.
    a. True
    b. False

40. What is a closed-circuit alarm system?
    a. One with all sensors connected in parallel
    b. One that includes heat detectors
    c. One with sensors connected in series
    d. A system that is monitored by a central station

41. What is a passive sensor?
    a. A sensor that has its own power source
    b. A sensor that can act as a self-contained alarm, because it doesn't need to be attached to any other components to work

   c. A sensor that makes no sound but detects sound
   d. A sensor that detects radiation or some disturbance, but doesn't depend on emitting anything itself to make the detection

42. A wire nut is used to cover and tightly connect two pig-tailed wires.
   a. True
   b. False

43. Which is an important consideration in choosing a camera for a CCTV system?
   a. The field of view (FOV) required by the application
   b. The purpose of the video system
   c. How much the customer is willing to pay
   d. All the above

44. What happens when a time-lapse recording is played back at normal speed?
   a. The playback skips every other frame.
   b. The playback shows events at speeds slower than real time.
   c. The playback shows events at a speed faster than real time.
   d. The playback skips every third frame.

45. A quad PIR design filters out internally generated "popcorn" noise.
   a. True
   b. False

46. What are the main causes of false alarms in intruder alarm systems?
   a. Faulty installation and operator errors
   b. Use of an end-of-the-line resistance loop
   c. Faulty resistors and relays
   d. Burglars running away too fast

47. What are three elements of the fire triangle?
   a. Oxygen, sparks, and hydrogen
   b. Heat, fuel, and oxygen
   c. Flint, sparks, and timber
   d. Hydrogen, gas, and sparks

48. The Bournelli principle is the principle used by ultrasonic detectors.
   a. True
   b. False

49. What are common wiring sizes for low-voltage systems?
   a. No. 38 to No. 45 AWG
   b. No. 22 to No. 18 AWG
   c. No. 30 to No. 35 AWG
   d. No. 5 to No. 10 AWG

50. What does power refer to?
   a. The amount of work being done
   b. The speed of work being done
   c. The rate of current increase
   d. The rate of resistance increase

51. The frequency range transmitted by PIRs is 10 to 50 MHz.

   a. True
   b. False
52. Which material is corrosion-resistant?
   a. Aluminum
   b. Plastic-coated steel
   c. Silicon-bronze alloy
   d. All the above
53. Which type of relay is commonly used in fire alarm systems?
   a. Unsealed wall-mount relays
   b. Heat density relays and smoke density relays
   c. Rate-of-rise relays and rate-of-drop relays
   d. Sealed plug-in relays and nonsealed plug-in relays
54. How high you mount a PIR has little to do with its protection coverage.
   a. True
   b. False
55. What is the purpose of a bell time-out feature in an alarm system?
   a. To notify the controller when the bell is malfunctioning
   b. To shut the bell off after a preset amount of time
   c. To let authorized persons shunt the bell
   d. To keep an audit trail of the number of times the system has been
      turned on or off, and whose code was used to do so
56. What does the National Fire Code prohibit?
   a. The use of telephone dialers to automatically call any emergency tele-
      phone number
   b. The use of tape telephone dialers to connect to central stations
   c. The use of telephone dialers to automatically call the fire department
   d. The use of digital communicators to connect to central stations
57. Electromagnetic locks are inherently fail-secure.
   a. True
   b. False
58. What is multiplex?
   a. Technology that sends two or more coded signals over the same wire
      or channel
   b. Technology that sends one coded signal over two or more wires or
      channels
   c. Technology that sends two or more coded signals over two or more
      wires or channels
   d. Technology that prevents garbled signals from being transmitted
59. What is transitional lighting?
   a. Lighting that turns off automatically at sunrise
   b. A path of lights leading to different rooms in a building
   c. A path of lights outdoors
   d. Lighting that gives a gradual light level change between bright and
      dim areas

60. By installing MOVs you can prevent EMI from damaging an access control panel.
    a. True
    b. False

Answers to the test

When you score the test, give yourself 2 points for each correctly answered multiple-choice question and 1 point for each correctly answered true/false question. In each case where you gave no answer to a question, or gave two or more answers to a question, give yourself no credit.

Scoring key: 75 percent is minimum for passing; 85 percent is good; 95 percent or better is excellent.

1. *a*	23. *c*	46. *a*
2. *c*	24. *b*	47. *b*
3. *b*	25. *c*	48. *b*
4. *d*	26. *c*	49. *b*
5. *c*	27. *a*	50. *a*
6. *b*	28. *a*	51. *b*
7. *d*	29. *c*	52. *d*
8. *d*	30. *a*	53. *d*
9. *b*	31. *d*	54. *b*
10. *a*	32. *a*	55. *b*
11. *d*	33. *a*	56. *c*
12. *a*	34. *d*	57. *b*
13. *b*	35. *a*	58. *a*
14. *c*	36. *a*	59. *d*
15. *b*	37. *b*	60. *a*
16. *a*	38. *a*	
17. *a*	39. *b*	
18. *b*	40. *c*	
19. *a*	41. *d*	
20. *d*	42. *a*	
21. *b*	43. *d*	
22. *b*	44. *c*	
	45. *a*	

15

Finding Job Openings and Getting Hired

Part 1 of this chapter tells how to find job openings and get interviews. Part 2 describes in detail how to do great in interviews and how to negotiate a top salary.

Part 1: Overview

Finding Jobs

A common way that people search for jobs is by looking though Help Wanted ads in newspapers or trade journals, and then sending letters or resumes to as many as possible. Many use expensive resume paper, and try to prepare it as "professionally" as possible, based on guidelines from a resume book. If they're lucky enough to get an interview, they turn into a bundle of nerves. If they're asked about pay, they are afraid that if they try to negotiate, they won't get the job. That common way of doing things is a good way of *not* getting a job, or of earning far less than the employer was willing to pay. There's a better way to get the job and salary you want.

Where to search

Good places to get leads for jobs include your local newspapers, trade journals, and the Internet. If you're willing to relocate, also look through out-of-town newspapers (you can find them at your library and sometimes online). Also, let your friends know you're looking for work. Referrals can be very helpful. If you're looking for a management position, you might find it useful to go through a private employment agency. Some charge you a fee; others charge the employer. I don't recommend going to one that you have to pay for, because chances are, you could have found and gotten the job without the agency.

I've had the greatest success by finding job openings before they're advertised. To do that, get a telephone directory for the city you want to work in and make a database of all the relevant companies. For each listing, get the name, address, and name of the owner. If the owner's name isn't listed, find it through the local Better Business Bureau or Chamber of Commerce or by calling the company and asking.

If you're already working in the electronic security industry and haven't told your boss that you're looking for a new job, be wary of blind ads—those with no name of the company placing the ad. Some employers place such ads to see who's thinking about leaving. If a blind ad has an address, you can use a reverse directory on the Internet to look up the company name.

I've never responded to a blind ad. I think directly doing so is tacky and is tantamount to groveling. How desperate do you have to be to send your name, address, phone number, and work history to an unknown company for a job you know nothing about? Doing so decreases your credibility and negotiating clout. I'm not saying that a blind ad can't result in a great job; only that the chances are slimmer. If I were to respond to a blind ad, I would do it indirectly.

I would first find out the name of the company behind the ad, and contact them as if I never saw the ad. I would contact a specific person by name. There are many ways to find out who placed the ad. If the ad has an address, you can use a reverse directory on the Internet to get the name of the company. If you have a friend at the newspaper, you may be able to get the information that way. Or you could use a ruse—whatever it takes. You're a security person—get creative and figure it out. The bottom line is, if you don't have a name, don't respond. That contact could taint you if you apply for a job with the company later.

Creating a Resume

A current resume can be very helpful in job hunting (see Figure 15.1). But that is not the canned resumes that you find in most general-purpose resume books. A good resume for an alarm systems technician is different from one that's good for, say, a chemist or banker. Creating a resume for the electronic security industry isn't about paper quality or fancy typefaces. It's about content. You're not being hired as a graphic designer, so don't be cute with the resume. Just use white $8\frac{1}{2} \times 11$ inch paper (24-pound bond) and black ink, with no illustrations. Employers see so-called professional resumes everyday—the expensive laid or watermarked papers with matching envelopes that all sound alike in the way they say nothing. Everyone who reads those books uses the same empty code words. The key to a good resume is to have something to say, and to say it in your own voice. That's what will make yours stand out.

Don't throw a resume together in a day or two. Give yourself at least a few days to write and rewrite it. Keep a small notebook with you so you can jot down ideas and corrections as they come to you. Your resume isn't a job application; it's a promotional piece that should appear to be thoughtful and honest. When you're writing your resume, you're selling yourself. A rule of thumb in deciding what to include is that if an item isn't something to help someone decide to hire you, then it doesn't belong on the resume. If you were recently fired, for

123 East 321 Street   Phone 123-456-7890
Any Town, Any State 01234   Fax 123-456-7890
                             E-mail daniel@iahssp.org

Resume of Daniel M. Phillips

Objective

Work experience
Position in Security Sales August 1997–Present
Automated Home Technologies, Sales Manager
Responsible for training and supervising home automation
sales team of 12 people

June 1992–August 1997
GAMER CCTV Company, Marketing Manager
In charge of creating promotional materials and marketing closed-cir-
cuit television systems to installation companies.
Duties included supervising a staff of four, and preparing articles and
media releases.

June 1985–June 1992
Western Burglar & Fire Alarm Systems,
Installer/salesperson
Sold and installed residential and commerical burglar and
fire alarm systems.

September 1982–June 1985
Security Lock, Safe & Alarm Company,
Installer/salesperson
Installed various physical and electronic security
systems and devices and worked in the store
making sales.

Education
1991 LTC Training Center   Davenport, IA
Application & Design of CCTV program
Installation/Field Service of CCTV program

1980–81 New York Alarm School   New York, NY
650 Hour Certificate in Alarm Installation

1975–79 Ohio State University   Columbus, OH
BA in Business Administration

Professional
memberships
International Association of Home Safety and
Security Professionals
National Burglar and Fire Alarm Assocation

Figure 15.1   Your resume should entice the reader to call you for an interview.

instance, don't write that, even if you have a good reason. Things like that can
be discussed in an interview. The most important thing that you want the
potential employer to consider should be at the top of the page, followed in
descending order by all the other important things. What's most important for
you may be different from what's most important for someone else. For that
and other reasons, it's important not to copy someone else's resume format and
just insert your information. Use a format that shows you in your best light.

Usually the headings *Experience* and *Education* are good choices for the first two listings. If you have more education than job experience (such as if you're a recent college graduate), then the education should come first. Other popular headings include *Capabilities* and *Certification*. But if you have something special to offer that will be a great selling point, make up a label for it and put it first (or high on your list). Don't restrict yourself to the headings or order of headings that you've seen on other resumes.

It's usually most effective to speak in the third person when you're speaking highly of yourself a lot. Writing in the first person usually comes off as arrogant after awhile when you write, "I can do this; I can do that. I have done this; I have done that." Using the third person makes it seem like someone else is writing all that good stuff about you.

Don't include references on your resume. And don't write "References available on request." That's a filler statement; it just takes up space without giving information. A prospective employer who wants references will ask for them whether you write that you have them or not.

If you have an exceptional reference letter, however, make a copy of it and send it with your resume. Also, if a related newspaper or magazine article has been written about you, you might want to send a clip. If you've written a technical article in an industry trade journal, send a copy. Remember, it's a sales piece. If an attachment will help sell you, then use it. But don't include such things as a copy of your driver's license, alarm installer's license, or certifications. Mentioning them on your resume is enough for now. If the potential employer needs copies or proof, you'll be asked for that later.

What if you don't have much to say? If you don't have a lot of experience or education, then you need to make the most out of other factors important to the employer. If the job requires you to drive a service vehicle, and you have a great driving record, considering pointing that out. You might state: "Have a perfect driving record; no accidents." If you had excellent attendance at your last job, you might say: "In 10 years on the job, was absent only 3 days." The main thing is to put your best foot forward.

The Cover Letter

In addition to your resume, you'll need to create a cover letter to each prospective employer. Figure 15.2 shows a cover letter. The cover letter should make the reader interested in reading the resume. The paper for the cover letter should be the same as the paper for the resume. Some people recommend using rag bond or laid paper, which does look and feel very nice—but I think that's overkill for a technician and tends to give a negative impression (sort of like wearing a tuxedo to a job interview). The letter should always be typed with black ink, be free of typographical errors and misspellings, and be addressed to a specific person. Never send it to a department only. If necessary, pick up the telephone and get the name of someone to send it to.

Daniel M. Phillips

123 East 321 Street
Any Town, Any State 01234

January 15, 2002

Ms. Merlyn Coles
Creakers Security Products, Inc.
321 West 123 Street
Any Town, Any State 43210

Dear Ms. Coles:

Having worked in the security field for over 10 years, and having spent most of that time in sales, I was happy to see your ad in *Security* magazine for the position of sales engineer. As my enclosed resume shows, I more than meet the listed criteria for the position.

It sounds like what I'm looking for. I'll call you in about a week to set up a meeting.

Sincerely,

Daniel M. Phillips

Figure 15.2 Your cover letter should entice the reader to read your resume.

Make the cover letter no longer than one page. Send your cover letter and resume in a 9 × 12 inch envelope so you don't have to fold them. That will make them look better when they are opened and passed around, and it will be helpful if the company runs them through a scanner.

After sending your cover letter and resume, wait about 10 days for a response. Then call the company and ask if it arrived. If you have one of the company's job applications, don't complete it. Write your name on the application, below that write "see attached resume," and then affix your resume to the application. (More than once I was able to use my resume as a job application.) If the company asks you to complete its application form, your resume will still be there to help guide the interview to your advantage.

Questions for review

1. What's the purpose of a cover letter?

2. What's the purpose of a resume?

3. Where are three places to find job listings?

4. What's a blind ad?

5. What kind of paper should be used to create your resume?

Part 2: Being Interviewed

Most jobs are not awarded on the basis of who has the most training, or the greatest work experience, but on who gets through the interview the best. If it were simply a matter of education or work history, there would be no need to meet with you. That information is on the resume and job application. It's about a gut reaction. The interviewer has to feel that you're right for the job. That involves you selling yourself. In some ways it's like selling anything else. But the interview is a special kind of game, like chess, with many standard rules and openings that have been developed over the years. If you understand the rules and don't take things personally, you'll do fine.

Get a good night's sleep before the interview. In the morning, bathe and put on clean clothes. Get there a few minutes early. Unless there's a verifiable dead body involved, being late is a bad sign, and will be held against you. Also, you'll do better with a few moments to catch your breath before you go into an interview.

From the moment you walk into the building until you get back into your car, you're performing. Never let down your guard between those times. When you walk in, don't smoke and don't accept anything to eat or drink. If the interviewer asks whether you want some coffee, politely say, "No thank you; I'm fine." You're not at a dinner party. You're there to do business. When you walk in, give a firm handshake and say hello. Wait for the interviewer to sit down first or to ask you to sit. Look her or him in the eyes if you can (if you can't, look at the forehead). Let the interviewer speak first.

Don't sit like a statue. Appear relaxed. Feel free to lean forward a bit, and to smile and laugh when appropriate. Try to look attentive. Don't interrupt the interviewer. Let the interviewer talk all he or she wants. The more the interviewer talks, the less you'll have to. If the interviewer reveals personal information, act interested and ask about it.

When you're asked a good question, pause a moment before answering, even if you've rehearsed the answer 100 times (which you should have). The pause will make you seem more thoughtful and will help the answer come off as spontaneous and sincere. Put your best foot forward, and start giving reasons why you're a great person to hire. Don't say anything negative about yourself or about anyone else.

Here are some questions you can expect to be asked, and you should have answers. Get comfortable with them so you can give similar answers without sounding as if you're reciting a book.

Q: How well do you take direction?

A: I take direction well. I'm a team player, and I respect the authority of my supervisor. I understand that some decisions may involve matters that I'm not fully aware of, so I don't need to fully agree with everything to follow directions.

Q: How do you feel about you last supervisor (or boss)?

A: He's a good person, with a great sense of humor. (Never criticize anyone. If the interviewer tries to get you to be critical, don't go for it. Stay positive.)

Q: How would you rate yourself on a scale of 1 to 10?

A: Probably an 8 or 9. I like myself, and I do my best. But there's always room for improvement.

Q: Do you prefer working alone or with others?

A: I can do either. I'm comfortable working alone when I need to, but I also enjoy working with people.

Q: Tell me a story.

A: What would you like me to tell you a story about? (Don't get suckered into rambling. If you don't know what the person is asking about, then find out before answering.)

Q: What are your weaknesses?

A: I enjoy working hard and probably need to slow down more. (Always turn a weakness into a strength. Never really say anything negative about yourself.)

Q: Do you now have or plan to have children?

A: No. (It doesn't matter if it's true. See my "balancing answer" theory below.)

Q: What do you plan to be doing 5 years from now?

A: (The answer should always be tied to the work you're applying for.)

Q: Sell me this pen.

A: (Pick up the pen and look at it. Notice any salable characteristics, and then start talking.) This is one of the finest ballpoint pens ever made. The ink is designed to flow evenly. The airtight cap snugly protects the tip. The material is designed for a comfortable grip. Your company's name can be imprinted on this pen at a cost lower than that for most unimprinted pens in office supply stores. We can do that for you because of the special manufacturing technology that we use. How many pens would you like?

Some questions are illegal for interviewers to ask you, but they might ask them anyway. You're not normally supposed to be asked about religion or politics, for example. If you mention those things on your resume, however (such as in telling about volunteer work), you may open the door to questions. In any case, when you're asked an illegal question, you can either answer it or not answer it. I think it's self-defeating and unfair for you to say, "That's an illegal question, and I will not answer it." That virtually guarantees you won't get the job, because you'll seem difficult (and perhaps litigious).

I know what I'm about to say may be controversial, but it's my belief that when an interviewer places you in such an untenable position by asking an illegal question, you have the right to say whatever the interviewer wants to hear—even if the answer isn't true. I say that because the question isn't supposed to be asked, much less be used to reject you. I don't consider the false answer to be a lie. I consider it a justified "balancing answer" that puts everything back in place to keep the interview fair.

I've used balancing answers and found them very effective. I recall a time when an interviewer was obviously of a different political bent from me, and he asked about my political leanings. I basically told him I was the same as he is (he had clearly telegraphed his leanings).

When you give a balancing answer, be sure to include a wrap-up statement—a comment that helps put an end to that line of questioning. You need to do that, because some interviewers may delve further into the matter with more and more personal and illegal questions that get harder and harder for you to answer. An atheist who's asked if he believes in God, for example, might say, "Yes, I believe in God. But I prefer to not discuss religion at work. I like to focus on my job while working." That balancing answer prevents the question from being used against the interviewee, and it puts the interviewer on notice that you are not interested in going into the matter further.

If you're asked illegal questions, as soon as you leave the interview, write down exactly what you were asked, by whom, and when, along with your answers. Those extemporaneous notes can be helpful if you decide to sue or file state or federal discrimination charges against the company. The notes can also be helpful if you get hired and the company tries to hassle you about the answers you gave. In addition to making notes, immediately after leaving the interview, tell someone what happened. That person may be useful as a witness.

If you don't get hired and want to take action against the company, speak to an attorney right away. You may then be advised to write a letter to the interviewer's supervisor complaining about the interviewer.

It might be helpful to send such a letter soon after the interview. Perhaps the interviewer's supervisor doesn't know about or agree with such interviewing tactics. You might get lucky that way. But I don't think so. I think it would more likely cause the company to see you as a troublemaker, or to close ranks against you in preparation for administrative or legal action you might take.

Special Types of Interviews

Some interviews are designed to create a lot of stress for you, to see how well you handle pressure. If you walk into a room with several interviewers sitting around, expect a stressful interview. Typically they will rapidly fire questions at you, not giving you enough time to answer one before asking another. If you get angry, curse them out, and storm out the door, you failed the interview. The appropriate response is to keep your composure, smile, look them in the eyes, and say, "You're asking some great questions. And I want to answer them all. But I need to take them one at a time."

In another kind of stressful interview, the interviewer comes in late, doesn't look you in the eyes, doesn't shake your hand, and acts disinterested in what you have to say. He or she will ask rude and intimidating (and perhaps illegal) questions. Again, don't take it personally. It's just a game. Don't let the interviewer know that you're onto him or her. Just stay calm, be polite, and answer the questions directly and positively.

A third type of stressful interview is more deceptive, because it doesn't involve continuous negativity. The interviewer starts by being polite and then all of a sudden hits you with something like "Why aren't you earning more money at your age?" Then the person will go back to softer questions to relax you, before giving another zinger. Your reaction to this type of interview should be the same as for the others. Don't let yourself get too relaxed by easy questions, or too stressed by tough ones. Take each question in stride. Keep in mind that the meeting won't last long, but could result in a job offer. If the interviewer seems especially obnoxious, tell yourself that she or he is really a nice person who's trying to do the job well.

Remember, the interview isn't officially over until you get into your car. Don't let your guard down just because the interviewer seems to be done asking questions. A common tactic is to hit with a tough question just at that point. No matter how tough the question, try to appear poised and give a simple and direct answer. Don't start rambling just because you feel as if you've said something wrong. Even if the interviewer gets quiet, don't start talking. Just enjoy the peace and think about what you'll eat for lunch on the first day of your new job. Before you leave, ask the interviewer when you can expect to hear something. Never act as if you believe the job is lost, no matter how badly you think you may have performed. Chances are, it wasn't nearly as bad as you think. Remember that you're being compared to other applicants. No one is perfect. (And if they didn't read this book, you have a better chance at the job than they do.)

Occasionally during a first interview you'll be asked about your salary requirements. Usually, when the question comes up at that time, it's just a feeler question and not meant to begin serious negotiations. Don't propose a salary. Just say, for example, "Right now, I mostly want you to know more about me and what I can offer your company, and I want to learn a little more about the position. If we decide we want to work together, I'm sure we can reach a fair salary." Usually salary negotiations take place during or after a second meeting.

Before the interview ends, the interviewer will ask if you have any questions. At that time, be sure to ask a few that you've prepared. Here are some possibilities:

What are the duties and responsibilities of the job?

Is it a new position?

What kind of person are you looking for?

Who are the direct supervisors for the position? Tell me a little about them.

It's good to ask thoughtful questions, but don't get wrapped up in little details. Don't ask how long your lunch break will be or how many paid sick days you'll get. You can find out those things after you're offered the job, and they may become part of your salary negotiations.

Negotiating a Salary

Before discussing salary, you need to figure out the minimum amount you can accept and how much you can reasonably hope for. To figure out the minimum amount, you might start with the amount you're making now and decide how much more (or less) you'll accept to take the new job. You might also start from the amount you need to pay your monthly bills. Consider any benefits (such as insurance) that you will be gaining or losing. To estimate what you can reasonably expect, start with any advertised salary range for the position. Another starting point is the average salary range for people in that position. You may be able to get that figure from trade journals or trade associations. One other way to estimate what you can reasonably expect is to know the ending salary of the last person to hold the job. He or she may not mind sharing that information with you.

With that information at hand, you'll be in a good position to begin negotiating. Rule number one: Never be first to propose a salary. When you're asked how much you're looking for, give a vague answer: "I don't have a specific figure in mind. I just want a fair salary that reflects my value to the company, and that allows me to spend all my work time doing the best I can for this company." The person may try to take control of the negotiations by asking you "put in your place" kinds of questions such as, "How much did you make in your last job?" or "How much are you earning now?" The idea is to make that figure a starting point for negotiations. Don't let the interviewer do that. Just respond with something like "Not enough, which is a big reason why I'm talking with you now." If the interviewer persists in trying to get a figure from you, point out that they're very different jobs with different responsibilities.

When a salary is proposed, don't blink and don't act happy, no matter how good it sounds. Keep a straight face, and realize that the negotiations have begun and that figure is the lowest the salary will go. For the next few minutes, forget about the issue of salary. Don't accept or reject the offer. Instead, ask about benefits. What percentage of insurance premiums does the company pay? Ask how much the last person in the job earned before leaving. If you're required to wear a uniform, ask who pays for them.

The person may try to pin you down on the issue of salary. Keep that issue open as long as possible, because doing so will give you more leverage on other issues. To deflect the issue a little longer, you might say, "Of course, I need to earn a decent living, but I see salary as a package and not just the amount written on the check. I'm trying to see what's being offered as a whole." If the company isn't offering any other benefits, you might try to propose some. Some things I've proposed and gotten include an extra week of paid vacation; free extra uniforms (they were tax-deductible to the company); use of the company vehicle at night; and the title "Manager." (An employer told me, "I don't care if you want to be called King of the company, as long as you know I'm the owner.")

After the talk about benefits is over, say to the employer, "I don't like to haggle. Can you just tell me what's the best salary you can pay me?" Listen intently as the employer whines about how much she or he is offering already; then give a counteroffer. The employer probably won't accept it, but that doesn't matter. (In fact, if it was accepted right away, your offer would have been too low.) Then stand up, shake hands, and thank him or her for meeting with you. Tell the interviewer you'll give the matter some thought, then leave. Now go to your next interview.

The secret to getting the most from negotiations is to know what parameters are reasonable, and to always be willing to walk away. If you're not prepared to walk away from an offer, then you're not negotiating—you're just bluffing.

You are a valuable commodity. People aren't offering you work because they're being nice. They've interviewed others, and you're one of the best. They want you because they believe you can contribute to their company. It's up to you to have enough self-respect to hold out for a good offer. Keep in mind, if that company wanted you, others are likely to want you also. Before you commit your time, your talents, your name, and your creativity to a company, make sure that the company appreciates you enough to pay you a decent wage.

Starting and Expanding a Business

Part 1 of this chapter describes the basics of starting an electronic security business, including writing a business plan, choosing a name, hiring employees, and buying insurance and equipment. Part 2 discusses proven promotional techniques for getting more business. Whether you're just starting out or have been in business for many years, you'll likely find something in this chapter to help you save or make more money.

Part 1: Basics

Starting a Security Business

To start an electronic security installation company, you'll need a place to operate from. There are advantages to working from a building that is used solely for your business (see Figure 16.1). But successful companies also operate out of office buildings that have various types of businesses (as shown in Figure 16.2), and out of buildings that can be used as both a business and a home (much like the style shown in Figure 16.3). The business/home combination can help keep initial costs to a minimum.

You'll also need at least one service vehicle (depending on the number of employees). Your service vehicle should have a design that's consistent with your building. The design should be professionally created and include a logo. Elements of that design should appear in all your stationery, literature, and advertisements. Creating and maintaining that visual identity is very important. It's best to use a graphic design firm if you can afford it. The next best option (which costs much less) is to hire a talented student from a local art school. To find one, just post Help Wanted notices on the school's bulletin boards or place an ad in its newspaper.

Be conservative in the beginning. Don't waste your money buying the newest and fanciest office furniture and service vehicles. Make sure you start with

Figure 16.1 Many of the larger security companies operate out of their own buildings.

Figure 16.2 Some electronic security companies operate out of an office building.

Figure 16.3 Some buildings can let you operate a security company in part of it (such as on the first floor), but live in another part of the building (such as upstairs).

enough money. Don't try to start on a shoestring. Develop a reasonable and conservative budget. Network with others in your community right away and often. Develop professional relationships with insurance agents, law enforcement officers, churches, local businesses, civic organizations, and others. Consider joining local and national trade associations. They can give you much needed information and training and can help establish your credibility with the public. Buy good books (like this one). Subscribe to security trade journals to help you stay updated with the industry. A list of associations and trade publications is given in Appendix F.

Don't try to sell systems at a lower price than everyone else does. That's a quick way to lose a lot of money and to lose all credibility with other alarm installers. Unless you're ADT, Brinks, or one of the other giants, you can't afford to profitably sell systems at lower costs than everyone around you. When some newcomer tries to do that, he or she goes out of business and consumers get stuck with poorly installed low-end alarm systems. Sell good-quality products and services, and a sense of security, rather than price.

Write a Business Plan

A written business plan is usually a must if you want to borrow money to start your business. Some landlords require one before they'll lease property to a new business. They want to assure themselves that the business has a realistic chance of being around a while. But even if no one else requires one, it's a good idea to have a written business plan. A good plan is like a road map that helps set you in the right direction and helps you stay on course. It will help you notice and correct problems before they get out of hand.

Business description.   Succinctly describe your business. What products and services will you provide, and how will you do it? What is your target market? Don't say, "Everyone." Be realistic and as specific as possible. Based on your strengths and weaknesses, which group is most likely to buy from you over your competitors (for example, residential, commercial, low-income, or high-end). How will you market your products and services? Where will your business be located? What hours will you work? Will you be paid only in cash and checks? Or will you accept credit cards?

Competition.   Look in your local telephone directory and find your competitors. Then gather all the information you can find about each of them: owners, size, length of time in business, annual revenue, number of employees, types of services offered, number of accounts, types of accounts (residential, commercial, both), number of locations, number of service vehicles, types of advertisements, promotional activities, company strong points, company weaknesses, and whatever else you can learn. To find out about a company, you have to do some digging. Go to your chamber of commerce, the company's website, licensing boards, Secretary of State's office, and newspaper archives (sometimes on the Internet). Get creative. The more details you can cite about each of your competitors, the more impressive your business plan will be. You need to be able to tell who they are, and why it's realistic to think a significant number of people will choose your company over theirs.

Personal.   Another question you need to answer is, "Why you?" What makes you qualified to run the business? What credentials and certifications do you have? How do they compare to those of your competitors? What associations do you belong to? How much do you love the work? Is it your life's passion or just a fast way to make some money? Do you plan to be doing this work for the next 10 years?

Future of the industry.   Include a statement about future trends that answers the following questions: Where is the industry going? What trends can you expect? What new technology will likely affect your business? Chapter 1 can help you with your statement.

Breakeven analysis.   One of the most important parts of a business plan is the date when you should make a profit. Making income alone doesn't mean much. Until your revenues exceed your costs, you haven't really made any money. Some people dump loads of money into a business and never make back what they put into it. That reminds me of a joke: What's the quickest way to a small fortune? Start out with a big one.

To make a break-even analysis forecast, you need to make four realistic estimates: fixed costs (overhead), sales revenue, gross profits from each sale (profits after costs), and break-even sales revenue (amount needed each week or month to cover all costs). Break-even sales revenue doesn't include profit.

Legal Entities

Every business is some type of legal entity. Either you can consciously choose the one that best meets your needs, or you'll be one by default. Which entity your business is will affect your tax rates, your liability, how you may legally take money from the business, and what kind of records you have to keep.

Sole proprietor. If you're the sole owner of your business and it isn't incorporated, it's a sole proprietorship—even if you have employees. The sole proprietorship is the easiest business form to start, and it is the most common. One drawback is that the owner has unlimited personal liability for the business, and when the owner dies, the business typically dies, too (unless the owner makes a provision in the will for the executor to keep the business going during the administration of the owner's estate).

General partnership. A general partnership is similar to two or more sole proprietors with equal interest and responsibility in the unincorporated business. If one of the partners dies or files bankruptcy, typically the general partnership is dissolved (unless all, or a majority, of the other partners agree to continue the business).

Limited partnership. The specific rights and obligations of partners in a limited partnership vary depending on statutes. Typically, however, in a limited partnership one or more partners invest money, but don't take part in the management of the business.

Corporation. In some states a corporation can be formed by one person, but whether it is formed by one person or twenty people, a corporation is significantly different from other forms of business. A corporation continues to exist even if one or more of the officers dies, resigns, files bankruptcy, or whatever. It is considered to be an entity distinct from each person holding office (even if it's one person). In law, a corporation is referred to as an *artificial person,* as opposed to a *natural person* (which is a human being). The corporation can enter into contracts, file lawsuits, and otherwise do business as an individual. Of course, human beings have to physically sign papers and carry out the tasks on behalf of the corporation. When doing so, however, persons must be properly authorized to do so, and need to follow protocols that make it clear that they are acting on behalf of the corporation. When you sign a document for a corporation, for instance, you need to include your corporate title. It's also a good idea to include *Incorporated* or *Inc.* with your company name on all stationery and literature. Your personal bank accounts must be separate from the corporate accounts.

Money can be taken out of a corporation in only two ways: salaries and dividends. Both have to be approved by the board of directors and entered into the minutes of the corporation. Your salary becomes your personal income, and it is taxed at your personal rates. Dividends may be made to shareholders only after taxes are paid, and the dividends become personal income and are taxed at personal rates.

S corporation.   An S corporation is a business corporation that opts to be taxed as a partnership under Subchapter S of the Internal Revenue Code, rather than according to the provisions of Subchapter C, which is the regular corporation tax section. That avoids double taxation at the corporate and then shareholder levels.

To be eligible for S corporation status, a corporation must *not* have more than 35 shareholders or more than one class of stock or own 80 percent or more of the stock of another corporation. As a general rule, all the shareholders much be natural persons (there are some exceptions, however) and must be U.S. citizens or resident aliens.

Any business or professional corporation that meets the requirements can choose to start being taxed under Subchapter S. To choose to be taxed as an S corporation, all shareholders must agree and sign a form. If you plan to opt for Subchapter S status, it's usually best to create your articles of incorporation with that in mind and to file Form 2553 immediately after filing the articles.

Limited liability company.   A limited liability company (LLC) is a hybrid between a general partnership and a corporation. It's a fairly new entity that was first enacted in the United States by Wyoming in 1977 and by Florida in 1982. It became popular after 1988 when the Internal Revenue Service decided it would be taxed as a partnership, rather than as a C corporation. More than two-thirds of states now have LLC statutes.

Members of an LLC may participate in the management of the business without risk of assuming the personal liability of a general partner. Members of an LLC may be individuals, corporations, partnerships, or other LLCs. A problem with LLCs is that not all states have LLC-compatible legislation. Some states tax LLCs as corporations; others impose license or franchise fees on them. Also, because LLCs are so new, there's still uncertainty regarding many technical federal and state legal issues.

Choosing a Name

Pick a name that quickly lets people know what your business is. Don't use a cute or clever name that people will have to think about too long before they get it. Stick to the basics. Use words such as *security, alarm,* and *systems* in your name. You may also want to incorporate your city or county name. Another consideration, especially if there are many electronic security companies in your area, is where it will be listed in your local telephone directory. Consider a name that will be listed close to the top of the category heading.

If you're not a corporation, you have to stick with your own name unless you file a fictitious name form with your state (usually with the corporations department). That form makes a public record of who you really are, in case someone decides to sue you. States don't want people running around making up new business names at will without any record of a real name behind the business.

Before you choose a name, make sure no one else in your state is using it. You can run a name check with your corporation's department. And avoid names that are deceptively similar to names used by famous companies, because they'll sue you. Even if your name is, say, John Brinks, don't even think about naming your company Brinks Security Systems or Brinks Alarms or Brinks anything. If your company's name is close enough to a famous brand name or company name that the average person (whoever that is) would think you are the same company or are affiliated with that famous company, you're in trouble. Even if you get the name accepted by your state's Secretary of State office, you won't be protected. That office can't be expected to know of every major brand and company name in every industry. It's your responsibility to choose a safe name.

Using Computers

A computer is virtually indispensable to competing in business today. You'll find it helpful for maintaining your customer database; keeping track of accounts receivables and accounts payable; keeping track of inventory; advertising; creating promotional materials; preparing letters, reports, and articles; printing payroll checks; and doing financial analysis.

Before you can do anything with the computer, you need the right software. For keeping track of inventories, get the kind that automatically increases and decreases your on-hand inventory account as you buy and sell products. All inventory programs require you to take the time to input all your inventory at least once. A stand-alone inventory program requires you to manually add and subtract from the recorded inventory each time you buy or sell a product. A more efficient program is one that seamlessly integrates several modules, such as accounts payable, accounts receivable, job costing, service tracking, and inventory.

That lets you enter information only once, and then each time you buy or sell inventory the software refers to the appropriate module to increase or decrease the inventory count.

PC or Mac?

A common question is, Which of the two major types of computer architecture should you buy? To run an electronic security business, an IBM PC (or just PC) is generally better. Apple Macintoshes (or Macs) are more often used by graphic design firms. With Apple's PowerMac you can work with both Mac and PC documents.

Insurance

You'll probably need various types of insurance: premises liability (for when people get hurt on your property), errors and omissions, property, automobile, workers' compensation, and indemnity bonds (which protect you from customers who claim you or an employee stole something from them). Look for an A-rated carrier (as rated by A. M. Best, a well-respected independent rating source). Companies with a B or C rating have less financial ability to pay a lot of claims. During tough times, those lower-rated companies are more likely to go bankrupt.

You'll save money by getting all the insurance from the same company under an umbrella policy, getting deductibles as high as you can reasonably afford, and paying annually. To keep your insurance, it may be best to not report some claims. If you have a minor accident in which no one is hurt and the claim is below your deductible, for instance, you'll have to pay the same amount whether you report it or not. So why have the insurance company put a blot on your record? Some insurance companies will cancel you for a single claim, no matter how small. If someone was hurt, however, or if the police or fire department was involved, then you should report it to the insurance company. That will protect you in case future claims are made. Sometimes people don't realize how hurt they are until they think about how much money they can get.

Hiring Employees

One of the toughest parts of business is to find and keep good employees. Ideally, you want someone who's intelligent, honest, well trained, and good-natured; who has a history of staying with companies for several years; and who has left each job on good terms. In the real world, however, job applicants usually fall short of perfect. Your job is much like that of a scout for a professional sports team. Out of the applicants you have to choose from, you need to make judgments about who will best fit into your team.

One way of finding new employees is to ask your current workers to recommend people. Another option is to place Help Wanted ads in trade journals, on the Internet, and in newspapers. In my experience, trade journals give the best results, mainly because the readers are usually more experienced. When jobs are scarce, your newspaper ad will likely bring in every unemployed person who's seen or heard an alarm system. Most people will require a lot of training. I've never tried to search for employees through the Internet; for some reason that method just doesn't feel right. It seems like a huge undertaking to weed the few serious applicants out of the tangled mass of anonymous e-mails. But it might work for you. If you decide to place ads in newspapers, consider using blind ads—those without your company name or address. Those ads can help you learn of dissatisfied employees who are looking around.

They can also help you in salary negotiations. By placing several blind ads with different starting salaries (or salary ranges), you can get a good idea about what salary a prospective employee is looking for. (However, never make willingness to accept a low salary a primary reason for hiring someone.)

A job application is often the most important paper tool for choosing a good employee. Make sure you use one that is at least two pages long and that asks for a lot of specifics, such as starting and ending dates and supervisor names. Never accept a resume in place of a job application, because with a resume the applicant has full control over what to include and exclude. It's too easy to make a resume look informative when it's actually hiding important information.

It's often helpful to give professionally designed written tests to job applicants. For salespersons, consider using the Contact Styles Survey (CSS). No special training is needed to administer the test. Always conduct a background check. Have the applicants give you written permission to do so, and then send letters requesting information to previous employers. They may not want to put much in writing out of concern over being sued. You can often get more useful information by following up your letter with a phone call. Get as much written information as you can on an applicant, but don't be a slave to paper. It's too easy for someone to look good on paper. No application, resume, or reference letter can take the place of a good face-to-face interview. If after an interview you think someone is a good candidate, have a second interview. That will give you time to receive more written information, and it will help you get a closer look at the person. Most likely there were questions you forgot to ask the first time that you should have asked. Also, the second interview is a good time to talk about salary.

Conducting the interview.   Don't waste your time trying to conduct a stressful interview. That's where you stomp into the room without looking at the applicant, act as if you're bored, and start firing off mean-spirited questions. Unless you're an interviewing expert, you'll look silly and will probably turn off your best job applicants. Instead, just be polite and ask good, open-ended questions. Let the interviewee do most of the talking. Start with the statement: "Tell me about yourself." If he or she responds, "What do you want to know?" say, "Just tell me anything you want me to know about you." Watch the person's face and body language. Be sure to ask about any apparent problems that you see on the resume or job application. Ask follow-up questions about what the interviewee tells you. Other important questions include these:

- Why do you want to work here?
- What did you like most about your last job?
- What did you like least about your last job?
- Why did you leave your last job?
- What's the best reason for hiring you?
- What would you most like to improve about yourself?
- What's the worst problem you've had with a former boss or supervisor?
- Under what circumstances would you quit a job?
- Do you have any questions about this company? (That should be your next-to-last question.)

After the interviewee asks a few questions about the company, or declines to ask, act as if you're done with the interview. Reach out to shake hands, and then ask "the question." That should be whatever question most concerns you about the application or resume. You might say, "One more thing. Where were you working between 1995 and 1999?" If the applicant is being honest, the sudden question shouldn't cause much of a problem. But if the person has a lot to hide, you'll probably notice sweat, trembling, rapid eye movement, and other signs of deception.

Questions for review

1. Why is it important to have a job applicant complete an application, instead of just providing you with a resume?

2. What are two requirements for a central station to be UL-listed?

3. What is an S corporation?

4. What kind of names shouldn't you use for your company?

5. What are two major differences between a corporation and a sole proprietorship?

Part 2: Expanding Your Business through Free Promotion

Anyone can hide behind advertisements. But to lead your company to new levels of profit, you need to come out from behind your desk and let the public know who you are. If you're proud of your company and have confidence in your knowledge of the field, then stand up and be a leader. There are many things you can do right now to greatly improve your company's image in the community without spending much money. I'm sharing this from experience, because I've done them all.

Public Speaking

Public speaking is a way to promote your services to 50 to 100 (or even to thousands) of prospects at one time, at virtually no cost. Nonprofit and service organizations such as the Kiwanis Clubs, Rotary, and Lion's or Optimist Clubs are always looking for professional speakers to talk to their groups. They get a speaker for free, and you get a forum for promoting your company and services. Public speaking will likely give you an advantage over your competitors, because they're probably afraid to do it.

Most people are deathly afraid of speaking to a group of strangers. I still get scared before I start. Some psychology professionals say the fear of public speaking that so many people have is due to childhood experiences, such as being laughed at when standing in front of a class. (Maybe that's why *scared* is spelled almost like *scarred*.)

In any case, face-to-face communication is one of the most cost-effective means of influencing people. There's power and honesty in a person looking you right in the eyes and talking that can't be replicated through e-mail, faxes, brochures, or magazine ads. By learning to speak in public, you can take advantage of that power. Even if you have been scarred by snickering classmates, you can quickly learn to be an effective speaker.

Being an *effective* speaker doesn't mean being a great speaker. You don't need to (and probably never will) give talks as a famous minister or stand-up comedian does. If you're comparing yourself to professional public speakers, that's part of the reason for your anxiety. Instead of comparing yourself to others, compare yourself to yourself—to a well-prepared version of you. Your audience knows you're not a professional speaker and won't expect you to sound like one.

Some fear is healthy and can be helpful. It will motivate you to properly prepare for your talk. Overconfidence isn't good. That might give you the illusion that you're good enough to just wing it, with no preparation. A little fear helps motivate you to properly prepare. Even the great speakers prepare their talks.

Practice a lot, at least with a tape recorder, preferably with a videocamera. Practice in front of friends, and listen to their criticisms. Try to learn how to do better. Pay particular attention to any annoying mannerisms you may have.

Preparing your speech

To prepare a speech, you need to actually write it out, and not just think it through. Start with a good opening. It may have the greatest impact of your speech, and it will help relax you. Don't say something hokey like "Hello, it's a pleasure to be here." Instead, show that it's a pleasure. Smile, and make an appropriate observation, tell a joke, or talk about something that happened just before your speech. When you tell jokes, keep in mind that they need to be in good taste for the audience as a whole. Avoid any jokes about women as a group or any race or any political party or religion. No matter how innocuous and funny such a joke may seem, it isn't worth the risk.

Think about your audience members. What is the information they want most from you? If you know your business, you'll be able to predict what their questions will be simply by experience. If you're not sure what a particular audience might want to hear, talk to the program chair and get that information from him or her.

Don't write your speech all at one sitting. Keep a notepad with you for a couple of weeks before the talk, and jot down ideas that come to mind. When you think of questions that you expect people will ask, or get ideas for comments or jokes, write them down. A few days before the speech, put it all together.

Some people suggest holding the paper and reading the speech straight through. That might be easier for you if you're really nervous. But it's harder on the audience. It's boring to watch someone read a piece of paper. An alternative is to write your speech word for word, and read it many times in practice. Then write down the key points of your speech, and place that on the podium. From there, use the notes as a guide and just talk to your audience. Don't worry about saying everything exactly word for word. Just remember to touch on all your key points.

On the day of your speech, arrive early and make sure the microphone works and any props are there. If possible, have someone introduce you. Having someone say some good things about you can put you at ease, and help give you credibility with your audience.

When you're speaking, look into the audience. If you don't feel comfortable looking into anyone's eyes, look at someone's forehead. Look at different parts of the audience. You may have heard the old advice about visualizing the audience members in their underwear. Marsha Brady used that on the Brady Bunch, and of course, it worked great for her. But I don't recommend it. It's too distracting (especially when you see someone who's attractive). You don't want to be ogling your audience.

Try to focus on a few people who are being attentive. You can deliver your speech in a competent manner if you use the following basic presentation skills: Speak clearly, enunciate well, raise and lower your voice occasionally, look up from your notes at the audience as often as you can (remember eye contact), smile once in a while, and draw on your natural enthusiasm or emotion in addressing the subject.

When you're behind the lectern, don't lean on it. Don't stand behind the lectern during most of the talk. That makes you look timid, as if you're afraid of the audience.

When you're almost ready to end, tell the audience and ask for questions. You could say, "Before I end this talk, are there any questions?" Then after you answer the questions, give your last comment and thank people for coming.

If you're prepared, you'll find that most questions are pretty simple to answer. If someone asks something that you don't know the answer to, just politely say, "I don't know." Don't guess at an answer, because that's often a trap to make you look like an idiot. The person asking the question may be another security professional or may have just finished doing a doctoral dissertation on the topic in question. Also, don't let anyone pull you into talking about matters outside the scope of your talk. If you're talking to homeowners about making their homes more secure and someone asks about the accuracy of campus crime statistics, for instance, say that it's beyond the scope of this talk, but you'd be happy to talk about that later. If people are making a lot of noise, you might stand still and say nothing until the room quiets. Then say, "Thank you," and continue the talk.

Handouts. Design handouts are of interest and value to your audience and include information about your company and its services. Don't make the handout look like nothing more than an advertisement, or few people will look at it, and it will make your speech seem suspect.

Business cards. If you're trying to develop business contacts, collect business cards from the audience. You can offer to send additional information or material to them. Or you can offer a door prize, such as a free home security inspection or electronic security-related item, to be given through a drawing of business cards at the end of your talk. The business cards give you prospects to follow up on.

Other Promotion Opportunities

Once you've spoken in public a few times and realize your world didn't come to an end, the sky's the limit for your promotional opportunities. You can then do television, radio, and print interviews.

Television

Your local television stations are great places to get interviewed. They probably have local programming on the weekends. You can also get interviewed for news stories and write your own articles. For me, doing television is about as scary as public speaking. You feel as though you're being watched by millions of people, and there will be a permanent record of how awkward you looked. But the reality is that you only get a few minutes of air time, the whole world isn't watching, and you don't look as bad as you feel.

Radio

For radio you can ask either to come on as a guest, which is usually pretty easy, or to do your own talk show. Getting a talk show can be hard, because it depends on how much time the station has available and on the interests of the audience. Also, doing a regular talk show will take a lot of your time. One of the advantages of radio is that you can be a guest without leaving your home. You have a set time to call in, and then you wait for the host to start talking to you.

News releases

Most of the popular word processing programs have news release templates you can use. If you don't have a template, just use an $8^1/_2 \times 11$-inch sheet of plain white paper. Set $1^1/_2$-inch margins on all sides. At the top left, write *Contact:* along with your name and address, so the editor can reach you with any questions. Drop down a few lines and type *For Immediate Release.* Then tell your story. Start with the most important information. Think as if you only have two sentences to make your point. Then expand with more details; pretend you have only four sentences. Then six sentences. Continue to write from most important to least important. Always assume that the editor is going to chop of a lot of your release from the bottom, but you're not sure how much will be chopped off. Type your release in double-space. Check it for accuracy. Don't have typographical errors or misspelled words. Use a dictionary.

Style is important, but the content of the release is critical. Write something interesting. Don't try to turn the news release into an advertisement. Don't use it to talk about your low, low prices. Try to put yourself in the position of a news editor. But isn't it supposed to be for promotion? Of course it is. But it's a sophisticated type of promotion—not a hard sell. By printing news stories about your company, the publication gives an implied endorsement. You are getting tremendous promotional value without ever mentioning your business hours or prices. A news release I received while writing this book is shown in Figure 16.4.

You'll increase your chance of getting the news release published if you include a usable quality photograph or illustration. It should be interesting, consistent with the release, and compatible with the news media's needs. If the news outlet only prints in black and white, for instance, don't send color photographs. That's more work for them. It is better to either take a new photograph or have it turned into a black-and-white.

Articles

A great way to build your company's credibility is to write short, informative articles for local publications. Use it to give people interesting, entertaining,

---

PRESS RELEASE

Brink's Home Security, Inc.
8880 Esters Boulevard, Irving, Texas 75063
Contact: Robert B. Allen
Phone: (972) 871-3824
FAX: (972) 871-3318

FOR IMMEDIATE RELEASE

BRINK'S HOME SECURITY, INC. ANNOUNCES THE APPOINTMENT OF STACEY RAPIER AS VICE PRESIDENT OF HUMAN RESOURCES

Irving, Texas, January 8, 2001—Peter A. Michel, President and Chief Executive Officer announces the appointment of Stacey Rapier as Vice President of Human Resources of Brink's Home Security, Inc., Irving, Texas.

Stacey brings over fourteen years of experience as a recognized senior-level human resources executive. Most recently, Stacey was Vice President, People & Corporate Services at The M/A/R/C Group. Previously, she was Vice President, People Development at AT&T Wireless Services and held various positions of increasing responsibility at NCR Corporation. Stacey received her Bachelor of Science degree in Business Administration from the University of Kansas.

Brink's Home Security, which was formed in 1983, has over 660,000 customers in over 98 markets in 42 states, Washington, D.C., British Columbia, and Alberta, Canada. The company installs and electronically monitors residential and light commercial security systems.

The Pittston Company (NYSE: PZB–news), is a diversified company with interests in security services through Brink's Incorporated and Brink's Home Security, Inc., global freight transportation and supply chain management services through BAX Global, and mining and minerals exploration through Pittston Coal Company and Pittston Mineral Ventures. Press releases are available on the World Wide Web at www.pittston.com, or by calling toll free 877-275-7488.

Figure 16.4 A sample news release.

and useful information. That will help them come to associate you with being a knowledgeable professional.

Don't worry about financial payment (it wouldn't be that much anyway). But always insist on a credit line. Squeeze what you can from a credit line, because it will seem as if the editor did it, instead of you. If you can, have them list your company name, address, and phone number in the credit line. Credit lines are free to the publisher but can be far more valuable to you than any amount they would have paid.

Get reprints or make copies of your better articles. Make them available to potential customers as flyers. Consider including the articles in your mailings. Your articles can also help you get television and radio interviews.

Conducting a Home Security Inspection

Even though you may specialize in electronic security, a good general knowledge of home security can be helpful to making sales. By offering free professional home security surveys, for instance, you can gain the confidence of potential customers. But you have to be able to tell customers more than that they need a new alarm system. This section shows what to consider when conducting a home security survey.

When you survey a house, it's best to start outside. Walk around the house and stand at the vantage points that passersby are likely to have. Many burglars will target a home because something catches their eye while driving or walking past it. When you look at the home from the street, note any features that might make someone think that no one is home, or that the home may be easy to break into. Keep in mind that burglars prefer to work in secrecy. They like heavy shrubbery and large trees that block or crowd an entrance, and they like homes that aren't well lighted at night. Other things that may attract burglars' attention include a ladder near the home, notes tacked to the door, and expensive things that can be seen through windows from outside.

As you walk around the home, note anything that might discourage burglars, such as a Beware of Dog sign that can be seen in the window. The customer will feel better if your survey results include some positive comments. Walk to each entrance and consider what burglars might like or dislike. Is the entrance well lighted? Can neighbors see someone who's at the entrance? Can someone climb through a window at the entrance?

After you survey the outside of the home, go inside and carefully examine each exterior door, window, and other opening. Consider whether each one is secure but allows occupants to get out quickly. Look for fire safety devices. Are there enough smoke detectors, and are they properly installed?

Surveying a high-rise apartment

High-rise apartments have special security concerns that don't apply to one- and two-floor homes. In a high-rise, more people have keys to the building, which means more people can carelessly allow unauthorized persons to enter.

The safest apartments have only one entrance for tenants to use, and that entrance is guarded 24 hours per day. An apartment that doesn't have guards should have a video intercom system outside the building. Video intercoms are better than audio intercoms because they let occupants see and hear who's at the door before buzzing the person in.

It's also important to consider the building's fire exits. Every fire exit door leading directly to apartments should stay locked from the exit side. In other words, a person who's in a fire exit stairwell should have to continue out of the building and reenter through the main entrance to get onto any floor. The fire exits should be only for getting out—not for getting in.

All fire exit doors on the main floor should be connected to an alarm that will sound if someone opens one of the doors and that can be heard by a guard or maintenance person.

Exterior fire escapes—the metal stairs on the outside of a building—present another problem. Many have ladders that can be reached from the ground. Burglars can use a stick to disengage the hook that holds the ladder, and make the ladder slide down. They can then climb the ladder to get into any apartment accessible via the fire escape. Apartments that can be accessed from an exterior fire escape should have grates inside that will prevent anyone from climbing through the windows. All exterior doors leading directly to a fire escape should be strong and equipped with good locks.

Elevators should have corner-mounted mirrors that let people to see who's on the elevator before getting on. Then if they see someone suspicious looking, they can avoid getting on. The mirrors should be positioned so that there's no hiding spot in the elevators.

Home Security Checklist

As you conduct your survey, note each potential problem.

Home exterior

- *Shrubbery.* It shouldn't be high enough for a burglar to hide behind—or too near windows or doors. If it is, the door or window should be protected.

- *Trees.* They shouldn't be positioned so a burglar can use them to climb into a window. If they are, the window should be protected.

- *House numbers.* They should be visible from the street to help police and firefighters quickly find the home in an emergency.

- *Main entrance visibility.* The entrance should be easily seen from the street or other public area.

- *Garage and other parking areas.* They should be well lighted.

- *Mailbox.* It should be locked or otherwise adequately secured, and should show either no name or only a first initial and last name.

- *Windows.* They should be secured against being forced open, but allow for easy emergency escape.

■ *Window air conditioners.* They should be bolted down or otherwise protected from removal.

Exterior doors and locks

■ *Door material.* It should be solid hardwood, fiberglass, PVC plastic, or metal.

■ *Door frames.* They should let doors fit snugly.

■ *Door glazing.* It shouldn't let someone gain entry by breaking it and reaching in.

■ *Door viewer* (without glazing in door). It should have a wide-angle door viewer or other device to see visitors.

■ *Hinges.* They should be on the interior side of the door or protected from outside removal.

■ *Stop molding.* This should be one piece or protected from being pried off.

■ *Deadbolts.* They should be the single-cylinder type with free-spinning cylinder guard and a bolt with a 1-inch throw and hardened steel insert. An alternative is a jimmyproof rimlock (or *interlocking deadbolt*), which is surface-mounted.

■ *Strike plates.* They should be securely fastened with hardened steel screws that penetrate the wall studs.

■ *Door openings* (mail slots, pet entrances, and other access areas). They shouldn't let a person gain entry by reaching through them.

■ *Sliding glass doors.* These should have a movable panel mounted on the interior side and a bar or other obstruction in the track.

Inside the home

■ *Smoke detectors.* They should be in working order, installed on every level of the home, and installed directly outside of each sleeping area.

■ *Burglar alarm.* It should be in good working order, with enough well-placed sensors, and adequately protected from vandalism.

Comments:

_____

_____

_____

_____

_____

_____

_____

Monitoring Services

Part 1 covers monitoring services. Offering your customers alarm monitoring services can be very profitable. If you have enough subscribers, you may want to start your own central station. Most alarm companies find it more cost-effective to have their customers monitored by another company. Part 2 covers central station monitoring contracts.

Part 1: Alarm Monitoring Services

When the alarm is triggered, the central station quickly receives a signal and then calls you to verify that there's a problem. If the person answering doesn't give the right code word, even if he or she has a great excuse for not giving it, the central station operator immediately calls the police. Use of the code word is evidence to the central station that the person isn't an intruder. It's also useful for a subscriber who is being held against her or his will. The subscriber can simply give a wrong code word, knowing that help will be summoned. That service involves paying a monthly fee, usually to the alarm installation company. Some installation companies do the monitoring directly, but most use the services of a third-party firm. Monitoring requires special training, takes a lot of time (24 hours per day), and has a lot of potential legal liability.

Not all central stations are alike. It's important for you to be careful in choosing one to use—not only because it affects your customers' satisfaction, but also because you could be held legally liable for making a negligent choice. Consider how long the service has been in business. When you consider which monitoring service to use, make sure yours has more than one telephone line and isn't being run by someone out of a bedroom. The alarm installation company who contracts with a shoddy central station could be held liable for mistakes the central station makes. It's best to use a central station that's listed with Underwriters Laboratories (UL) or is a member of the Central Station Alarm Association (CSAA).

To get a UL listing, a central station must have adequate equipment and software to handle its accounts. Its building must be fire-resistant and have sprinklers, a dual-generator system, and a backup battery system. That helps ensure that the monitoring service won't be interrupted. The CSAA is more than 50 years old. To join, a monitoring company must be UL-listed or meet comparable standards. And CSAA has professional standards for its members and provides members with continuing education.

Because it's a valuable service that can bring in substantial recurring revenues, installers should try to sell monitoring services with every installation. In fact, some companies install alarm systems for little profit, or at a loss, just to get the monitoring service contract.

When you sign up with a monitoring service, you'll need to complete several documents: a *monitoring agreement* (describes the relationship between the monitoring company and the installing dealer); *dealer information form* (for dealer contact information, names of officers or owners, and technical system information); and an *alarm monitoring service agreement* (tells in detail the terms and conditions of service and includes redundant disclaimers). The names of the documents differ among monitoring companies. Some call a *dealer agreement* an *installer agreement,* for instance. Sample dealer agreements are shown in Figures 17.1 and 17.2. As you'll learn in part two of this chapter, it's important to understand your contracts.

Questions for review

1. What is the purpose of a code word when a central station responds to an alarm?

2. What is the CSAA?

3. Why do some alarm installers use third-party central stations, instead of monitoring their customers in-house?

4. What is an important factor in choosing a central station?

5. What are two documents that central stations require alarm dealers to complete before providing monitoring service?

Figure 17.1 Monitoring companies require dealers to sign a "Dealer Agreement."

DEALER AGREEMENT

Agreement made this _____ day of _____, 20_____ by and between Blaakman Monitoring Services. A corporation duly organized under the laws of the state of Pennsylvania and having a place of business at 123 East Grinnell Blvd., Pittsford, PA 14596 (hereinafter called BMS) and _____, a (hereinafter called "the Dealer").

In consideration of the mutual promises and covenants hereinafter specified, and for other good and valuable consideration the parties hereto do, for themselves, their successors, and assigns mutually agree as follows:

1. BMS recognizing that the Dealer will be entering into agreements with its customers (hereinafter called "Subscriber" or "Subscribers") for the monitoring of protective systems at Subscriber's premises, agrees to provide the monitoring of protective systems as set forth in this agreement for such Subscribers as the Dealer may direct.

2. The fee to be paid by the Dealer to BMS for such services shall be specified by the Company's Price List in effect at the time such services are rendered. The Dealer acknowledges having received the current Price List and specifically agrees that same and/or any amendment hereof, be incorporated by reference as part of this agreement as if set out in full herein. Such fees shall be paid to BMS by the Dealer in advance, commencing with the rendering of service by BMS to the Subscriber. All subsequent fees shall be paid by the Dealer within thirty (30) days of invoice date. Any delinquent accounts for amounts due under this Agreement shall be subject to a late payment or finance charge of one and one-half percent (1 1/2%) per month, or eighteen percent (18%) per annum until paid.

3. In the event that amounts due by Dealer to BMS hereunder are not paid by the Dealer within thirty (30) days of the date of the invoice BMS may terminate this agreement at its option, and all monitoring services by notice given under Paragraph 14 below. Such termination shall be effective upon mailing pursuant to Paragraph 14. It is the responsibility of the Dealer to notify all his/her Subscribers of termination of services.

4. In the event the Dealer's check for service under this agreement is returned by the Dealer's bank for reason of insufficient funds or otherwise, BMS's obligations under this agreement shall immediately terminate until any outstanding balance owed BMS by the Dealer and the non-sufficient funds or bad check fee permitted by law is paid in full by certified check or money order.

5. Each Alarm Monitoring Service Agreement to be performed for any Subscriber shall be automatically renewed yearly unless BMS or the Dealer gives written notice to the other of its intention not to renew as to any particular Subscriber at least 30 days before the commencement of said renewal period. The Dealer specifically agrees that its failure to make payments herein provided as to any particular Subscriber shall automatically terminate BMS's obligation to render its service to such Subscriber, but the failure to render its service shall not be considered an election of remedies. Any fees paid by the Dealer for service to a Subscriber shall not be refundable whether service to such Subscriber is terminated by actions of the Dealer or the Subscriber. However, the Dealer may request within thirty (30) days of termination of service, that fees paid for a Subscriber whose service has been terminated be applied to services rendered by BMS to other Subscriber of the Dealer. In the event that the Dealer notifies BMS of its termination of service for Subscriber for any reason, all BMS responsibilities hereunder for such Subscriber shall come to an end as of the date fixed in such notice.

6. The Dealer and Subscriber understand that a system is in temporary service for thirty (30) days, until BMS's current form of Alarm Monitoring Service Agreement signed by Subscriber and the Dealer and payment for said system, together with a fully signed copy of such agreement, is received by BMS. Systems not paid for within thirty (30) days are taken out of service.

(Continued)

7. The Dealer and BMS agree that BMS's sole and only obligation under this Agreement and/or under any Agreement between the Dealer and the BMS shall be to monitor signals received by means of the Alarm system and to respond thereto. BMS, upon receipt at the Central Station of an Alarm signal from the Subscriber's Premises, shall endeavor to notify promptly the appropriate municipal authority and/or any designated representative of the Subscriber whose name and telephone number are set forth in Notification Instructions of the alarm monitoring service agreement, by telephone call or as same may be changed in writing by the Subscriber from time to time, unless there is reasonable cause to assume that an emergency condition does not exist.

8. It is understood that BMS owns none of the electro-protective equipment in the Subscriber's premises and has no responsibility for the condition and/or the functioning thereof and that maintenance, repair, service, replacement, or insurance of the electro-protective equipment are not the obligation of BMS.

9. BMS shall not be obligated to perform any monitoring service during any time when Customer's telephone or telephone equipment shall not be working or disabled by any means since signals to BMS are received solely by means of telephone communication.

10. This agreement may be suspended or canceled as to any particular Subscriber should the equipment at the premises of such Subscriber become so disabled or so substantially damaged including repeated false alarms that further service to such Subscriber is impracticable or if the rendering of such service is due to strikes, riots, floods, fires, malfunctions of telephone lines or telephone equipment, acts of God, or any other causes beyond the control of BMS.

11(*a*). IT IS UNDERSTOOD AND AGREED BY THE PARTIES HERETO THAT BMS OR ITS AGENTS IS NOT AN INSURER AND THAT INSURANCE, IF ANY, COVERING PERSONAL INJURY AND PROPERTY OR DAMAGE ON OR TO SUBSCRIBER'S PREMISES SHALL BE OBTAINED BY SUBSCRIBER; THAT THE CONSIDERATION PROVIDED FOR HEREIN IS BASED SOLELY ON THE VALUE OF THE EQUIPMENT AS SET FORTH HEREIN AND IS UNRELATED TO THE VALUE OF THE SUBSCRIBER'S PROPERTY OR THE PROPERTY OF OTHERS LOCATED ON SUBSCRIBER'S PREMISES; THAT BMS OR ITS AGENTS MAKES NO GUARANTEE OR WARRANTY INCLUDING ANY IMPLIED WARRANTY OF MERCHANTABILITY OR FITNESS THAT THE SYSTEM OR SERVICES SUPPLIED WILL AVERT OR PREVENT OCCURRRENCES OR THE CONSEQUENCES THEREFROM WHICH THE SYSTEM OR SERVICE MAY BE INTENDED TO DETECT OR AVERT.

11(*b*). DEALER ACKNOWLEDGES THAT IT IS IMPRACTICAL AND EXTREMELY DIFFICULT TO FIX THE ACTUAL DAMAGES, IF ANY, WHICH MAY PROXIMATELY RESULT FROM A FAILURE OF BMS OR ITS AGENTS TO PERFORM ANY OF ITS OBLIGATIONS OR A FAILURE OF THE SYSTEM TO OPERATE BECAUSE OF, AMONG OTHER THINGS: THE UNCERTAIN AMOUNT OR VALUE OF SUBSCRIBER'S PROPERTY OR THE PROPERTY OF OTHERS WHICH MAY BE LOST OF DAMAGED; THE UNCERTAINTY OF THE RESPONSE TIME OF THE POLICE OR FIRE DEPARTMENT; THE INABILITY TO ASCERTAIN WHAT PORTION, IF ANY, OF ANY LOSS WOULD BE PROXIMATELY CAUSED BY BMS OR ITS AGENTS' FAILURE TO PERFORM ANY OF ITS OBLIGATIONS OR FAILURE OF ITS EQUIPMENT TO OPERATE; THE NATURE OF THE SERVICES TO BE PERFORMED BY BMS OR ITS AGENTS.

11(*c*). IT IS AGREED THAT BMS OR ITS AGENTS IS NOT AN INSURER AND THAT PAYMENTS BY DEALER ARE BASED SOLELY UPON THE VALUE OF THE SERVICES HEREIN DESCRIBED AND IT IS NOT THE INTENTION OF THE PARTIES THAT BMS OR ITS AGENTS ASSUME RESPONSIBILITY FOR ANY LOSS OCCASIONED BY MALFEASANCE, MISFEASANCE, OR NONFEASANCE IN THE PERFORMANCE OF THE EQUIPMENT PURCHASED OR THE SERVICES UNDER THIS AGREEMENT OR FOR ANY LOSS OR DAMAGE SUSTAINED THROUGH BURGLARY, THEFT, ROBBERY, FIRE, OR OTHER CAUSE OR ANY LIABILITY EXCEPT AS SPECIFICALLY SET FORTH HEREIN BY VIRTUE OF THIS AGREEMENT OR BECAUSE OF THE RELATION HEREBY ESTABLISHED. IF THERE SHALL, NOTWITHSTANDING THE ABOVE PROVISIONS, AT ANY

TIME BE OR ARISE ANY LIABILITY ON THE PART OF BMS OR ITS AGENTS BY VIRTUE OF THIS AGREEMENT OR BECAUSE OF THE RELATION HEREBY ESTABLISHED, DUE TO THE NEGLIGENCE, INCLUDING GROSS NEGLIGENCE, ACTIVE OR PASSIVE, OF BMS OR ITS AGENTS OR OTHERWISE, SUCH LIABILITY IS AND SHALL BE LIMITED TO THE SUM OF _____ MONTH'S SERVICE FEES OR _____ DOLLARS ($_____), WHICHEVER IS THE LESSER, WHICH SUM SHALL BE PAID AND RECEIVED AS LIQUIDATED DAMAGES. SUCH LIABILITY AS HEREIN SET FORTH IS FIXED AS LIQUIDATED DAMAGES AND NOT AS A PENALTY, AND THIS LIABILITY SHALL BE COMPLETE AND EXCLUSIVE. IN THE EVENT DEALER OR SUBSCRIBER DESIRES BMS OR ITS AGENTS TO ASSUME GREATER LIABILITY FOR THE PERFORMANCE OF ITS SERVICES HEREUNDER, A CHOICE IS HEREBY GIVEN OF OBTAINING FULL OR LIMITED LIABILITY BY PAYING AN ADDITIONAL AMOUNT UNDER A GRADUATED SCALE OF RATES PROPORTIONED TO THE RESPONSIBILITY, AND AN ADDITIONAL RIDER SHALL BE ATTACHED TO THIS AGREEMENT SETTING FORTH THE ADDITIONAL LIABILITY OF BMS OR ITS AGENTS AND ADDITIONAL CHARGE. ANY RIDER AND ADDITIONAL OBLIGATION SHALL IN NO WAY BE INTERPRETED TO HOLD BMS OR ITS AGENTS AS AN INSURER. UNLESS A LONGER PERIOD IS REQUIRED BY APPLICABLE LAW, ANY ACTION AGAINST BMS IN CONNECTION WITH ITS SERVICE MUST BE COMMENCED WITHIN ONE YEAR AFTER THE CAUSE OF ACTION HAS OCCURRED.

11(*d*). DEALER AGREES TO AND SHALL INDEMNIFY, DEFEND, AND HOLD HARMLESS BMS, ITS EMPLOYEES AND AGENTS, FOR AND AGAINST ALL CLAIMS, LAWSUITS, AND LOSSES WHICH CLAIM AND DAMAGES IS BROUGHT OR LOSS SUSTAINED BY PARTIES OR ENTITIES OTHER THAN THE PARTIES TO THIS AGREEMENT. THIS PROVISION SHALL APPLY TO ALL CLAIMS, LAWSUITS, OR _____ ALLEGED TO BE CAUSED BY BMS OR ITS AGENTS NEGLIGENT PERFORMANCE, WHETHER ACTIVE OR PASSIVE AND TO ALL CLAIMS BASED UPON DEFECTS IN DESIGN, INSTALLATION, MAINTENANCE, OPERATION, OR NONOPERATION OF THE ALARM SYSTEM, WHETHER THOSE CLAIMS BE BASED UPON NEGLIGENCE (ACTIVE OR PASSIVE), WARRANTY, OR STRICT PRODUCT LIABILITY ON THE PART OF BMS, ITS AGENTS, SERVANTS, OR EMPLOYEES.

12. IN THE EVENT ANY PERSON, NOT A PARTY TO THIS AGREEMENT, INCLUDING DEALER OR SUBSCRIBER'S INSURANCE COMPANY SHALL MAKE ANY CLAIM OR FILE ANY LAWSUIT AGAINST BMS OR AGENTS FOR ANY REASON WHATSOEVER, INCLUDING BUT NOT LIMITED TO THE INSTALLATION, DESIGN, MAINTENANCE, OPERATION, OR NONOPERATION OF THE ALARM SYSTEM, THE DEALER AGREES TO INDEMNIFY, DEFEND, AND HOLD BMS OR ITS AGENTS, ASSIGNS, AND EMPLOYEES HARMLESS FROM ANY AND ALL CLAIMS AND LAWSUITS INCLUDING THE PAYMENT OF ALL DAMAGES, EXPENSES, COSTS, AND ATTORNEY'S FEES, WHETHER THESE CLAIMS BE BASED UPON ALLEGED INTENTIONAL CONDUCT, ACTIVE OR PASSIVE NEGLIGENCE, WARRANTY, STRICT OR PRODUCT LIABILITY, ON THE PART OF BMS, ITS AGENTS, ASSIGNS, OR EMPLOYEES.

13. DEALER HEREBY RELEASES, DISCHARGES, AND AGREES TO HOLD BMS, ITS AGENTS, ASSIGNS, OR EMPLOYEES HARMLESS FROM ANY AND ALL CLAIMS, LIABILITIES, DAMAGES, LOSSES, EXPENSES, OR LAWSUITS RISING FROM OR CAUSED BY ANY HAZARD COVERED BY INSURANCE IN OR ON THE PREMISES OF SUBSCRIBER WHETHER SAID CLAIM IS MADE BY SUBSCRIBER, HIS AGENTS OR INSURANCE COMPANY, OR ANY OTHER PARTIES CLAIMING UNDER OR THROUGH DEALER OR SUBSCRIBER, DEALER AGREES TO INDEMNIFY BMS, ITS ASSIGNS, AGENTS, OR EMPLOYEES AGAINST DEFEND AND HOLD HARMLESS BMS FROM ANY CLAIMS FOR SUBROGATION WHICH MAY BE BROUGHT AGAINST BMS OR ITS AGENTS BY ANY INSURER OR INSURANCE COMPANY OR ITS AGENTS OR ASSIGNS, INCLUDING THE PAYMENT OF ALL DAMAGES, EXPENSES, COSTS AND ATTORNEYS' FEES.

(Continued)

14. DOES NOT MAKE ANY REPRESENTATION OR WARRANTY INCLUDING ANY IMPLIED WARRANTY OF MERCHANTABILITY OR FITNESS THAT THE SYSTEM OR SERVICE SUPPLIED MAY NOT BE COMPROMISED OR THAT THE SYSTEM OR SERVICES WILL IN ALL CASES PROVIDE THE PROTECTION FOR WHICH IT MAY BE INTENDED. THERE ARE NO IMPLIED WARRANTIES WHATSOEVER.

15. The parties specifically agree that any notices required to be given under this agreement shall be made in writing and mailed by certified mail, return receipt requested, to the address of each party indicated herein or such other address as from time to time may be made known by either party; that this agreement contains the entire understanding and final expression of agreement between the parties and that no prior statements or representations of any type shall be received in evidence or otherwise used to vary the express terms set forth herein. The parties hereby further agree that this agreement may be amended only in a writing signed by the parties; that no oral modification of this agreement shall be enforceable; that this agreement, as to any particular Subscriber, shall not be assignable by the Dealer except upon the express written consent of BMS.

16. The Dealer acknowledges that BMS is the owner of all right, title, and interest together with all the goodwill of the corporate name and trade name *BMS Monitoring* and the trademark. The Dealer agrees that the Dealer's right to use this name and mark is derived solely from this Agreement and is limited to the conduct of business by the Dealer pursuant to and in compliance herewith and all applicable operating procedures prescribed by BMS. Any unauthorized use of this name and mark by the Dealer is a breach of the agreement and an infringement of the rights of BMS in and to such name and mark. The Dealer shall not use the name and mark (or part thereof) as part of any corporate or trade name, nor may the Dealer use such name and mark with the sale of any unauthorized product or service or in any other manner not expressly authorized in writing by BMS.

17. This agreement is valid only when signed by an officer of BMS at its Home Office in Pittsford, Pennsylvania.

18. This Agreement is made in, and shall be governed by, the laws of the State of Pennsylvania. In the event Dealer shall violate any term, covenant, or Agreement hereunder and BMS shall incur any legal expenses as a result thereof, Dealer agrees to pay reasonable attorney's fees so incurred by BMS, including court costs and appellate proceedings. Dealer stipulates that venue for the purposes of enforcing this Agreement should be found in the Twelfth Judicial Circuit in and for Trisha County, Pennsylvania.

19. All changes and/or cancellations must be sent in writing unless a signed release form is on file, which releases BMS from all liability and monitoring responsibilities.

20. In the event of a default by the dealer of the terms and conditions of this agreement, BMS at its option may terminate this agreement and all BMS's responsibilities hereunder shall come to an end as of the date fixed in such notice.

21. Dealer and BMS agree that upon termination of this Agreement, Dealer, within 30 days, will cause to be removed all customer accounts from dialing into BMS's central station. In the event Dealer, within 30 days of termination of this Agreement, fails to cause all customers to be removed from dialing and accessing to BMS's central monitoring station, Dealer agrees that it shall continue to accrue charges for every month that the customer continues to access BMS's central monitoring station. In addition, Dealer agrees that BMS may at its option, contact each customer, individually, to advise them that their account has been taken offline and will no longer be providing support services and in the event of an emergency of fire, theft, or the like, will not be provided monitoring services. BMS will continue to have the right to provide any additional notices and to charge additional fees each month until such time as Dealer does in fact remove the customer and prohibits their access to central monitoring station phone lines.

22. In the event any of the terms or provisions of this Agreement shall be invalid or inoperative, all of the remaining terms and provisions shall remain in full force and effect.

IN WITNESS WHEREOF, the parties have executed this agreement on the date and year first above written and specifically represent that the person executing same in behalf of each party is fully authorized to do so, and is subject to all terms and provisions of this agreement.

BY MY SIGNATURE BELOW I PERSONALLY AND INDIVIDUALLY GUARANTEE PAYMENT OF THIS ACCOUNT PROMPTLY.

DEALER

_____   _____

Signature as corporate officer and individually   Date

_____   _____

Print Name   Title   SS#

_____   _____

Signature of Partner/Spouse   Title   SS#

Federal Tax ID

#_____

Figure 17.2 Some dealer agreements are called *installer agreements.*

INSTALLER AGREEMENT

AGREEMENT made this day of _____, 20____, by and between Smith-Cole Monitoring Services, Inc. of 321 Merlin Avenue, Gavin, New York 14909 (hereafter called "SMS") and

Company Name_____

President/Owner_____

Address_____ City_____

State_____Telephone_____

(hereinafter called "the installer").

1) The installer is engaged in the business of equipping, furnishing, and installing electronic security systems and devices and intends to enter into agreements with his customers (hereinafter called "the Subscribers" or, individually hereinafter called "the Subscriber") for monitoring systems for Subscribers' electronic security systems and devices to provide the services and notifications set forth in Schedule "A" annexed hereto. As to each of the services and notifications set forth in Schedule "A," the installer will advise SMS, in writing, of those to be provided for each individual Subscriber at the time the installer enters into an agreement to furnish such services and notifications.

2) SMS agrees to provide the monitoring and notification services set forth in Schedule "A" for the annual fees therein set forth for each such service. Each contract which the installer enters into with a Subscriber shall be for an initial period of two years or more and such term shall be the term of this agreement as to each Subscriber for whom the installer requests services. The fees to be paid by the installer to SMS for services to be performed for each Subscriber shall be those set forth in the then current Price List. Such annual fee shall be paid to SMS by the installer, in advance, at the time of notification by the installer to SMS of a Subscriber for whom services are requested. The annual fee for the second year of each agreement and for any subsequent years thereof, for any Subscriber shall be paid by the installer to SMS during the eleventh month of the preceding year for which services are to be performed. Each agreement for services to be performed for any Subscriber shall be automatically renewed for an additional year and from year to year, beginning the second year, unless SMS or the installer gives notice to the other of its intention not to renew as to any Subscriber during the eleventh month before the anniversary date of the commencement of service for such Subscriber. In the event of automatic renewal after the initial contract period, the fees as to each Subscriber shall be in accordance with the price schedule which SMS then has in effect. The failure of the installer to make payment of the fees herein provided for, as to any Subscriber, shall automatically terminate this agreement as to such Subscriber.

3) The agreement as to any Subscriber shall become effective only (*a*) when SMS shall have received a completed agreement signed by such Subscriber in the form annexed as Schedule "B" (Alarm Monitoring Service Agreement) and SMS has accepted payment of the fee to be paid for services to be provided to such Subscriber and (*b*) when the installer shall have sent an acceptable test signal on the monitoring equipment provided by the installer for such Subscriber for each condition which it is proposed be monitored for such Subscriber.

4) Any fees paid by the installer for services to a Subscriber shall not be refundable. Notwithstanding the foregoing, if the installer shall, for any reason, terminate its agreement with a Subscriber or if a Subscriber shall, for any reason, terminate its agreement with the installer, the installer shall, upon written notification to SMS of such termination have the option (a) within 60 days of such termination, and upon payment of the then prevailing registration fee, to substitute another Subscriber for the same services and obtain full credit for the unexpired portion of any Subscriber's contract or (b) after 60 days of such termination, and upon payment of the then prevailing registration fee, to substitute another Subscriber for the same services and obtain credit for the remaining term of the terminated Subscriber's agreement.

5) SMS and the installer agree that SMS's sole and only obligation under this agreement and/or under any agreement between the Subscribers and the installer shall be to monitor signals received by means of the security system and to respond thereto.

   SMS, upon receipt of a signal from a Subscriber's premises shall make every reasonable effort to transmit notification of the alarm promptly to the police, fire, or other authorities and/or the person or persons whose names and telephone numbers are set forth on the Notification Instruction received by SMS as to each Subscriber, or as the same may be changed on written notification by the Subscriber from time to time, unless there is just cause to assume that an emergency condition does not exist.

6) It is understood that SMS owns none of the electronic security equipment in the Subscriber's premises and has no responsibility for the condition and/or the functioning thereof and that maintenance, repair, service, replacement, or insurance of the electronic security equipment are not the obligation or responsibility of SMS.

7) This agreement may be suspended, at SMS's option, as to any Subscriber, should the electronic security equipment on the premises of such Subscriber become so disabled or so substantially damaged that further service to such Subscriber is impracticable. In such event, SMS will make a pro rata refund to the installer for the fees during such period of suspension.

   SMS assumes no liability for delay in installation of the system, or interruption of service due to strike, riots, floods, fires, acts of God, or any causes beyond the control of SMS, including interruption in telephone service. SMS will not be required to supply service to the Subscriber while interruption of service due to any such cause shall continue.

8) SMS shall not be liable for any loss or damage caused by defects or deficiencies in the electronic security equipment of any Subscriber nor shall SMS incur any liability for any delay in response time or nonresponse of Police, Fire, or other authorities, institutions, or individuals notified by SMS.

9) SMS shall not be obligated to perform any monitoring service hereunder during any time when any Subscriber's telephone or telephone equipment shall not be working since signals to SMS are received solely by means of telephonic communication.

10) SMS hereby disclaims all warranties, express or implied, including those of merchantability or fitness that its services will avert, deter, or prevent any loss which monitoring might alleviate or mitigate.

11) The installer shall notify SMS immediately of any modification, alteration, termination, or discharge of any agreement between any Subscriber and the installer. Failure to so notify will result in discharge and termination of this agreement as to such Subscriber but such termination shall not affect the installer's obligation to make payments hereunder.

12) The installer agrees to pay any and all sales, use, or business taxes or imposition by municipal, state, and/or federal authorities in connection with the services to be performed by SMS, and the installer agrees to hold SMS harmless from, and to indemnify it against, any claims for the foregoing.

(Continued)

13) It is understood and agreed by the parties hereto that Company is not an insurer and that insurance, if any, covering personal injury and property loss or damage on any Subscriber's premises shall be obtained by the Subscriber; that SMS is being paid to monitor a system designed to reduce certain risks of loss and that the amounts being charged by SMS are not sufficient to guarantee that no loss will occur; that SMS is not assuming responsibility for any losses which may occur even if due to Company's negligent performance or failure to perform any obligation under this agreement. SMS does not make any representation or warranty, including any implied warranty of merchantability or fitness, that the system installed by the installer or service supplied by SMS may not be compromises, or that the services will in all cases provide the protection for which it is intended.

Since it is impractical and extremely difficult to fix actual damages which may arise due to the failure of services provided, if, notwithstanding the above provisions, there should arise any liability on the part of SMS, such liability shall be limited to an amount equal to the annual service charge provided in any agreement between the installer and Subscriber or _____ ($_____ whichever is greater. This sum shall be complete and exclusive and shall be paid and received as liquidated damages and not as a penalty. In the event that the installer wishes to increase the maximum amount of such liquidated damages as to any Subscriber, the installer may, as a matter of right, obtain from SMS higher limits by paying an additional amount under a graduated scale of rates relating to the higher limits of liquidated damages.

14) It is understood and agreed by and between the parties hereto, that if there is any conflict between this contract and Installer's purchase order, or any other document, this contract will govern.

15) The agreement as to any Subscriber shall not be assignable by the installer except upon the written consent of SMS first obtained.

16) This agreement is made in, and shall be governed solely by, the laws of the State of New York.

17) Any notice required to be given hereunder by either party shall be in writing sent by certified mail, return receipt requested, addressed to such party at the address at the head of this agreement or at such other address as either party shall notify the other hereof, in the same manner. This shall not apply, however, to the initial request for the provision of services to any Subscriber, which shall be governed by Clause "3" hereof.

18) This agreement contains the entire understanding between the parties. It becomes valid only when and if signed by a duly authorized representative of SMS. No representations of any kind not contained herein or those made by some third party shall in any way bind SMS. This agreement may only be altered or modified by an agreement in writing signed by both parties hereto.

IN WITNESS WHEREOF, the parties have executed this agreement the _____day of 20____.

By _____   _____
    Installing Company Signature   Title

By _____   _____
    Smith-Cole Monitoring Services, Inc.   Title

Part 2: Central Station Monitoring

**Understanding Central Station Monitoring
Contracts—by Kenneth Kirschenbaum, Esq.**

Both central stations providing third-party, or "wholesale," monitoring and the installing company are often referred to as the *dealer*. Although both are in the alarm business and share the goal of providing the most reliable monitoring services possible, the two have some obvious adverse interests and concerns. These differences are typically noted in the contract that central stations require the installing company to sign.

Central stations providing third-party monitoring should use two contracts. (1) The *installer contract* is a one-time agreement between the central station and the dealer. (2) The *three-party contract* is between the central station, dealer, and each subscriber monitored. What provisions should you be looking for in these contracts; which can you, if you are a dealer, ask to be omitted; and which, if you are the central station, can you permit to be omitted?

The Installer Contract

Let's start with the installer contract. It requires that the dealer commit each account for a specific duration. If the subscriber defaults, the dealer should be able to replace the account or at least pay for monitoring until the service and all signals coming into the central station are stopped. The contract requires the dealer to indemnify the central station for monitoring failures. Since the central station has or should have insurance, errors and omissions, it does not need your indemnity. A dealer should ask to have it waived, and the central station should have no problem with that request.

Often central stations will permit the dealer to pay late and build up an amount past due. If the dealer ultimately defaults in making payment, the installer contract should provide that the central station can communicate with the subscribers and offer them monitoring services directly. This is something that the central station can do without the contract provision, but the contract provision would eliminate a successful lawsuit by the dealer for interference of contracts with the subscribers. This provision enables the central station to recoup some of or all its losses. The dealer should ask for notice provisions and an opportunity to cure a default before the central station can notify the subscribers of a monetary default.

The Three-Party Contract

The three-party contract is sometimes the only monitoring contract used by the dealer. That's a big mistake for the dealer. Years ago I added a provision that extended the protection of the exculpatory clause and limitation-of-liability clause to the dealer. But make no mistake about it, the three-party contract is designed to protect the central station. It, too, will have an indemnity clause, and as in the installer contract, a dealer should argue that the central station carries insurance and does not need the indemnity. Read contract provisions carefully. Not all contracts are the same, and it should not be only when there is a problem that the contract gets a close reading.

If you, a dealer, have your monitored subscribers sign a three-party monitoring contract provided by your central station, do you need to have your own monitoring contract? The answer is, unequivocally, yes.

There are so many reasons; let me mention just a few to convince you. The three-party contract provided by the central station is drafted for the protection of the central station, not the dealer. The provisions protect the central station. Years ago I did add some protection for the dealer to the three-party contract I offer to central stations; but you can't be sure the three-party contract your central station is using is mine, or that the protection designed for the dealer has been copied in that contract.

The three-party contract generally makes no mention of the amount of money the subscriber is to pay, or that payments are to be made to the dealer, or what happens if the subscriber doesn't pay the dealer. Nonpayment pertains to the dealer's failing to pay the central station. So the typical three-party contract provides no protection against liability for the dealer (unless it is mine or the provision in mine is copied); it contains no collection provisions for the dealer if the subscriber defaults; it will not be a *salable* contract if you go to sell your business. You need your own monitoring contract. Your central station, if it is smart, will want you to have a three-party contract signed also. You will have to have your subscriber sign two monitoring contracts, yours and the central station's. But only yours contains all the protective clauses you need and the collection provisions you need to enforce the contract if necessary.

Consenting to Your Terms

An alarm company recently purchased a standard form contract, and apparently its sales division is concerned that prospective subscribers would be reluctant to sign it. This alarm company's typical subscriber is a large commercial real estate concern in New York City that usually insists on signing its own forms. It is unlikely this type of client would sign any form contract presented by the alarm company—according to the alarm company's salespeople. The alarm company owners ask if there is a "watered down" version of the contract, one without many of the provisions found in the standardized form contract.

There are several essential considerations regarding alarm contract terms: (1) The alarm company's errors and omissions insurer may require a particular approved contract for coverage. (2) Each contract provision was inserted for a reason and designed for the alarm company's protection, protecting the company form liability or assisting the company in enforcing the contract in the event of the subscriber's default, thus protecting the asset of the contract. (3) From the subscriber's perspective, the contract expresses in clear, unambiguous terms the intent of the alarm company. Thus, the contract spells out the fact that the alarm company is not liable for damages if the system fails to prevent a loss, and it expresses what is expected of the subscriber and what happens if there is a subscriber default.

Usually, once subscribers and their counsel understand why the contract has these particular provisions, they accept the contract with few or no changes. Before you delete or modify any provision, carefully consider why it is there in the first place. Remember that it is your contract. You need to understand what's in it and why.

Getting a Jump on Renewals

One of the staple provisions in an alarm contract that calls for periodic payments is a renewal clause. Contracts that provide for a 3- or 5-year term have a renewal clause that automatically renews for an additional term (sometimes for an another 3 or 5 years, typically, or year to year). Some states, such as New York, require that a notice be served reminding the subscriber that the contract will self-renew. The penalty for not serving notice is that the contract is unenforceable.

Many alarm companies do not rely on the renewal clause, even though it is in their contracts. Instead, they have a practice of sending new contracts to their subscribers. This practice is okay, but it needs to be handled properly, especially if your state requires a renewal notice.

Here's a recommendation you may want to consider: One year prior to the expiration of the original term of the contract, send your subscriber a new contract for a new term. Offer whatever incentives you think appropriate to get your subscriber's attention and encourage him or her to sign a new contract, starting a new term. This is *not* a renewal contract, and *do not* call it that. It's a new contract. To add consideration on your part you should offer something, such as an inspection, price freeze, or free home security check (see Chapter 16 for more details about conducting a home security check).

If the subscriber signs and returns the new contract, you have a fresh new contract for the full term. Although it may not be necessary (the future service beyond the original expiring contract may be sufficient consideration), it will strengthen your chances if you have to sue to recover payments owed under the new contract.

If the subscriber does not sign the contract, then you still have another year on the original contract. When the contract is about to self-renew, make sure you comply with any statutes requiring notice of the renewal. Generally, the contract itself will not have any notice requirement, so the contract will self-renew unless the subscriber cancels in a timely fashion.

One caveat: When (if) you send out a contract, do not make any reference to the expiration date of the original contract or suggest that service will terminate if the subscriber fails to sign the new contract. If anything, you may remind the subscriber that he or she is under contract but that you are offering an incentive to lock in a price, or get some other incentive, if the new contract is entered into.

You might be thinking that all this sounds like additional and maybe unnecessary work on your part. Reconsider. At least the perception is that your business is selling and accumulating contracts with recurring revenue, and you know how valuable it is to be able to show recurring revenue streams.

18

Final Thoughts

In this chapter I share some opinions of mine and of other industry professionals that you may find helpful or entertaining. There are no review questions here, because there are no right or wrong answers. If you've read the rest of this book, you're qualified to create your own Part 2, which is your own thoughtful opinions about the comments in this chapter.

Uniting the Industry Associations

There's been a lot of talk about the major electronic security associations, including the National Burglar and Fire Alarm Association, the Central Station Alarm Association, and the Security Industry Association, joining together to create "one voice" for the industry. I don't like that idea. *One voice* sounds like a code word for monopoly. To be the official representative for all security dealers and installers is too much power for one group. Many companies that are in the same industry have incompatible interests. Some interests of the larger alarm installation companies, for instance, are incompatible with those of the smaller companies. The industry benefits from having multiple autonomous voices. There may be times when it's in everyone's best interest to work together and to speak as one, but that should be done on a case-by-case basis. If the major associations were to merge, soon many members would break away and form or join other associations, defeating the alleged purpose of the merger.

More Licensing Laws

Every time I turn around, I hear about new legislation being proposed to further regulate alarm dealers and installers—ostensibly to improve the image of the industry and to protect consumers. The industry is overregulated as it is. In all but a minority of cases, the regulation serves one or both of two purposes: to keep out new competitors or to increase an association's power and income. Associations who push new legislation make it a point to include their certification tests as a prerequisite for licensing. To say that the push for new licensing requirements is mainly about public safety is disingenuous. It is driven by perceived self-interest. But unnecessary fees and regulations cause more harm than good to the industry. People need to stop relying on laws to keep out competitors, and instead learn to run a better business. More competition helps the public far more than unnecessary restraint of trade.

Why Aren't You Incorporated?
by Kenneth Kirschenbaum, Esq.

Some of you are still doing business in your own name, under an assumed name, or as a partnership—in other words, not as a corporation or other legal form of entity that shields you from liability (such as the overrated LLC). Why?

There can be only one reason (and that's because I am being kind at the moment): You don't want to go to the expense of incorporating, or the expense of filing separate tax returns for the corporation. It's a lame excuse. Here are some easy reasons not to do business in a way that exposes you, your assets, and your family's security to risk from your business activities. Well, first, there is personal liability for the obligations of your business—not just contractual obligations to your suppliers, your central station monitoring company, Yellow Pages, computer consultants, insurance premiums, and your employees, but also to your subscribers for negligence and breach of contract. All claims, all lawsuits.

Another reason is that corporations permit you to tax various tax liberties that may not be deductible, or wise to deduct, as an individual. Talk to your accountant about this issue (unless he or she recommended an LLC). Even though it might cost a little more to do business as a corporation, the benefits outweigh the minimal cost. It's really such an obvious choice that I am finding it difficult to discuss.

Some of you who are just starting out, or who do security work on a part time basis, may believe that the cost and effort to form a corporation just aren't warranted. You are wrong. It only takes one subscriber with a loss. Even if you have errors and omissions insurance (and my contracts), you won't be happy to pay the deductible and the claim may very well exceed the coverage. Worse, the likelihood is that if you do business in your own name you don't carry insurance (or have my contracts—sorry I couldn't help that self-promotion). One claim exposes you and all your assets. It makes no sense.

Once you incorporate, be sure to assign the contracts you have with your subscribers, and your suppliers for that matter, to the corporation. Be formal about it. And once incorporated, be sure to always use the proper corporate name on all literature, business cards, and contracts. If your name is StrongArm Security Corp. (I just made that up and it's not intended to be you if it's your name) and you go around as StrongArm Security, you could be accused of acting as a "principal for a nonentity or nonexistent entity," since there is no StrongArm Security (without the *Corp.*). And you could be held personally liable on the theory that an agent for a nondisclosed principal is personally liable.

The Silence Is Deafening
by John "Jack" Fay

I am really surprised by the relative lack of public comment by the security industry to the Buford Furrow incident. Spokespersons from law enforcement, the mental health industry, and human rights organizations were quick and loud in making their positions known, and the antigun groups were especially vocal about guns falling too easily into the hands of nuts. Interestingly (and to my dismay), very little was heard from the security industry. A marvelous opportunity seems not to have been seized. At a minimum, I expected Burns, Pinkerton, and others to use the dialogue on Furrow to educate the public generally and property owners and managers particularly.

To refresh your memory, Buford Furrow is the white supremacist killer of a postal worker and the attempted killer of five children at the North Valley Jewish Community Center in Los Angeles. Furrow told authorities that prior to his shooting rampage, he had scouted three other Jewish institutions but decided not to attack there because they were protected by security officers. He ended up choosing North Valley because the absence of security officers made it an easy target.

Talk about a door opener and a chance to get a message across! The Furrow case proves the deterrant power of a visible security presence. Furrow went shopping for a place to kill. He backed away from three places where guards were present, and he attacked where there were no guards. The media went wild with the story, and properly so. Anybody with even a random thought on the matter was afforded his or her 15 minutes of fame. But hardly a squeak came out of the security industry. It causes one to wonder if the contract guard companies were asleep at the switch.

Perhaps because I am not an insider to the guard business I am simply unaware that guard companies have opted to take a different tack—one in which their sales representatives are, at this very moment, saying to property managers, "Remember when you told me you could see no value in hiring security officers? Well, let me tell you about this guy Furrow." A thought-provoking question deserves to be presented to property managers: How many deranged individuals and outright criminal opportunists have changed their minds, as Furrow did, after seeing their potential targets protected by security officers? Granted, there is no way to accurately quantify in dollars the value of uncommitted criminal acts, but there is indeed a value. The value has to be enormous; the Furrow case makes the point and then some.

Guard companies can and should cite Furrow as an example of what happens when preventive steps are not taken to offset anticipated crime. No sane person can say that crime is not present in Los Angeles and that children are not assets to be safeguarded.

And it is not just the guard business that should be carrying the message. Companies in access control, intrusion detection, metal detection, and CCTV should be interested as well. Indeed, I would venture to say that Furrow is an issue for the entire security industry, both for the positive light it casts upon security overall and for the negative outcomes that result when management fails to take reasonable security precautions. The fact that the American Society for Industrial Security (ASIS), our industry's advocate, did not immediately jump on this issue is disappointing. The ASIS obligation, at least as I see it, is to let the public know what the industry is doing to protect public safety. The fundamental, underlying rationale for speaking out on Furrow is not to sell more security services and products, but to inform the public of risks and of how risks can be countered. I call it an obligation to society.

Property managers at the three locations rejected by Furrow must be thanking their lucky stars they had the foresight to hire guards. In retrospect, the caretakers of those properties seem brilliant. The North Valley management is viewed differently. The parents of the wounded children are surely asking, "Could you not anticipate that a criminal, much less a madman, would enter the premises with evil in mind? Are my children not worthy of protection?" If experience proves right, the same questions will be asked of North Valley in civil suits alleging negligent security.

A Final Final Thought

Thank you for taking the time to look at this book. I hope it has been helpful to you and prompts you to check out more of my books and tapes. If you have ideas for making this book better, please let me know. I may be able to use them in the next edition!

Bill Phillips
C/o Box 2044
Erie, PA 16512-2044
E-mail: billphillips@iahssp.org

Manufacturers

Adams Rite Manufacturing Co.
260 Santa Fe St.
Pomona, CA 91767
Phone: 800-872-3267; 909-632-2300
Fax: 909-632-2370
Website: www.Adamsrite.com
Maker of electric strikes.

ADEMCO Group
165 Eileen Way
Syosset, NY 11791
Phone: 800-645-7568; 516-921-6704
Website: www.ademco.com

With an impressive history beginning nearly 70 years ago, the companies of the
ADEMCO Group have emerged as leaders in nearly every facet of electronic security
technology. Important breakthroughs by ADEMCO Group companies have helped fuel
the growth of the electronic security industry, by making security systems more
flexible and easier to install, use, and service. The company's breakthrough
developments include reliable supervised wireless technology, featuring Q.E.D.
programming for quick use of wireless devices; the first custom English language
keypads; affordable two-wire multiplex; and the first CCD camera for security
applications. ADEMCO Group companies include ADEMCO, AlarmNet, Apex, ASC
(ADEMCO Sensor Company), Fire Burglary Instruments, Javelin Systems, and
Northern Computers.

ADEMCO Sensor Company (ASC)
165 Eileen Way
Syosset, NY 11791
Phone: 800-645-7568; 516-921-6704
Fax: 800-921-6704
Website: www.ademco.com

AW SPERRY
245 Marcus Blvd.
Hauppauge, NY 11788
Phone: 800-645-5398; 631-231-7050
Fax: 631-434-3128
Website: www.awsperry.com

AW Sperry is a manufacturer of professional-quality test and measuring instruments, such as analog and digital multimeters, circuit breaker finders, and EMF finders.

CADDX Controls, Inc.
1420 N. Main St.
Gladewater, TX 75647
Phone: 800-727-2339

Continental Instruments (a Napco Security Company)
355 Bayview Ave.
Amityville, NY 11701
Phone: 631-842-9400
Fax: 631-842-9135

Access control systems and equipment.

Corby Industries, Inc.
1501 E. Pennsylvania St.
Allentown, PA 18103
Phone 800-652-6729; 610-433-1412
Fax: 610-435-1963

Dynalock Corporation
705 Emmett St.
P.O. Box 9470
Forestville, CT 06011-9470
Phone: 860-582-4761
Fax: 860-585-0338
Website: www.dynalock.com

George Risk Industries, Inc.
GRI Plaza
802 S. Elm St.
Kimball, NE 69145
Phone: 800-523-1227; 308-235-4645
Fax: 308-235-3561
Website: www.grisk.com

George Risk Industries manufactures high-quality security products, including recessed and surface-mount magnetic contacts, pushbutton and proximity (encapsulated reed) switches, water sensors, and assorted adapters, plugs, and accessories.

Highpower Security Products
290 Pratt St., 4th floor
Meriden, CT 06450
Phone: 800-991-3646; 203-634-3900
Fax: 203-238-2425
Website: www.highpowersecurity.com

Makers of Thunderbolt electromagnetic locks and push plates.

Labor Saving Devices
5678 Eudora St.
Commerce City, CO 80022-3809
Phone: 800-648-4714; 303-287-2121
Fax: 303-287-9044
Website: www.lsdinc.com

NAPCO Security Systems, Inc.
333 Bayview Ave.
Amityville, NY 11701
Phone: 631-842-9400
FAX: 631-842-9137
Website: www.napcosecurity.com

The NAPCO Security Group is one of the world's most diversified manufacturers of
security products, encompassing intruder and fire alarms, access control systems and
electronic digital and proximity locks, as well as panic exit hardware. Since 1969,
NAPCO has enjoyed a reputation in the security industry for advanced technology
and high quality, building many of the industry's best-known brand names, such as
NAPCO, Alarm Lock, and Continental Instruments. Because of NAPCO Security
Group's strengths in various security technologies, including alarms, sensors, locks,
and access control, its product offerings are among the most innovative and reliable on
the market.

Northern Computers Inc.
5007 S. Howell Ave.
Milwaukee, WI 53207
Phone: 800-323-4576; 414-769-5980
Fax: 414-769-5989
Website: www.nciaccess.com

Panasonic Security Group
One Panasonic Way
Secaucus, NJ 07094
Phone: 877-733-3689
Website: cctv.panasonic.com

Radionics
340 El Camino Real-South, Building 36
P.O. Box 80012
Salinas, CA 93912-0012
Phone: 800-538-5807; 831-757-8877
Fax: 831-757-6093
Website: www.radionicsinc.com

Rainbow CCTV/ISO
2495 Da Vinci
Irvine, CA 92614
Phone: 800-654-5367; 949-260-1599
Fax: 949-260-1594
Website: www.isorainbow.com

ROFU International Corp.
2004 48th Ave., Ct. E.
Tacoma, WA 98424
Phone: 800-255-7638; 253-922-1828
Fax: 253-922-1728
Website: www.rofu.com

Maker of electric strikes.

Rokonet
5 Westchester Plaza
Elmsford, NY 10523
Phone: 800-344-2025; 914-592-1068
Fax: 914-592-1271

Samsung Opto-Electronic America Inc.
40 Seaview Dr.
Secaucus, NJ 07094
Phone: 800-762-7746; 201-902-0347
Fax: 201-902-9342
Website: www.simplyamazing.com

Sony Security Systems
2 Paragon Dr.
Montvale, NJ 07645
Phone: 201-358-4954
Fax: 201-358-4943

Tane Alarm Products
249-50 Jericho Turnpike
Bellerose Village, NY 11001
Phone: 800-852-5050; 516-328-3351
Fax: 516-326-9125
Website: www.magneticcontacts.com

Trine Products
1430 Ferris Pl.
Bronx, NY 10461
Phone: 718-829-4796
Fax: 718-518-7022

Ultrak, Inc.
1301 Waters Ridge Dr.
Lewisville, TX 75057
Website: www.ultrak.com

Ultrak, Inc. designs, manufactures, and services innovative electronic products and systems for the security and surveillance, industrial video, and professional audio markets. Its goal is to be the preferred worldwide provider of end-user focused security solutions while upholding the fundamental principle of meeting and exceeding customer expectations. Headquartered in Lewisville (Dallas), Texas, Ultrak has multiple locations throughout the United States, Europe, Asia, and South Africa.

Vicon Industries
89 Arkay Dr.
Hauppauge, NY 11788
Phone: 800-645-9116; 631-952-2288
Fax: 631-951-2288

CCTVs and related equipment and supplies.

Visonic Inc.
10 Northwood Dr.
Bloomfield, CT 06002-1911
Phone: 800-223-0020; 860-243-0833
Fax: 860-242-8094
Website: www.visonic.com

Established in 1973, the Visonic Group's wired and wireless security and home automation systems and products include complete access control and home automation systems. Individual components are also available, including smart control panels, state-of-the-art detectors and transceivers, and software and readers. Visonic Group's parent company is Visonic Ltd., headquartered in Tel Aviv with production facilities in Kiryat Gat, Israel. Its wholly owned subsidiaries include Visaccess Ltd. (access control systems), located in Carmiel, Israel, and sales and marketing companies in the United States, United Kingdom, Spain, and Germany. In addition there are three sales offices in Norway, Singapore, and Australia. Together, they serve a network of distributors and technical support teams in more than 50 countries worldwide, with an installed base of millions of systems.

Wheelock Inc.
273 Branchport Ave.
Long Beach, NJ 07740
Phone: 732-222-6880
Fax: 732-222-2588
Website: www.wheellockinc.com

Maker of fire safety products.

Winsted
10901 Hampshire Ave. S.
Minneapolis, MN 55438-2385
Phone: 800-447-2257
Fax: 800-421-3839
Website: www.winsted.com

Makers of high-technology furniture for command center, security, and multimedia applications. Since its inception in 1963, Winsted Corporation has been a pioneer in product design and development. The company's modular design systems have become an industry standard. Development of specialized products for the security and surveillance industry helped to further broaden its product line and expansion into new markets.

A dominant factor in U.S. markets for many years, Winsted Corporation began expansion into overseas markets in 1975. Winsted's international distribution was firmly established in 1984 with the formation of Winsted, Ltd., in England. Since then, Winsted, Ltd., has grown into an ongoing marketing and manufacturing facility serving the European, Middle East, and African markets. In 1986 distributor agreements were established in Australia and Japan. As the growing video markets in Hong Kong, Taiwan, and Korea became apparent, additional distribution was established in those areas.

X-10 (USA) Inc.
91 Ruckman Rd.
Closter, NJ 07624
Phone: 800-526-0027; 201-784-9700
Fax: 201-784-9464

Central Stations and Suppliers

Central Stations

Alarm Tech Central Station Inc.
Phone: 800-729-8324; 516-232-0900
Website: www.alarmtechcentral.com

All American Monitoring
1375 East Ave., N.
Sarasota, FL 34237
Phone: 800-318-9486
Fax: 941-366-8032
Website: www.allamericanmonitoring.com

Amcest
1017 Walnut St.
Roselle, NJ 07203
Phone: 800-631-7370; 908-241-6500
Website: www.amcest.com

Americom Central Station
1355 Fairfax Ave.
San Francisco, CA 94124-1735
Phone: 888-211-9853; 415-821-9500
Fax: 415-824-5476
Website: www.americomcs.com

C.M.S. Monitoring Inc.
P.O. Box 184
Medford, NY 11763
Phone: 631-289-2800
Fax: 631-289-2496

Digital Monitoring Products, Inc.
2841 E. Industrial Dr.
Springfield, MO 65802
Phone: 800-641-4281; 417-831-9362
Fax: 417-831-1325
Website: www.dmpnet.com

Nationwide Digital Alarm Monitoring System, Inc.
P.O. Box C-651
Brooklyn, NY 11209-0651
Phone: 800-221-0826; 800-522-5177 (NY State)

Suppliers

ADI
263 Old Country Rd.
Melville, NY 11747
Phone: 800-233-6261
Website: www.adilink.com

Atlas Wire and Cable Corp.
133 S. Van Norman Rd.
Montebello, CA 90640
Phone: 800-423-4659
Fax: 562-692-9202

Supplier of wire and cable.

AWCCTV Corp.
60 E. 42 St., Suite 2123
New York, NY 10165
Phone: 800-396-2288; 212-983-1820

Supplier of CCTV cameras, monitors, and equipment.

Bi-Tronics
10 Skyline Dr.
Hawthorne, NY 10532
Phone: 800-666-0996; 914-592-1800
Fax: 800-569-4244

Suppliers of connectors, cables, power supplies, and installation accessories.

Biometric Identification
5000 Van Nuys Blvd., Suite 300
Sherman Oaks, CA 91403
Phone: 818-501-3908
Fax: 818-461-0843
Website: www.biometricid.com

Suppliers of biometric access control systems.

Canadian Flexi Drills
395 Steelcase Rd., E.
Markham, Ontario
Canada L3R 163

Supplier of specialty drill bits, installation tools, and accessories.

D&H
2525 N. Seventh St.
Harrisburg, PA 17110-0967
Phone: 800-340-1008
Website: www.dandh.com

A national distributor of a wide range of security, fire and home automation systems, and products.

Decal Factory
P.O. Box 28056
Spokane, WA 99228
Phone: 800-369-5331; 509-465-8931
Fax: 509-482-8934

Supplies decals and signs.

Highpower Security Products LLC
290 Pratt St., 4th floor
Meriden, CT 06450
Phone: 800-991-3646;
 203-634-3900;
Fax: 203-238-2425
Website: www.highpowersecurity.com

Suppliers of electromagnetic locks. keypads, contacts and switches, CCD cameras, and accessories.

Hirsch Electronics
1900 Carnegie Ave., Bldg. B
Santa Ana, CA 92705
Phone: 949-250-8888
Fax: 949-250-7372

Home Automation
5725 Powell St.
New Orleans, LA 70123
Phone: 800-229-7256; 504-736-9810
Fax: 504-736-9890
Website: www.homeauto.com

LRC Electronics
Charlie Pierce, President
930 South Rolff St.
Davenport, IA 52802
Phone: 319-324-2199
Fax: 319-324-7938
Website: lrc-inc.com

Supplier of CCTV equipment, books, and courses.

Supercircuits
One Supercircuits Plaza
Leander, TX 78641
Phone: 512-260-0333
Website: www.supercircuits.com

Source for overt and covert video security products, including cameras, monitors, brackets, lenses, and accessories. Has color catalog.

Supply Dog
81 E. Jefryn Blvd.
Deer Park, NY 11729-9939
Phone: 800-933-3824
Website: www.supplydog.com

Source for closed-circuit television equipment, intruder and fire alarm systems, access control components, annunciators, and sensors. Has color catalog.

Electronic Schematic Symbols

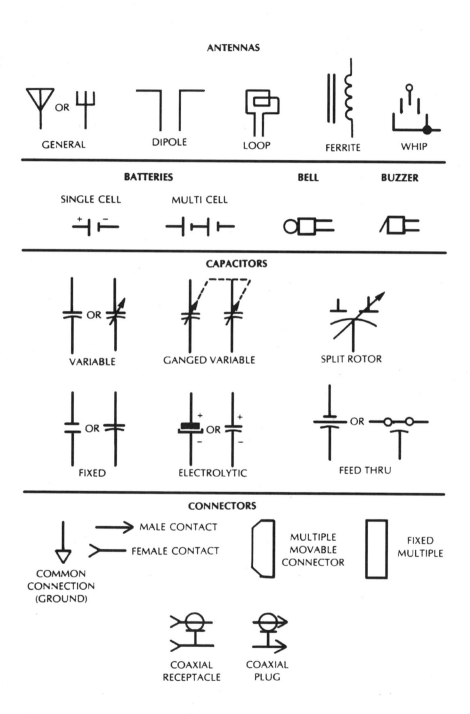

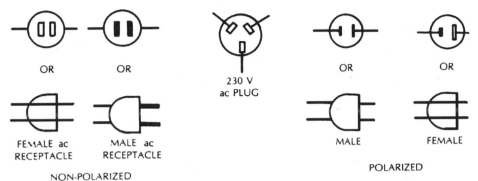

OR   OR

230 V
ac PLUG

OR   OR

FEMALE ac   MALE ac
RECEPTACLE   RECEPTACLE

MALE   FEMALE

NON-POLARIZED

POLARIZED

CRYSTALS

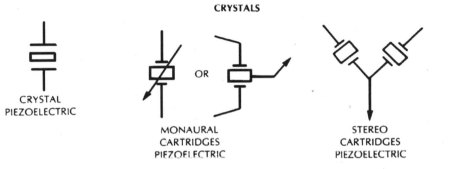

CRYSTAL
PIEZOELECTRIC

OR

MONAURAL
CARTRIDGES
PIEZOELECTRIC

STEREO
CARTRIDGES
PIEZOELECTRIC

DIODES

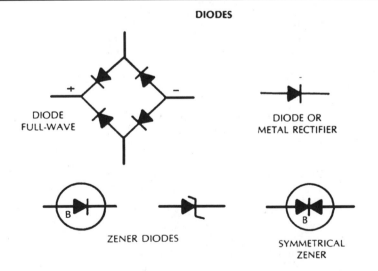

DIODE
FULL-WAVE

DIODE OR
METAL RECTIFIER

ZENER DIODES

SYMMETRICAL
ZENER

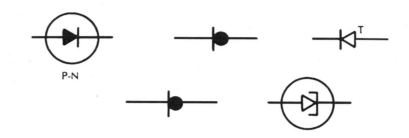

P-N

TUNNEL DIODES

VARACTOR
DIODES

SILICON-CONTROLLED
RECTIFIER

FUSES

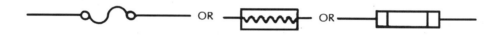

GROUNDS

CHASSIS GROUND
(NOT NECESSARILY
AT GROUND)

EARTH
GROUND

HEADPHONES

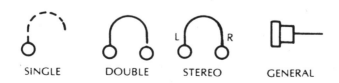

SINGLE   DOUBLE   STEREO   GENERAL

READOUT INDICATOR

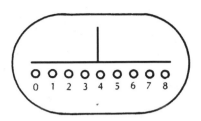

INDUCTORS (COILS)

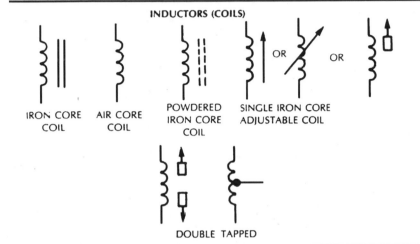

IRON CORE COIL   AIR CORE COIL   POWDERED IRON CORE COIL   SINGLE IRON CORE ADJUSTABLE COIL

DOUBLE TAPPED

JACKS

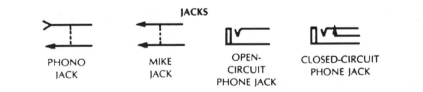

PHONO JACK   MIKE JACK   OPEN-CIRCUIT PHONE JACK   CLOSED-CIRCUIT PHONE JACK

LAMPS

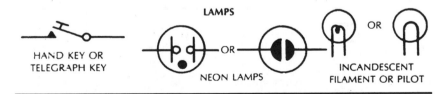

HAND KEY OR TELEGRAPH KEY   NEON LAMPS   INCANDESCENT FILAMENT OR PILOT

METERS

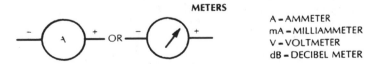

A = AMMETER
mA = MILLIAMMETER
V = VOLTMETER
dB = DECIBEL METER

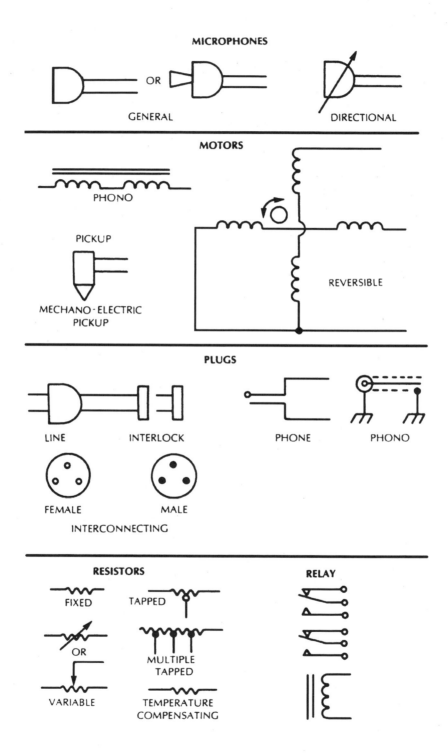

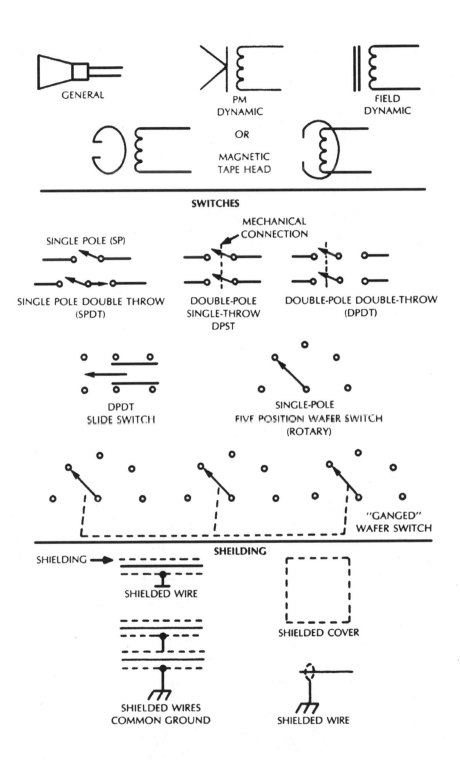

GENERAL

PM
DYNAMIC

OR

MAGNETIC
TAPE HEAD

FIELD
DYNAMIC

SWITCHES

SINGLE POLE (SP)

SINGLE POLE DOUBLE THROW
(SPDT)

MECHANICAL
CONNECTION

DOUBLE-POLE
SINGLE-THROW
DPST

DOUBLE-POLE DOUBLE-THROW
(DPDT)

DPDT
SLIDE SWITCH

SINGLE-POLE
FIVE POSITION WAFER SWITCH
(ROTARY)

"GANGED"
WAFER SWITCH

SHEILDING

SHIELDING ➔

SHIELDED WIRE

SHIELDED WIRES
COMMON GROUND

SHIELDED COVER

SHIELDED WIRE

TRANSFORMERS

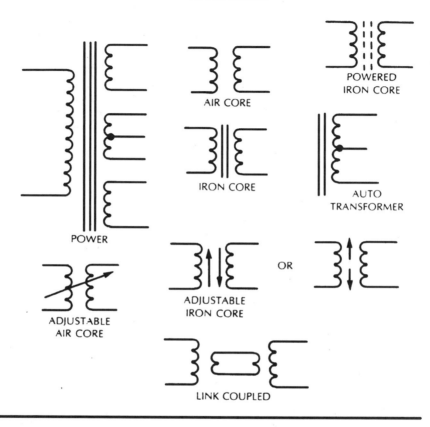

AIR CORE

POWERED
IRON CORE

IRON CORE

AUTO
TRANSFORMER

POWER

ADJUSTABLE
AIR CORE

ADJUSTABLE
IRON CORE

OR

LINK COUPLED

TRANSISTORS

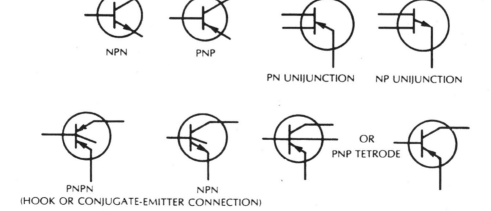

NPN

PNP

PN UNIJUNCTION

NP UNIJUNCTION

PNPN
(HOOK OR CONJUGATE-EMITTER CONNECTION)

NPN

OR
PNP TETRODE

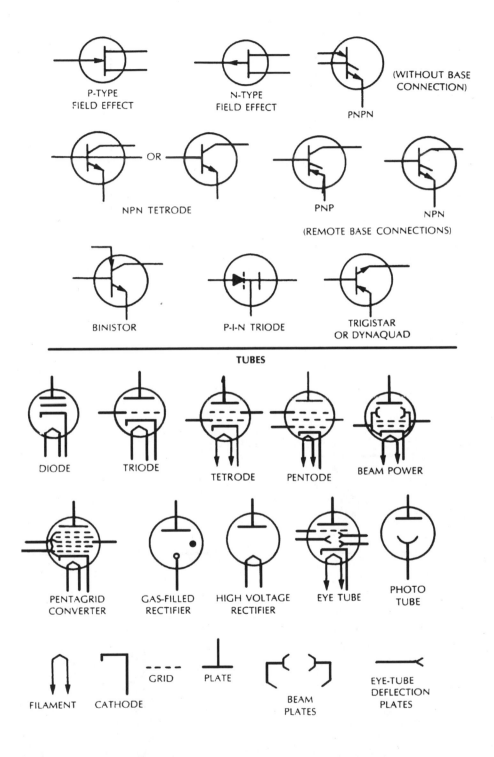

P-TYPE
FIELD EFFECT

N-TYPE
FIELD EFFECT

PNPN

(WITHOUT BASE
CONNECTION)

NPN TETRODE

PNP

NPN

(REMOTE BASE CONNECTIONS)

BINISTOR

P-I-N TRIODE

TRIGISTAR
OR DYNAQUAD

TUBES

DIODE   TRIODE   TETRODE   PENTODE   BEAM POWER

PENTAGRID
CONVERTER

GAS-FILLED
RECTIFIER

HIGH VOLTAGE
RECTIFIER

EYE TUBE

PHOTO
TUBE

FILAMENT   CATHODE   GRID   PLATE   BEAM
PLATES

EYE-TUBE
DEFLECTION
PLATES

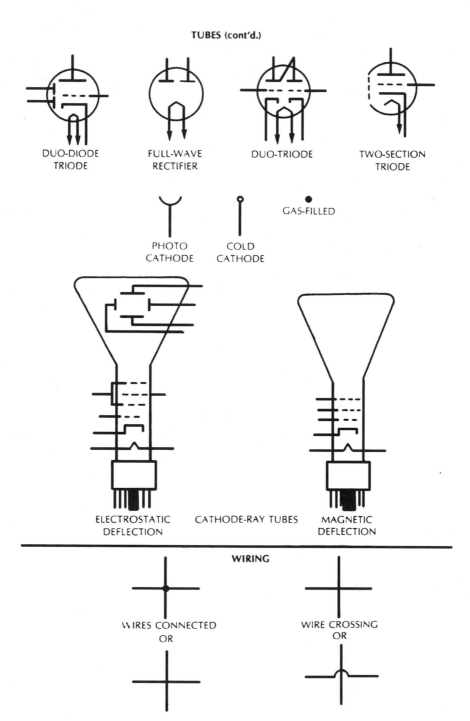

TUBES (cont'd.)

DUO-DIODE
TRIODE

FULL-WAVE
RECTIFIER

DUO-TRIODE

TWO-SECTION
TRIODE

PHOTO
CATHODE

COLD
CATHODE

GAS-FILLED

ELECTROSTATIC
DEFLECTION

CATHODE-RAY TUBES

MAGNETIC
DEFLECTION

WIRING

WIRES CONNECTED
OR

WIRE CROSSING
OR

License Requirements
for New York,
North Carolina,
and Utah

Figure D.1 outlines the license requirements for New York State; Figure D.2, for North Carolina; and Figure D.3, for Utah.

New York State Department of State
SECURITY OR FIRE ALARM INSTALLERS
FREQUENTLY ASKED QUESTIONS

What does an alarm installer do?

An alarm installer installs, services, or maintains security or fire alarm systems to detect intrusion, break-in, movement, sound, or fire. Any entity which engages in the business of providing any of these services must be licensed by the Department as an alarm installer.

Do I need a license to install an alarm system in a motor vehicle?

No. A license is not required to install systems on motor vehicles, boats, or airplanes.

Do I need a license to install a battery-operated smoke detector?

No. A license is not required to install a battery-operated smoke detection device. However, a person who is in the business of installing hardwired smoke detectors must be licensed.

Does my employee need a license to install a system on my property?

No. If a purchaser or owner personally installs the alarm system, or has it installed by an employee on his or her own property or place of business, a license is not required.

I am new to the industry. How do I become licensed?

If you are at least 18 years of age, and new to the industry, you must submit an application to the Department which shows:

- Completion of at least 60 hours of qualifying education
- Passing of an alarm installer examination
- Freedom from disqualifying criminal convictions

What are the educational requirements, and where can I go for courses?

Applicants are required to submit evidence of education which demonstrates sufficient training in installing, servicing, or maintaining of security or fire alarm systems. The 60 hours of coursework may be completed in any course of study which has been approved by the Department. The courses may be given by trade associations or other private entities. You may obtain a list of approved course providers upon request.

Must I submit fingerprints?

Yes. You will be required to submit fingerprint cards and a $50 fee with your application.

How long is the license term?

Two years.

What are the fees for licensure?

The application fee is $200. Additionally, a fee of $50 is charged for the fingerprint submission.

I am a master electrician. Do I need an alarm installer license?

A master electrician who practices only within his or her local jurisdiction must register with the Department. However, all licensing requirements are waived, including the submission of fingerprints. A master electrician who wishes to engage in the business of alarm installation outside of her or his local jurisdiction must be licensed by the Department. Education, experience, and exam requirements are waived for applicants, but each applicant must submit fingerprints.

How do I renew?

Approximately 90 days prior to the expiration of your original, 2-year term of licensure, a computer-generated renewal form will be sent to you. Simply complete the form, enclose the renewal fee of $100, and return it as directed.

How do I obtain application materials and/or a list of approved course providers?

Applications and lists of approved course providers may be requested from the Division of Licensing Services by e-mail, by telephone at (518) 474-4429 or by fax at (518) 473-6648.

Figure D.1

North Carolina Alarm Installer Registration Requirements

Job Description: Alarm installers sell or attempt to sell alarm system devices by engaging in a personal solicitation at a residence or business, combined with personal inspection of the interior of the residence or business to advise on specific types and specific locations of alarm system devices. Alarm installers also install, service, monitor, or respond to electrical, electronic, or mechanical alarm signal devices, burglar alarms, television cameras or still cameras used to detect burglary, breaking or entering, intrusion, shoplifting, pilferage, or theft.

Education and Experience Requirements: There are no defined education and experience requirements for this registration.

Application: Applicants must be at least 18 years old, of good moral character and a U.S. citizen or resident alien. Candidates are required to submit an alarm registration application with one set of classifiable fingerprints, two recent head and shoulders color photographs (1 inch by 1 inch), and a statement of the results of the local criminal history records searched by the city and county where the applicant has resided in the past 48 months. The applicant must be employed by a licensed alarm system licensee before making application for the registration card.

Examination: No examination is required for the registration.

Fees: Initial fee: $20.00, application; $10.00, multiple registration fee; $5.00, SBI fee.*

Duration: Biannual

Renewal Fee: $20.00

Continuing Education: Continuing education is not required upon renewal of this registration.

DOT: 822.361-022
Registration Authority:
NC Alarm Systems Licensing Board
P.O. Box 29500
Raleigh, NC 27626
Phone: (919) 662-4387

_____

*Applies to initial applicants or expired registration.

Figure D.2

Figure D.3

Utah Construction Trades Licensing Act Burglar Alarm Licensing Rules

R156-55d-102. Definitions.

In addition to the definitions in Title 58, Chapters 1 and 55, as used in Title 58, Chapters 1 and 55, or these rules:

(1) "Individual employed" as used in Subsection 58-55-102(2), means an individual who has an agreement with an alarm business or company to perform alarm systems business activities under the direct supervision or control of the alarm business or company and for whose alarm system business activities the alarm company is legally liable and who has or could have access to knowledge of specific applications.

(2) "Knowledge of specific applications" as used in Subsection R156-55d-102(1), means obtaining specific information about any premises which is protected or is to be protected by an alarm system. This knowledge is gained through access to records, on-site visits or otherwise gathered through working for an alarm business or company.

(3) "Unprofessional conduct" as defined in Title 58, Chapters 1 and 55, is further defined, in accordance with Subsection 58-1-203(5), in Section R156-55-502.

R156-55d-103. Authority—Purpose.

These rules are adopted by the division under the authority of Subsection 58-1-106(1) to enable the Division to administer Title 58, Chapter 55.

R156-55d-104. Organization—Relationship to Rule R156-1.

The organization of this rule and its relationship to Rule R156-1 is as described in Section R156-1-107.

R156-55d-302a. Qualifications for Licensure—Application Requirements.

(1) An application for licensure as an alarm company shall include:
   (a) A record of criminal history or certification of no record of criminal history with respect to the applicant's qualifying agent, issued by the Bureau of Criminal Identification, Utah Department of Public Safety;
   (b) Two fingerprint cards containing:
      (i)   The fingerprints of the applicant's qualifying agent;
      (ii) The fingerprints of each of the applicant's officers, directors, shareholders owning more than 5% of the stock of the company, partners, and proprietors; and
      (iii) The fingerprints of each of the applicant's management personnel who will have responsibility for any of the company's operations as an alarm company within the state;
   (c) A fee established in accordance with Section 63-38-3.2 equal to the cost of conducting a check of records of the Federal Bureau of Investigation, and the Bureau of Criminal Identification, Utah Department of Public Safety, for each individual for whom fingerprints are required under Subsection (1)(b); and
   (d) A copy of the driver's license or Utah identification card for each individual for whom fingerprints are required under Subsection (1)(b).
(2) An application for license as an alarm company agent shall include:
   (a) A record of criminal history or certification of no record of criminal history with respect to the applicant, issued by the Bureau of Criminal Identification, Utah Department of Public Safety;
   (b) Two fingerprint cards containing the fingerprints of the applicant;
   (c) A fee established in accordance with Section 63-38-3.2 equal to the cost of conducting a check of records of the Federal Bureau of Investigation, and the Bureau of Criminal Identification, Utah Department of Public Safety, regarding the applicant; and
   (d) A copy of the driver's license or Utah identification card for the applicant.

R156-55d-302c. Qualifications for Licensure—Experience Requirements.
In accordance with Subsections 58-1-203(2) and 58-1-301(3) the experience requirements for an alarm company applicant's qualifying agent in Subsection 58-55-302(3)(h)(i) are defined, clarified, or established in that an individual to be approved as a qualifying agent of an alarm company shall:

(1) Have not less than 6,000 hours of experience in the alarm company business of which not less than 2,000 hours shall have been in a management, supervisory, or administration position; or

(2) Have not less than 6,000 hours of experience in the alarm company business combined with not less than 2,000 hours of management, supervisory, or administrative experience in a lawfully and competently operated construction company.

R156-55d-302d. Qualifications for Licensure—Examination Requirements.
In accordance with Subsections 58-1-203(2) and 58-1-301(3), the examination requirements for an alarm company applicant's qualifying agent in Subsection 58-55-302(3)(h)(i)(C) are defined, clarified, or established in that an individual to be approved as a qualifying agent of an alarm company shall:

(1) Pass the Utah Burglar Alarm Law and Rules Examination with a score of not less than 75%; and

(2) Pass the Burglar Alarm Qualifier Examination with a score of not less than 75%.

R156-55d-302e. Qualifications for Licensure—Insurance Requirements.
In accordance with Subsections 58-1-203(2) and 58-1-301(3), the insurance requirements for licensure as an alarm company in Section 58-55-302(3)(h)(ix)(A) are defined, clarified, or established as follows:

(1) An applicant for an alarm company license shall file with the Division a "certificate of insurance" issued by an insurance company or agent licensed in the state demonstrating the applicant is covered by comprehensive public liability coverage in an amount of not less than $300,000 for each incident, and not less than $1,000,000 in total;

(2) The terms and conditions of the policy of insurance coverage shall provide that the Division shall be notified if the insurance coverage terminates for any reason; and

(3) All licensed alarm companies shall have available on file and shall present to the Division upon demand, evidence of insurance coverage meeting the requirements of this section for all periods of time in which the alarm company is licensed in this state as an alarm company.

R156-55d-303. Renewal Cycle—Procedure.

(1) In accordance with Subsection 58-1-308(1), the renewal date for the two year renewal cycle applicable to licensees under Title 58, Chapter 55, is established by rule in Section R156-1-308.

(2) Renewal procedures shall be in accordance with Section R156-1-308.

R156-55d-304. Renewal Requirement—Demonstration of Clear Criminal History.

(1) In accordance with Subsections 58-1-203(7), 58-1-308(3)(b), and 58-55-302(4), there is created as a requirement for renewal or reinstatement of any license of an alarm company or alarm company agent a demonstration of clear criminal history for each alarm company qualifying agent and for each alarm company agent.

(2) Each application for renewal or reinstatement of a license of an alarm company shall be accompanied by a record of criminal history or certification of no record of criminal history with respect to the alarm company's qualifying agent, issued by the Bureau of Criminal Identification, Utah Department of Public Safety, within 120 days prior to submission of the application for renewal or reinstatement to the Division.

(3) Each application for renewal or reinstatement of a license of an alarm company agent shall be accompanied by a record of criminal history or certification of no record of

(Continued)

criminal history with respect to the alarm company agent, issued by the Bureau of Criminal Identification, Utah Department of Public Safety, within 120 days prior to submission of the application for renewal or reinstatement to the Division.

R156-55d-306. Change of Qualifying Agent.
In accordance with Subsection 58-55-304(6), an alarm company whose qualifier has ceased association or employment shall file with the Division an application for change of qualifier on forms provided by the Division accompanied by a record of criminal history or certification of no record of criminal history, fee, fingerprint cards, and copy of an identification as required under Subsection R156-55d-302a(1).

R156-55d-502. Unprofessional Conduct.
"Unprofessional conduct" includes:

(1) Failing as an alarm company to notify the Division of the cessation of performance of its qualifying agent or failing to replace its qualifying agent as required under Section R156-55d-306;

(2) Failing as an alarm company agent to carry or display a copy of the licensee's license as required under Section R156-55d-601;

(3) Failing as an alarm agent to carry or display a copy of his National Burglar and Fire Alarm Association (NBFAA) level one certification or equivalent training as required under Section R156-55d-603;

(4) Employing as an alarm company qualifying agent or alarm company agent knowing that individual has engaged in conduct inconsistent with the duties and responsibilities of an alarm company agent;

(5) Failing to comply with operating standards established by rule;

(6) A judgment on, or a judicial or prosecutorial agreement concerning a felony, or a misdemeanor involving moral turpitude, entered against an individual by a federal, state or local court, regardless of whether the court has made a finding of guilt, accepted a plea of guilty or nolo contendere by an individual, or a settlement or agreement whereby an individual has entered into participation as a first offender, or an action of deferred adjudication, or other program or arrangement where judgment or conviction is withheld;

(7) Making false, misleading, deceptive, fraudulent, or exaggerated claims with respect to the need for an alarm system, the benefits of the alarm system, the installation of the alarm system or the response to the alarm system by law enforcement agencies; and

(8) An alarm business or company having a residential or commercial false alarm rate 100% above the average of the residential or commercial false alarm rate of the municipality or county jurisdiction in which the alarm business or company's alarm systems are located.

R156-55d-601. Display of License.
An alarm company agent shall carry on his person at all times while acting as an alarm company agent a copy of his license and shall display that license upon the request of any person to whom the agent is representing himself as an alarm company agent, and upon the request of any law enforcement officer or representative of the Division.

R156-55d-602. Operating Standards—Alarm Equipment.
In accordance with Subsection 58-55-308(1), the following standards shall apply with respect to equipment and devices assembled as an alarm system:

(1) An alarm system installed in a business or public building shall utilize equipment equivalent to or exceeding minimum Underwriters Laboratories, or the National Electrical Code standards for alarm system equipment.

(2) An alarm system installed in a residence shall utilize equipment equivalent to or exceeding minimum Underwriters Laboratories, or the National Electrical Code standards for residence alarm systems.

R156-55d-603. Operating Standards—Alarm Installer.
In accordance with Subsection 58-55-308(1), the operating standards for the installer of an alarm system include the following:

(1) An alarm agent must be fully trained in the installation of an alarm system in accordance with the National Burglar and Fire Alarm Association (NBFAA) level one certification or equivalent training requirements prior to the alarm agent installing any alarm system in any residence, business, or public building within the state.

(2) An alarm agent upon receiving initial licensure may work under the direct supervision of an alarm agent who has level one certification for a period of 6 months from the time of initial licensure without being required to hold a level one certificate.

(3) An alarm agent shall carry evidence of the NBFAA level one certification or equivalent training with him at all times.

(4) An alarm agent holding licensure under Title 58, Chapter 55, shall have until January 1, 2001, to comply with the NBFAA level one certification or equivalent training requirement.

R156-55d-604. Operating Standards—Alarm System User Training.
In accordance with Subsection 58-55-308(1), the operating standards for the installation of an alarm system include the following:

(1) Upon completion of the installation of an alarm system by an alarm business or company, the installing alarm agent shall review with the alarm user, or in the case of a company, its employees, the operation of the alarm system to ensure that the user understands the function of the alarm system.

(2) The alarm business or company shall maintain training records, including installer and user false alarm prevention checklists, the dates of the training and the location of the training on each alarm system installed. These records shall be maintained in the files of the alarm business or company for at least 3 years from the date of the training.

KEY
Licensing, alarm company,* burglar alarms*
Date of Enactment or Last Substantive Amendment
September 18, 2000
Authorizing, Implemented, or Interpreted Law
58-55-101; 58-1-106(1); 58-1-202(1); 58-55-302(3)(h); 58-55-302(3)(i); 58-55-302(4); 58-55-308

For questions regarding the content or application of rules under Title R156, please contact the promulgating agency (Commerce, Occupational and Professional Licensing). A list of agencies with links to their homepages is available at http://www.state.ut.us/government/agencylist.html.

For questions about the rulemaking process, please contact the Division of Administrative Rules at rulesonline@state.ut.us. Please note: The Division of Administrative Rules is not able to answer questions about the content or application of these rules.

Laws and regulations are subject to change at any time, through legislation, court action, or otherwise. The information in this appendix may not be current and isn't meant to be accepted as legal advice.

Certification and Training Programs

Many colleges, vocational schools, and state and regional trade associations offer safety and security certification programs. You can find out about them by calling and asking for a catalog or literature. Programs listed here are from national associations, private training programs, and manufacturers. Typically, college or vocational school programs require you to attend classes for several months or years. Manufacturers' programs focus on their own models and are often conducted in conjunction with trade shows.

Burglar Alarms and Home Automation

CEDIA
9202 N. Meridian St., Suite 200
Indianapolis, IN 46260-1810
Phone: 800-669-5329
Fax: 317-571-5603
Website: http://www.cedia.org

Digital Security Controls, Ltd. (DSC)
3301 Langstaff Rd.
Concord, Ontario
Canada L4K 4L2
Phone: 888-888-7838; 905-760-3000
Fax: 905-760-3040
Website: www.dsc.com

IQ
8300 Colesville Rd., Suite 750
Silver Spring, MD 20910
Phone: 301-585-1855
Website: http://www.alarm.org/iq/iq.html

National Training School
8300 Colesville Rd., Suite750
Silver Spring, MD 20910
Phone: 888-702-1687
Fax: 301-585-1866
Website: http://www.alarm.org/nts/index.html

Sponsored by the National Burglar and Fire Alarm Association (NBFAA)

NMFOTC World Class Training Labs
Division of Wright Communications Corp.
P.O. Box 560099
Montverde, FL 34756
Phone: 407-469-0071; 800-333-6456
Fax: 407-469-3991

World Institute for Security Enhancement
P.O. Box 770727
Miami, FL 33177
Phone: 305-773-0048
Website: http://www.worldinstitute.org

Closed-Circuit Television

The Gamewell Company
60 Pleasant St.
Ashland, MA 01721
Phone: 508-231-1400
Fax: 508-231-0900
Website: http://www.gamewell.com

LTC Training Center
Charlie Pierce, President
930 S. Rolff St.
P.O. Box 4475
Davenport, IA 52808

Panasonic Security & Digital Imaging Company
Security Systems Group
Secaucus, NJ
Phone: 877-733-3689
Website: http://cctv.panasonic.com.

Fire Systems

Fire-lite Alarms
One Fire-Lite Pl.
Northford, CT 06472
Phone: 203-484-1200
Fax: 203-484-1036
Website: http://www.firelite.com

NICET
1420 King St.
Alexandria, VA 22314-2794
Phone: 888-476-4238
Website: http://www.nicet.org/index.html

Trade Organizations and Publications

Organizations

American Fire Sprinkler Association
12959 Jupiter Rd., Suite 142
Dallas, TX 75238-3200
Phone: 214-349-5965
Fax: 214-343-8898
E-mail: afsainfo@firesprinkler.org

American National Standards Institute
1819 L Street, NW
Washington, DC 20036
Phone: 212-642-4980 or 212-642-4900
Website: www.ansi.org

American Society for Industrial Security
1625 Prince St.
Alexandria, VA 22314-2818
Phone: 703-519-6200
Fax: 703-519-6299
E-mail: asis@asisonline.org
Website: www.asisonline.org

American Society for Testing and Materials
100 Barr Harbor Dr.
West Conshohocken, PA 19428-2959
Phone: 610-832-9585
Fax: 610-832-9555
Website: www.astm.org

Automatic Fire Alarm Association (AFAA), Inc.
P.O. Box 951807
Lake Mary, FL 32795-1807
Phone: 407-322-6288
Fax: 407-322-7488
Website: www.afaa.org

Building Officials and Code Administrators International, Inc. (BOCA)
4051 W. Flossmoor Rd.
Country Club Hills, IL 60478
Phone: 708-799-2300
Fax: 708-799-4981
Website: www.bocai.org/

Canadian Alarm and Security Association (CANASA)
610 Alden Rd., Suite 100
Markham, Ontario
Canada L3R 9Z1
Phone: 905-513-0622 or toll free in Canada 1-800-538-9919
Fax: 905-513-0624
Website: www.canasa.org

Canadian Society for Industrial Security Inc.
2700 Lancaster Rd., Unit 102
Ottawa, Ontario
Canada K1B 4T7
Phone: 613-738-1744; 1-800-461-7748
Fax: 613-738-1920
Website: www.csis-scsi.org

Central Station Alarm Association
440 Maple Ave. E., Suite 201
Vienna, VA 22180
Phone: 703-242-4670
Fax: 703-242-4675
Website: www.csaaul.org

Fire Protection Association Australia
13 Ellingworth Parade
P.O. Box 1049
Box Hill, Victoria, 3128
Australia
Phone: 161(0)3 9890-1544
Fax: 161(0)3 9890-1577
Website: www.fpaa.com.au

International Association of Home Safety and Security Professionals
Box 2044-E
Erie, PA 16512-2044
Website: www.iahssp.org

International Organization for Standardization (ISO)
1, rue de Varembé, Case postale 56
CH-1211 Geneva 20
Switzerland
Phone: 141-22-749-01-11
Fax: 1 41-22-733-34-30
E-mail: central@iso.ch
Website: www.iso.ch/

National Association of Home Builders
1201 15th St., NW
Washington, DC 20005
Phone: 800-368-5242; 202-822-0200
Website: www.nahb.com

National Burglar and Fire Alarm Association (NBFAA)
8300 Colesville Rd., Suite 750
Silver Spring, MD 20910
Phone: 301-585-1855
Fax: 301-585-1866
Website: www.alarm.org

National Fire Protection Association
1 Batterymarch Park
P.O. Box 9101
Quincy, MA 02269-9101
Phone: 617-770-3000
Fax: 617-770-0700
Website: www.nfpa.org

The National Fire Sprinkler Association
P.O. Box 1000
Patterson, NY 12563
E-mail: Info@nfsa.org
Website: www.nfsa.org

National Security Institute
116 Main St., Suite 200
Medway, MA 02053
Phone: 508-533-9099
Fax: 508-533-3761
Website: nsi.org

National Systems Contractors Association
625 First St. SE, Suite 420
Ccdar Rapids, IA 52401
Phone: 800-446-6722; 319-366-6722
Fax: 319-366-4164
Website: www.nsca.org

National Institute of Standards and Technology (NIST)
100 Bureau Dr., Stop 3460
Gaithersburg, MD 20899-3460
Phone: 301-975-NIST (6478)
TTY: 301-975-8295
Website: www.nist.gov/

Underwriters Laboratories Inc. (UL)
333 Pfingsten Rd.
Northbrook, IL 60062-2096
Phone: 847-272-8800
Fax: 847-272-8129
E-mail: northbrook@us.ul.com
Website: www.ul.com

Publications

Access Control & Security Systems Integration Magazine
6151 Powers Ferry Rd. NW
Atlanta, GA 30339

For security and facilities directors of commercial, industrial, and institutional organizations covering door entry, CCTV, sensors, gates and operators, and perimeter security, including fencing and guard services and hardware.

Buildings Magazine
Stamats Communications, Inc.
Stamats Buildings Group
615 5th St. SE
P.O. Box 1888
Cedar Rapids, IA 52406-1888
Phone: 319-364-6167
E-mail: linda-monroe@buildings.com
Website: www.buildingsmag.com

Commercial Building
Stamats Communications, Inc.
Stamats Buildings Group
615 5th St. SE
P.O. Box 1888
Cedar Rapids, IA 52406-1888
Phone: 319-364-6167
E-mail: craig-rieks@buildings.com
Website: www.buildingsmag.com

Professional Security Magazine
JTC Associates Ltd.
4 Elms Lane
Shareshill, Wolverhampton WV10 7JS

For security officers, consultants, directors, and law enforcement officers.

Security Dealer
445 Broad Hollow Rd.
Melville, NY 11747

Monthly magazine for security dealers and installers.

Security Distributing & Marketing (SDM)
1050 Rte. 83, Suite 200
Bensenville, IL 60106-1096

A leading industry trade journal.

Security Management
1625 Prince St.
Alexandria, VA 22314-2818

Published by ASIS.

Security Sales Magazine
21061 S. Western Ave.
Torrance, CA 90501
E-mail: info@securitysales.com
Website: www.securitysales.com

For the professional installing dealer.

Glossary

AC See *Alternating current.*

Access Control The control of pedestrian and vehicular traffic through entrances and exits of a protected area or premises.

Access Mode The operation of an alarm system such that no alarm signal is given when the protected area is entered; however, a signal may be given if the sensor, annunciator, or control unit is tampered with or opened.

Access/Secure Control Unit See *Control unit.*

Access Switch See *Authorized access switch.*

Accumulator A circuit which accumulates a sum. For example, in an audio alarm control unit, the accumulator sums the amplitudes of a series of pulses, which are larger than some threshold level; subtracts from the sum at a predetermined rate to account for random background pulses; and initiates an alarm signal when the sum exceeds some predetermined level. This circuit is also called an integrator; in digital circuits it may be called a counter.

AC Induction Unwanted ac signals picked up when wiring (such as alarm system wiring) is too close to other wiring, transformers, generators, motors, and other ac power sources.

Active Intrusion Sensor An active sensor which detects the presence of an intruder within the range of the sensor. Examples are an ultrasonic motion detector, a radio-frequency motion detector, and a photoelectric alarm system. See also *Passive intrusion sensor.*

Active Sensor A sensor that detects the disturbance of a radiation field which is generated by the sensor. See also *Passive sensor.*

Activity Detection A form of video motion detection, often used with video multiplexers to improve the camera update times. It also gives a relay closure.

Actuating Device See *Actuator.*

Actuator A manual or automatic switch or sensor such as holdup button, magnetic switch, or thermostat which causes a system to transmit an alarm signal when manually activated or when the device automatically senses an intruder or other unwanted condition.

AF See *Audio frequency.*

Air Gap The distance between two magnetic elements in a magnetic or electromagnetic circuit, such as between the core and the armature of a relay.

Alarm Circuit An electric circuit of an alarm system which produces or transmits an alarm signal.

Alarm Condition A threatening condition, such as an intrusion, fire, or holdup, sensed by a detector.

Alarm Device   A device which signals a warning in response to an alarm condition, such as a bell, siren, or annunciator.

Alarm Discrimination   The ability of an alarm system to distinguish between those stimuli caused by an intrusion and those that are a part of the environment.

Alarm Line   A wired electric circuit used for the transmission of alarm signals from the protected premises to a monitoring station.

Alarm Receiver   See *Annunciator.*

Alarm Screen   A window covering made with fine wires and connected to an alarm system's protective loop so that an alarm condition occurs when there's a break in the screen.

Alarm Sensor   See *Sensor.*

Alarm Signal   A signal produced by a control unit indicating the existence of an alarm condition.

Alarm State   The condition of a detector which causes a control unit in the secure mode to transmit an alarm signal.

Alarm Station   (1) A manually actuated device installed at a fixed location to transmit an alarm signal in response to an alarm condition, such as a concealed holdup button in a bank teller's cage. (2) A well-marked emergency control unit, installed in fixed locations usually accessible to the public, used to summon help in response to an alarm condition. The control unit contains either a manually actuated switch or telephone connected to fire or police headquarters, or a telephone answering service. See also *Remote station alarm system.*

Alarm System   An assembly of equipment and devices designated and arranged to signal the presence of an alarm condition requiring urgent attention such as unauthorized entry, fire, and temperature rise. The system may be local, police connection, central station, or proprietary. (For individual alarm systems, see alphabetical listing by type, e.g., intrusion alarm system.)

Alternating Current (AC)   Electric current that continually reverses direction.

Ammeter   A meter for measuring the amount of electric current flow.

Ampere (Amp)   A unit for measuring electric current flow.

Analog (or Analogue)   A nondigital signal in which any level is represented by a directly proportional electrical voltage.

Angle of View   The maximum viewing area of a camera/lens.

Annunciator   An alarm monitoring device which consists of a number of visible signals such as flags or lamps indicating the status of the detectors in an alarm system or systems. Each circuit in the device is usually labeled to identify the location and condition being monitored. In addition to the visible signal, an audible signal is usually associated with the device. When an alarm condition is reported, a signal is indicated visibly, audibly, or both. The visible signal is generally maintained until reset either manually or automatically. Common annunciators include sirens, bells, and strobe lights.

Answering Service   A business which contracts with subscribers to answer incoming telephone calls after a specified delay or when scheduled to do so. It may also provide other services such as relaying fire or intrusion alarm signals to the proper authorities.

Aperture   The lens opening that controls the light-gathering capability of a lens. The maximum aperture is the minimum *f*-stop of a lens.

Area Protection   Protection of the inner space or volume of a secured area by means of a volumetric sensor.

Area Sensor   A sensor with a detection zone which approximates an area, such as a wall surface or the exterior of a safe.

Armored Cable   Two or more wires grouped together in a protective metal covering.

Aspect Ratio   The ratio of the width to the height of a picture frame's image size. For a standard TV system the aspect ratio is 4 horizontal units over 3 vertical units, or 4:3.

Aspherical Lens   A lens designed with a nonspherical shape to refract light passing through it, decreasing barrel distortion on wide-angle lenses, or to lower the lens aperture so that it passes more light.

Attenuation   A decrease or loss in a video signal magnitude when it is transmitted from one point to another, usually measured in decibels.

Audible Alarm Device   (1) A noise-making device such as a siren, bell, or horn used as part of a local alarm system to indicate an alarm condition. (2) A bell, buzzer, horn, or other noise-making device used as a part of an annunciator to indicate a change in the status or operating mode of an alarm system.

Audio Detection System   See *Sound-sensing detection system.*

Audio Frequency (Sonic)   Sound frequencies generally regarde to be within the range of human hearing, about 20 Hz to 20,000 kHz.

Audio Monitor   An arrangement of amplifiers and speakers designed to monitor the sounds transmitted by microphones located in the protected area. Similar to an annunciator, except that supervisory personnel can monitor the protected area to interpret the sounds.

Authorized Access Switch   A device used to make an alarm system or some portion or zone of a system inoperative in order to permit authorized access through a protected port. A shunt is an example of such a device.

Auto White Balance   A feature that lets the camera constantly monitor the light and adjusts its color to maintain white areas.

Automatic Frequency Control (AFC)   An electronic circuit in which the frequency of an oscillator is automatically maintained within specified limits.

Automatic Gain Control (AGC)   An electronic circuit in which the gain of a signal is automatically adjusted as a function of its input or other specified parameter.

Auto-Iris Lens   A lens with an aperture that automatically adjusts to maintain proper light levels on the imaging device.

Auto-Terminating   Feature whereby the equipment automatically selects the correct termination depending on whether the video output BNC is connected.

B.A.   See *Burglar alarm.*

Back Focus.   The mechanical focusing adjstment for a camera. It aligns the imaging sensor with the focal point of the lens to adjust for different different back focal lenths of lenses. Very important on zoom lenses to ensure the image stays in focus throughout the zoom range.

Backlight Compensation (BLC)   A CCD camera feature that electronically compensates for high background lighting to give detail that would normally be silhouetted.

Balanced Signal   The transmission of two video signals equal to each other in voltage but opposite in polarity, usually sent over twisted-pair cable.

Bandwidth   The span that an information-bearing signal requires or allows, or the value expressing the difference between the upper and lower limits through a range of allowable frequencies.

Baseband Video   Unmodulated video signal that can be displayed on a monitor but not on a domestic TV.

Beam Divergence   In a photoelectric alarm system, the angular spread of the light beam.

BLC   See *Backlight compensation.*

BNC   The most common type of video connector used for CCTVs.

Box   See *Junction box.*

Break Alarm   (1) An alarm condition signaled by the opening or breaking of an electric circuit. (2) The signal produced by a break alarm condition (sometimes referred to as an open-circuit alarm or trouble signal, designed to indicate possible system failure).

Bug   (1) To plant a microphone or other sound sensor or to tap a communication line for the purpose of surreptitious listening or audio monitoring; loosely, to install a sensor in a specified location. (2) The microphone or other sensor used for the purpose of surreptitious listening.

Building Security Alarm System   The system of protective signaling devices installed at a premise.

Burglar Alarm (B.A.) Pad   A supporting frame laced with fine wire or a fragile panel located with foil or fine wire and installed so as to cover an exterior opening in a building, such as a door or skylight. Entrance through the opening breaks the wire or foil and initiates an alarm signal. See also *Grid.*

Burglar Alarm System   See *Intrusion alarm system.*

Burglary   The unlawful entering of a structure with the intent to commit a felony or theft therein.

BX   See *Armored cable.*

Cabinet-for-Safe   A wooden enclosure having closely spaced electrical grids on all inner surfaces and contacts on the doors. It surrounds a safe and initiates an alarm signal if an attempt is made to open or penetrate the cabinet.

Cable   Two or more wires grouped together within a protective jacket or sheath.

Capacitance   The property of two or more objects which enables them to store electric energy in an electric field between them. The basic measurement unit is the farad. Capacitance varies inversely with the distance between the objects; hence the change of capacitance with relative motion is greater, the nearer one object is to the other.

Capacitance Alarm System   An alarm system in which a protected object is electrically connected as a capacitance sensor. The approach of an intruder causes sufficient change in capacitance to upset the balance of the system and initiate an alarm signal. Also called a proximity alarm system.

Capacitance Detector   See *Capacitance sensor.*

Capacitance Sensor   A sensor which responds to a change in capacitance in a field containing a protected object or in a field within a protected area.

Capacitor   An electronic component designed to store an electric charge.

Carrier Current Transmitter   A device which transmits alarm signals from a sensor to a control unit via the standard ac power lines.

CCTV   See *Closed-circuit television.*

Central Station   A control center to which alarm systems in a subscriber's premises are connected, where circuits are supervised, and where personnel continuously record and investigate alarm or trouble signals. Facilities are provided for the reporting of alarms to police and fire departments or to other outside agencies.

Central Station Alarm System   An alarm system, or group of systems, the activities of which are transmitted to, recorded in, maintained by, and supervised from a central station. This differs from proprietary alarm systems in that the central station is owned and operated independently of the subscriber.

Circuit   A continuous loop of electric flow from a power source to a load and back to the power source.

Circuit Breaker   A safety device for breaking a circuit in cases of circuit overloads and shorts.

Circumvention   The defeat of an alarm system by the avoidance of its detection devices, such as by jumping over a pressure sensitive mat, entering through a hole cut in an unprotected wall rather than through a protected door, or keeping outside the range of an ultrasonic motion detector. Circumvention contrasts with *Spoofing.*

Closed-Circuit Alarm   See *Cross-alarm.*

Closed-Circuit System   A system in which the sensors of each zone are connected in series so that the same current exists in each sensor. When an activated sensor breaks the circuit or the connecting wire is cut, an alarm is transmitted for that zone.

Closed-Circuit Television (CCTV) System   A nonbroadcast on-premises television system used to watch certain areas. At a minimum, it consists of a camera, transmission link (usually cable), and monitor (which may be a television set).

Clutch Head Screw   A mounting screw with a uniquely designed head for which the installation and removal tool is not commonly available. They are used to install alarm system components so that removal is inhibited.

C-mount   An industry standard for mounting a $^2/_3$-inch and a 1-inch lens on a camera. The C-mount lens has a 17.5-mm diameter. The distance from the flange surface to the focal point is 17.52 mm. A C-mount lens can be used on a CS-mount camera with a 5-mm adapter ring; however, a CS-mount lens can't be used on a C-mount format camera.

Coded-Alarm System   An alarm system in which the source of each signal is identifiable. This is usually accomplished by means of a series of current pulses which operate audible or visible annunciators or recorders or both, to yield a recognizable signal. This is usually used to allow the transmission of multiple signals on a common circuit.

Coded Cable   A multiconductor cable in which the insulation on each conductor is distinguishable from all others by color or design. This assists in identification of the point of origin or final destination of a wire.

Coded Transmitter   A device for transmitting a coded signal when manually or automatically operated by an actuator. The actuator may be housed with the transmitter, or a number of actuators may operate a common transmitter.

Coding Siren   A siren which has an auxiliary mechanism to interrupt the flow of air through its principal mechanism, enabling it to produce a controllable series of sharp blasts.

Combination Sensor Alarm System   An alarm system which requires the simultaneous activation of two or more sensors to initiate an alarm signal.

Compromise   See *Defeat.*

Conductor   Material that lets electric current flow through it. Generally the term is used only when referring to materials through which current flows easily, such as copper wire.

Conduit   Metal or plastic tubing used for protecting wires.

Constant Ringing Drop (CRD)   A relay which, when activated even momentarily, will remain in an alarm condition until reset. A key is often required to reset the relay and turn off the alarm.

Constant Ringing Relay (CRR)   See *Constant ringing drop.*

Contact   (1) Each of the pair of metallic parts of a switch or relay which by touching or separating make or break the electric current path. (2) Switch-type sensor.

Contact Device   A device which, when actuated, opens or closes a set of electric contacts; a switch or relay.

Contact Microphone   A microphone designed for attachment directly to a surface of a protected area or object; usually used to detect surface vibrations.

Contact Vibration Sensor   See *Vibration sensor.*

Contactless Vibrating Bell   A vibrating bell whose continuous operation depends upon application of an alternating current, without circuit-interrupting contacts such as those used in vibrating bells operated by direct current.

Continuity   An unbroken path from one point to another.

Control Box   See *Control unit.*

Control Cabinet   See *Control unit.*

Control Panel   See *Control unit.*

Control Unit (or Control Box or Control Panel)   A device, usually electronic, which provides the interface between the alarm system and the human operator and produces an alarm signal when its programmed response indicates an alarm condition. Some of or all the following may be provided for: power for sensors, sensitivity adjustments, means to select and indicate access mode or secure mode, monitoring for line supervision and tamper devices, timing circuits for entrance and exit delays, transmission of an alarm signal, etc.

Covert   Hidden or disguised.

CRD   See *Constant ringing drop.*

Cross-Alarm   (1) An alarm condition signaled by crossing or shorting an electric circuit. (2) The signal produced due to a cross-alarm condition.

Crossover   An insulated electric path used to connect foil across window dividers, such as those found on multiple-pane windows, to prevent grounding and to make a more durable connection.

Crosstalk   An undesired electric signal that interferes with the desired signal, and is caused by electromagnetic or electrostatic coupling by conductors in close proximity or external sources.

CRR   Constant ringing relay. See *Constant ringing drop.*

CS-Mount   An industry standard for mounting a lens on a camera. It has a 12.5-mm diameter and uses the same thread as the C-mount, but requires the lens to be 5 mm closer to the image sensor.

Current   The flow of electrons.

Dark Current   The current output of a photoelectric sensor when no light is entering the sensor.

Day Setting   See *Access mode.*

DC   See *Direct current.*

Defeat   The frustration, counteraction, or thwarting of an alarm device so that it fails to signal an alarm when a protected area is entered. Defeat includes both circumvention and spoofing.

Detection Range   The greatest distance at which a sensor will consistently detect an intruder under a standard set of conditions.

Detector   (1) A sensor such as those used to detect intrusion, equipment malfunctions or failure, rate of temperature rise, smoke, or fire. (2) A demodulator, a device for recovering the modulating function or signal from a modulated wave, such as that used in a modulated photoelectric alarm system. See also *Photoelectric alarm system, modulated.*

Dialer   See *Telephone dialer, automatic.*

Differential Pressure Sensor   A sensor used for perimeter protection which responds to the difference between the hydraulic pressures in two liquid-filled tubes buried just below the surface of the earth around the exterior perimeter of the protected area. The pressure difference can indicate an intruder walking or driving over the buried tubes.

Digital Telephone Dialer   See *Telephone dialer, digital.*

Diode   An electrical component designed to serve as a one-way valve for electric current.

Direct Connect   See *Police connection.*

Direct Current (DC)   Electric current that flows in one direction only. Batteries are a source of direct current.

Direct Wire Burglar Alarm (DWBA) Circuit   See *Alarm line.*

Direct Wire Circuit   See *Alarm line.*

Door Cord   A short, insulated cable with an attaching block and terminals at each end, used to conduct current to a device, such as foil, mounted on the movable portion of a door or window.

Door Trip Switch   A mechanical switch mounted so that movement of the door will operate the switch.

Doppler Effect (Shift)   The apparent change in frequency of sound or radio waves when reflected from or originating from a moving object. It is utilized in some types of motion sensors.

Double-Circuit System   An alarm circuit in which two wires enter and two wires leave each sensor.

Double Drop   An alarm signaling method often used in central station alarm systems in which the line is first opened to produce a break alarm and then shorted to produce a cross-alarm.

Drop   (1) See *Annunciator*. (2) A light indicator on an annunciator.

Duress Alarm Device   A device which produces either a silent alarm or a local alarm under a condition of personnel stress such as holdup, fire, illness, or other panic or emergency. The device is normally manually operated and may be fixed or portable.

Duress Alarm System   An alarm system which employs a duress alarm device.

DWBA   Direct wire burglar alarm. See *Alarm line*.

E-Field Sensor   A passive sensor which detects changes in the earth's ambient electric field caused by the movement of an intruder. See also *H-field sensor*.

Electrical Box (or Box or Junction Box)   A container, usually metal or plastic, used to house wiring connections.

Electromagnetic   Pertaining to the relationship between current flow and magnetic field.

Electromagnetic Interference (EMI)   Impairment of the reception of a wanted electromagnetic signal by an electromagnetic disturbance. This can be caused by lightning, radio transmitters, power line noise, and other electrical devices.

Electromechanical Bell   A bell with a prewound spring-driven striking mechanism, the operation of which is initiated by the activation of an electric tripping mechanism.

Electronic   Related to, or pertaining to, devices which utilize electrons moving through a vacuum, gas, or semiconductor, and to circuits or systems containing such devices.

EMI   See *Electromagnetic interference*.

End-of-Line Resistor   See *Terminal resistor*.

Entrance Delay   The time between actuating a sensor on an entrance door or gate and the sounding of a local alarm or transmission of an alarm signal by the control unit. This delay is used if the authorized access switch is located within the protected area and permits a person with the control key to enter without causing an alarm. The delay is provided by a timer within the control unit.

EOL   End of line.

Exit Delay   The time between turning on a control unit and the sounding of a local alarm or transmission of an alarm signal upon actuation of a sensor on an exit door. This delay is used if the authorized access switch is located within the protected area and permits a person with the control key to turn on the alarm system and to leave through a protected door or gate without causing an alarm. The delay is provided by a timer within the control unit.

Fail-Safe   A feature of a system or device which initiates an alarm or trouble signal when the system or device either malfunctions or loses power.

False Alarm   An alarm signal transmitted in the absence of an alarm condition. These may be classified according to causes: environmental, e.g., rain, fog, wind, hail, lightning, temperature; animals, e.g., rats, dogs, cats, insects; human-made disturbances, e.g., sonic booms, EMI, vehicles; equipment malfunction, e.g., transmission errors, component failure; operator error; and unknown.

False-Alarm Rate, Monthly   The number of false alarms per installation per month.

False-Alarm Ratio   The ratio of false alarms to total alarms; may be expressed as a percentage or as a simple ratio.

Feed Wire   A conductor that carries 120-volt current uninterrupted from the service panel.

Fence Alarm   Any of several types of sensors used to detect the presence of an intruder near a fence or any attempt to climb over, go under, or cut through the fence.

Field   The space or area in which there exists a force such as that produced by an electrically charged object, a current, or a magnet.

Fire Detector (Sensor)   See *Heat sensor* and *Smoke detector.*

Floor Mat   See *Mat switch.*

Floor Trap   A trap installed to detect the movement of a person across a floor space, such as a trip wire switch or mat switch.

Foil   Thin metallic strips which are cemented to a protected surface (usually glass in a window or door) and connected to a closed electric circuit. If the protected material is broken so as to break the foil, the circuit opens, initiating an alarm signal. Also called *tape.* A window, door, or other surface to which foil has been applied is said to be taped or foiled.

Foil Connector   An electrical terminal block used on the edge of a window to join interconnecting wire to window foil.

Foot Rail   A holdup alarm device, often used at cashiers' windows, in which a foot is placed under the rail, lifting it, to initiate an alarm signal.

Frequency-Division Multiplexing (FDM)   See *Multiplexing, frequency-division.*

Fuse   A safety device that interrupts electric current flow during an overload or short circuit. It's often used in older homes.

Glass-Break Vibration Detector   A vibration detection system which employs a contact microphone attached to a glass window to detect the cutting or breakage of the glass.

Greenfield   See *Armored cable.*

Grid   (1) An arrangement of electrically conducting wire, screen, or tubing placed in front of doors or windows or both which is used as part of a capacitance sensor. (2) A lattice of wooden dowels or slats concealing fine wires in a closed circuit which initiates an alarm signal when forcing or cutting the lattice breaks the wires. Used over accessible openings, it is sometimes called a protective screen. See also *Burglar alarm pad.* (3) A screen or metal plate, connected to earth ground, sometimes used to provide a stable ground reference for objects protected by a capacitance sensor. If placed against the walls near the protected object, it prevents the sensor sensitivity from extending through the walls into areas of activity.

Grounding Wire   A wire in an electric circuit that conducts current to the earth during a short circuit. It's usually a bare copper wire.

Heat Detector   See *Heat sensor.*

Heat Sensor   (1) A sensor which responds to a local temperature above a selected value, to a local temperature increase which is at a rate of increase greater than a preselected rate (rate of rise), or to both. (2) A sensor which responds to infrared radiation from a remote source, such as a person.

Hi-Field Sensor   A passive sensor which detects changes in the earth's ambient magnetic field caused by the movement of an intruder. See also *E-field sensor.*

Holdup   A robbery involving the threat to use a weapon.

Holdup Alarm Device   A device which signals a holdup. The device is usually surreptitious and may be manually or automatically actuated, fixed or portable. See *Duress alarm device.*

Holdup Alarm System, Automatic   An alarm system which employs a holdup alarm device, in which the signal transmission is initiated solely by the action of the intruder, such as a money clip in a cash drawer.

Holdup Alarm System, Manual   A holdup alarm system in which the signal transmission is initiated by the direct action of the person attacked or of an observer of the attack.

Holdup Button   A manually actuated mechanical switch used to initiate a duress alarm signal; usually constructed to minimize accidental activation.

Hood Contact   A switch which is used for the supervision of a closed safe or vault door. It is usually installed on the outside surface of the protected door.

Hot wire   A wire that carries voltage. In an electric circuit, such wires are usually covered with red or black insulation.

Impedance   The opposition to the flow of alternating current in a circuit. It may be determined by the ratio of an input voltage to the resultant current.

Impedance Matching   Making the impedance of a terminating device equal to the impedance of the circuit to which it is connected, in order to achieve optimum signal transfer.

Infrared (IR) Motion Detector   A sensor which detects changes in the infrared light radiation from parts of the protected area. Presence of an intruder in the area changes the infrared light intensity from that direction.

Infrared (IR) Motion Sensor   See *Infrared motion detector.*

Infrared Sensor   See *Heat sensor, Infrared motion detector,* and *Photoelectric sensor.*

Inking Register   See *Register, inking.*

Insulator   Material that resists the flow of electric current, such as plastic and rubber. For safety, such materials are used to cover electric wires, cables, and tools.

Integrated Circuit (IC)   A microscopic electronic circuit etched onto a computer chip.

Interior Perimeter Protection   A line of protection along the interior boundary of a protected area including all points through which entry can be effected.

Intrusion   Unauthorized entry onto the property of another.

Intrusion Alarm System An alarm system for signaling the entry or attempted entry of a person or an object into the area or volume protected by the system.

Ionization Smoke Detector A smoke detector in which a small amount of radioactive material ionizes the air in the sensing chamber, thus rendering it conductive and permitting a current to flow through the air between two charged electrodes. This effectively gives the sensing chamber an electrical conductance. When smoke particles enter the ionization area, they decrease the conductance of the air by attaching themselves to the ions, causing a reduction in mobility. When the conductance is less than a predetermined level, the detector circuit responds.

IR Infrared.

Jack An electrical connector which is used for frequent connect and disconnect operations, for example, to connect an alarm circuit at an overhang door.

Junction Box See *Electrical box.*

Lacing A network of fine wire surrounding or covering an area to be protected, such as a safe, vault, or glass panel, and connected into a closed-circuit system. The network of wire is concealed by a shield such as concrete or paneling in such a manner that an attempt to break through the shield breaks the wire and initiates an alarm.

Light-Emitting Diode (LED) A diode that emits light.

Light Intensity Cutoff In a photoelectric alarm system, the percentage reduction of light which initiates an alarm signal at the photoelectric receiver unit.

Line Amplifier An audio amplifier which is used to provide preamplification of an audio alarm signal before transmission of the signal over an alarm line. Use of an amplifier extends the range of signal transmission.

Line Sensor (Detector) A sensor with a detection zone which approximates a line or series of lines, such as a photoelectric sensor which senses a direct or reflected light beam.

Line Supervision Electronic protection of an alarm line accomplished by sending a continuous or coded signal through the circuit. A change in the circuit characteristics, such as a change in impedance due to the circuit's having been tampered with, will be detected by a monitor. The monitor initiates an alarm if the change exceeds a predetermined amount.

Local Alarm An alarm which, when activated, makes a loud noise (see *Audible alarm device*) at or near the protected area or floods the site with light or does both.

Local Alarm System An alarm system which, when activated, produces an audible or visible signal in the immediate vicinity of the protected premises or object. This term usually applies to systems designed to provide only a local warning of intrusion and not to transmit to a remote monitoring station. However, local alarm systems are sometimes used in conjunction with a remote alarm.

Loop An electric circuit consisting of several elements, usually switches, connected in series.

Magnetic Alarm System An alarm system which will initiate an alarm when it detects changes in the local magnetic field. The changes could be caused by motion of ferrous objects such as guns or tools near the magnetic sensor.

Magnetic Contact A switch unit that consists of two separate units: a magnetically actuated switch and a magnet. The switch is usually mounted in a fixed position (door jamb or window frame) opposing the magnet, which is fastened to a hinged or sliding door, window, etc. When the movable section is opened, the magnet moves with it, actuating the switch.

Magnetic Sensor   A sensor which responds to changes in magnetic field. See also *Magnetic alarm system.*

Magnetic Switch   See *Magnetic contact.*

Magnetic Switch, Balanced   A magnetic contact that operates using a balanced magnetic field in such a manner as to resist defeat with an external magnet. It signals an alarm when it detects either an increase or a decrease in magnetic field strength.

Matching Network   A circuit used to achieve impedance matching. It may also allow audio signals to be transmitted to an alarm line while blocking direct current used locally for line supervision.

Mat Switch   A flat area switch used on open floors or under carpeting. It may be sensitive over an area of a few square feet or several square yards.

McCulloh Circuit (Loop)   A supervised single-wire loop connecting a number of coded transmitters located in different protected areas to a central station receiver.

Mechanical Switch   A switch in which the contacts are opened and closed by means of a depressible plunger or button.

Mercury Fence Alarm   A type of mercury switch which is sensitive to the vibration caused by an intruder climbing on a fence.

Mercury Switch   A switch operated by tilting or vibrating that causes an enclosed pool of mercury to move, making or breaking physical and electrical contact with conductors. These are used on tilting doors and windows, and on fences.

Microwave Alarm System   An alarm system which employs radio-frequency motion detectors operating in the microwave frequency region of the electromagnetic spectrum.

Microwave Frequency   Radio frequencies in the range of approximately 1.0 to 300 GHz.

Microwave Motion Detector   See *Radio-frequency motion detector.*

Modulated Photoelectric Alarm System   See *Photoelectric alarm system, modulated.*

Monitor Cabinet   An enclosure which houses the annunciator and associated equipment.

Monitor Panel   See *Annunciator.*

Monitoring Station   The central station or other area at which guards, police, or commercial service personnel observe annunciators and registers reporting on the condition of alarm systems.

Motion Detection System   See *Motion sensor.*

Motion Detector   See *Motion sensor.*

Motion Sensor   A sensor which responds to the motion of an intruder. See also *Radio-frequency motion detector, Sonic motion detector, Ultrasonic motion detector,* and *Infrared motion detector.*

Multiplexing   A technique for the concurrent transmission of two or more signals in either or both directions, over the same wire, carrier, or other communication channel. The two basic multiplexing techniques are time-division multiplexing and frequency-division multiplexing.

Multiplexing, Frequency-Division (FDM) The multiplexing technique which assigns to each signal a specific set of frequencies (called a channel) within the larger block of frequencies available on the main transmission path in much the same way that many radio stations broadcast at the same time but can be separately received.

Multiplexing, Time-Division (TDM) The multiplexing technique which provides for the independent transmission of several pieces of information on a timesharing basis by sampling, at frequent intervals, the data to be transmitted.

National Electrical Code (NEC) Widely accepted safety rules and regulations for working with electricity. It's the bible of the electrical construction industry and is published by the National Fire Protection Association (NFPA).

NEC See *National Electrical Code.*

Neutralization See *Defeat.*

Neutral Wire (or Grounded Wire) A wire that returns current at zero voltage to the electric power source. It's usually covered with light gray or white insulation.

NICAD (Nickel Cadmium) A high-performance, long-lasting rechargeable battery, with electrodes made of nickel and cadmium, which may be used as an emergency power supply for an alarm system.

Night Setting See *Secure mode.*

Nonretractable (One-Way) Screw A screw with a head designed to permit installation with an ordinary flat bit screwdriver but which resists removal. These screws are used to install alarm system components so that removal is inhibited.

Normally Closed (NC) Switch A switch in which the contacts are closed when no external forces act upon the switch.

Normally Open (NO) Switch A switch in which the contacts are open (separated) when no external forces act upon the switch.

Nuisance Alarm See *False alarm.*

Object Protection See *Spot protection.*

Open-Circuit Alarm See *Break alarm.*

Open-Circuit System A system in which the sensors are connected in parallel. When a sensor is activated, the circuit is closed, permitting a current which activates an alarm signal.

Panic Alarm See *Duress alarm device.*

Panic Button See *Duress alarm device.*

Passive Intrusion Sensor A passive sensor in an intrusion alarm system which detects an intruder within the range of the sensor. Examples are a sound-sensing detection system, a vibration detection system, an infrared motion detector, and an E-field sensor.

Passive Sensor A sensor which detects natural radiation or radiation disturbances, but does not itself emit the radiation on which its operation depends.

Passive Ultrasonic Alarm System An alarm system which detects the sounds in the ultrasonic frequency range caused by an attempted forcible entry into a protected structure. The system consists of microphones, a control unit containing an amplifier, filters, an accumulator, and a power supply. The unit's sensitivity is adjustable so that ambient noises or normal sounds will not initiate an alarm signal; however, noise above the preset level or a sufficient accumulation of impulses will initiate an alarm.

Percentage Supervision   A method of line supervision in which the current in or resistance of a supervised line is monitored for changes. When the change exceeds a selected percentage of the normal operating current or resistance in the line, an alarm signal is produced.

Perimeter Alarm System   An alarm system which provides perimeter protection.

Perimeter Protection   Protection of access to the outer limits of a protected area, by means of physical barriers, sensors on physical barriers, or exterior sensors not associated with a physical barrier.

Permanent Circuit   An alarm circuit which is capable of transmitting an alarm signal whether the alarm control is in access mode or secure mode. It is used, for example, on foiled fixed windows, tamper switches, and supervisory lines. See also *Supervisory alarm system, supervisory circuit,* and *Permanent protection.*

Permanent Protection   A system of alarm devices such as foil, burglar alarm pads, or lacings connected in a permanent circuit to provide protection whether the control unit is in the access mode or secure mode.

Photoelectric Alarm System   An alarm system which employs a light beam and photoelectric sensor to provide a line of protection. Any interruption of the beam by an intruder is sensed by the sensor. Mirrors may be used to change the direction of the beam. The maximum beam length is limited by many factors, some of which are the light source intensity, number of mirror reflections, detector sensitivity, beam divergence, fog, and haze.

Photoelectric Alarm System, Modulated   A photoelectric alarm system in which the transmitted light beam is modulated in a predetermined manner and in which the receiving equipment will signal an alarm unless it receives the properly modulated light.

Photoelectric Beam-Type Smoke Detector   A smoke detector which projects a light beam across the area to be protected onto a photoelectric cell. Smoke between the light source and the receiving cell reduces the light reaching the cell, causing actuation.

Photoelectric Detector   See *Photoelectric sensor.*

Photoelectric Sensor   A device which detects a visible or invisible beam of light and responds to its complete or nearly complete interruption. See also *Photoelectric alarm system* and *Photoelectric alarm system, modulated.*

Photoelectric Spot-Type Smoke Detector   A smoke detector that contains a chamber with covers which prevent the entrance of light but allow the entrance of smoke. The chamber contains a light source and a photosensitive cell placed so that light is blocked from it. When smoke enters, the smoke particles scatter and reflect the light into the photosensitive cell, causing an alarm.

Point Protection   See *Spot protection.*

Police Connection   The direct link by which an alarm system is connected to an annunciator installed in a police station. Examples of a police connection are an alarm line and a radio communications channel.

Police Panel   See *Police station unit.*

Police Station Unit   An annunciator which can be placed in operation in a police station.

Portable Duress Sensor   A device carried on a person which may be activated in an emergency to send an alarm signal to a monitoring station.

Portable Intrusion Sensor   A sensor which can be installed quickly and which does not require the installation of dedicated wiring for the transmission of its alarm signal.

Positive Noninterfering (PNI) and Successive Alarm System   An alarm system which employs multiple alarm transmitters on each alarm line (like McCulloh loop) such that in the event of simultaneous operation of several transmitters, one of them takes control of the alarm line, transmits its full signal, then releases the alarm line for successive transmission by other transmitters which are held inoperative until they gain control.

Potentiometer   An adjustable resistor.

Pressure Alarm System   An alarm system which protects a vault or other enclosed space by maintaining and monitoring a predetermined air pressure differential between the inside and outside of the space. Equalization of pressure resulting from opening the vault or cutting through the enclosure will be sensed and will initiate an alarm signal.

Printing Recorder   An electromechanical device used at a monitoring station which accepts coded signals from alarm lines and converts them to an alphanumeric printed record of the signal received.

Proprietary Alarm System   An alarm system which is similar to a central station alarm system except that the annunciator is located in a constantly guarded room maintained by the owner for internal security operations. The guards monitor the system and respond to all alarm signals or alert local law enforcement agencies or do both.

Protected Area   An area monitored by an alarm system or guards, or enclosed by a suitable barrier.

Protected Port   A point of entry such as a door, window, or corridor which is monitored by sensors connected to an alarm system.

Protection Device   (1) A sensor such as a grid, foil, contact, or photoelectric sensor connected into an intrusion alarm system. (2) A barrier which inhibits intrusion, such as a grille, lock, fence, or wall.

Protection, Exterior Perimeter   A line of protection surrounding but somewhat removed from a facility. Examples are fences, barrier walls, or patrolled points of a perimeter.

Protection Off   See *Access mode.*

Protection On   See *Secure mode.*

Protective Screen   See *Grid.*

Protective Signaling   The initiation, transmission, and reception of signals involved in the detection and prevention of property loss due to fire, burglary, or other destructive conditions. Also the electronic supervision of persons and equipment concerned with this detection and prevention. See also *Line supervision* and *Supervisory alarm system.*

Proximity Alarm System   See *Capacitance alarm system.*

Punching Register   See *Register, punch.*

Radar Alarm System   An alarm system which employs radio-frequency motion detectors.

Radar (Radio Detecting and Ranging)   See *Radio-frequency motion detector.*

Radio-Frequency Interference (RFI)   Electromagnetic interference in the radio-frequency range.

Radio-Frequency Motion Detector   A sensor which detects the motion of an intruder through the use of a radiated radio-frequency electromagnetic field. The device operates by sensing a disturbance in the generated RF field caused by intruder motion, typically a modulation of the field referred to as a Doppler effect, which is used to initiate an alarm signal. Most radio-frequency motion detectors are certified by the FCC for operation as field disturbance sensors at one of the following frequencies: 0.915 GHz (L band), 2.45 GHz (S band), 5.8 GHz (X band), 10.525 GHz (X band), and 22.125 GHz (K band). Units operating in the microwave frequency range are usually called microwave motion detectors.

Reed Switch   A type of magnetic switch consisting of contacts formed by two thin, movable, magnetically actuated metal vanes or reeds, held in a normally open position within a sealed glass envelope.

Register   An electromechanical device which makes a paper tape in response to signal impulses received from transmitting circuits. A register may be driven by a prewound spring mechanism, an electric motor, or a combination of these.

Register, Inking   A register which marks the tape with ink.

Register, Punch   A register which marks the tape by cutting holes in it.

Register, Slashing   A register which marks the tape by cutting V-shaped slashes in it.

Relay   A mechanical switch that closes when current flows through its wire coil.

Remote Alarm   An alarm signal which is transmitted to a remote monitoring station. See also *Local alarm.*

Remote Station Alarm System   An alarm system which employs remote alarm stations usually located in building hallways or on city streets.

Reporting Line   See *Alarm line.*

Resistance Bridge Smoke Detector   A smoke detector which responds to the particles and moisture present in smoke. These substances reduce the resistance of an electric bridge grid and cause the detector to respond.

Resistor   An electronic component designed to resist current flow.

Retard Transmitter   A coded transmitter in which a delay period is introduced between the time of actuation and the time of signal transmission.

RFI   See *Radio-frequency interference.*

RF Motion Detector   See *Radio-frequency motion detector.*

Romex   A popular brand of plastic-sheathed electric cable that's often used for indoor wiring.

Screw Terminal   A place on a switch, receptacle, or fixture to connect wire to the device.

Secure Mode   The condition of an alarm system in which all sensors and control units are ready to respond to an intrusion.

Security Monitor   See *Annunciator.*

Seismic Sensor   A sensor, generally buried under the surface of the ground for perimeter protection, which responds to minute vibrations of the earth generated as an intruder walks or drives within its detection range.

Sensor   A device which is designed to produce a signal or offer indication in response to an event or stimulus within its detection zone.

Sensor, Combustion   See *Ionization smoke detector, Photoelectric beam-type smoke detector, Photoelectric spot-type smoke detector,* and *Resistance bridge smoke detector.*

Sensor, Smoke   See *Ionization smoke detector, Photoelectric beam-type smoke detector, Photoelectric spot-type smoke detector,* and *Resistance bridge smoke detector.*

Shunt   (1) A deliberate shorting out of a portion of an electric circuit. (2) A key-operated switch which removes some portion of an alarm system for operation, allowing entry into a protected area without initiating an alarm signal. A type of authorized access switch.

Shunt Switch   See *Shunt.*

Signal Recorder   See *Register.*

Silent Alarm   A remote alarm without an obvious local indication that an alarm has been transmitted.

Silent Alarm System   An alarm system which signals a remote station by means of a silent alarm.

Single-Circuit System   An alarm circuit which routes only one side of the circuit through each sensor. The return may be through either ground or a separate wire.

Single-Stroke Bell   A bell which its struck once each time its mechanism is activated.

Slashing Register   See *Register, slashing.*

Smoke Detector   A device which detects visible or invisible products of combustion. See also *Ionization smoke detector, Photoelectric beam-type smoke detector, Photoelectric spot-type smoke detector,* and *Resistance bridge smoke detector.*

Solid State   (1) An adjective used to describe a device such as a semiconductor transistor or diode. (2) A circuit or system which does not rely on vacuum or gas-filled tubes to control or modify voltages and currents.

Sonic Motion Detector   A sensor which detects the motion of an intruder by her or his disturbance of an audible sound pattern generated within the protected area.

Sound-Sensing Detection System   An alarm system which detects the audible sound caused by an attempted forcible entry into a protected structure. The system consists of microphones and a control unit containing an amplifier, accumulator, and a power supply. The unit's sensitivity is adjustable so that ambient noises or normal sounds will not initiate an alarm signal. However, noises above this preset level or a sufficient accumulation of impulses will initiate an alarm.

Sound Sensor   A sensor which responds to sound; a microphone.

Space Protection   See *Area protection.*

Spoofing   The defeat or compromise of an alarm system by tricking or fooling its detection devices such as by short-circuiting part or all of a series circuit, cutting wires in a parallel circuit, reducing the sensitivity of a sensor, or entering false signals into the system. Spoofing contrasts with *Circumvention*.

Spot Protection   Protection of objects such as safes, art objects, or anything of value which could be damaged or removed from the premises.

Spring Contact   A device employing a current-carrying cantilever spring which monitors the position of a door or window.

Standby Power Supply   Equipment which supplies power to a system in the event the primary power is lost. It may consist of batteries, charging circuits, auxiliary motor generators, or a combination of these devices.

Strain Gauge Alarm System   An alarm system which detects the stress caused by the weight of an intruder as he or she moves about a building. Typical uses include placement of the strain gauge sensor under a floor joist or under a stairway tread.

Strain Gauge Sensor   A sensor which, when attached to an object, will provide an electrical response to an applied stress upon the object, such as a bending, stretching, or compressive force.

Strain-Sensitive Cable   An electric cable which is designed to produce a signal whenever the cable is strained by a change in applied force. Typical uses including mounting it in a wall to detect an attempted forced entry through the wall, or fastening it to a fence to detect climbing on the fence, or burying it around a perimeter to detect walking or driving across the perimeter.

Subscriber's Equipment   That portion of a central station alarm system installed in the protected premises.

Subscriber's Unit   A control unit of a central station alarm system.

Supervised Lines   Interconnecting lines in an alarm system which are electrically supervised against tampering. See also *Line supervision*.

Supervisory Alarm System   An alarm system which monitors conditions or persons or both and which signals any deviation from an established norm or schedule. Examples are the monitoring of signals from guard patrol stations for irregularities in the progression along a prescribed patrol route and the monitoring of production or safety conditions, such as sprinkler water pressure, temperature, or liquid level.

Supervisory Circuit   An electric circuit or radio path which sends information on the status of a sensor or guard patrol to an annunciator. For intrusion alarm systems, this circuit provides line supervision and monitors tamper devices. See also *Supervisory alarm system*.

Surreptitious   Covert, hidden, concealed, or disguised.

Surveillance   (1) Control of premises for security purposes through alarm systems, closed-circuit television (CCTV), or other monitoring methods. (2) Supervision or inspection of industrial processes by monitoring those conditions which could cause damage if not corrected. See also *Supervisory alarm system*.

Tamper Device   (1) Any device, usually a switch, which is used to detect an attempt to gain access to intrusion alarm circuitry, such as by removing a switch cover. (2) A monitor circuit to detect any attempt to modify the alarm circuitry, such as by cutting a wire.

Tamper Switch   A switch which is installed in such a way as to detect attempts to remove the enclosure of some alarm system components such as control box doors, switch covers, junction box covers, or bell housings. The alarm component is then often described as being tampered with.

Tape   See *Foil*.

Tapper Bell   A single-stroke bell designed to produce a sound of low intensity and relatively high pitch.

Telephone Dialer, Automatic   A device which, when activated, automatically dials one or more preprogrammed telephone numbers (e.g., police, fire department) and relays a recorded voice or coded message giving the location and nature of the alarm.

Telephone Dialer, Digital   An automatic telephone dialer which sends its message as a digital code.

Terminal Resistor   A resistor used as a terminating device.

Terminating Capacitor   A capacitor sometimes used as a terminating device for a capacitance sensor antenna. The capacitor allows the supervision of the sensor antenna, especially if a long wire is used as the sensor.

Terminating Device   A device which is used to terminate an electrically supervised circuit. It makes the electric circuit continuous and provides a fixed impedance reference (end-of-line resistor) against which changes are measured to detect an alarm condition. The impedance changes may be caused by a sensor, tampering, or circuit trouble.

Time Delay   See *Entrance delay* and *Exit delay*.

Time-Division Multiplexing (TDM)   See *Multiplexing, time-division*.

Timing Table   That portion of central station equipment which provides a means for checking incoming signals from McCulloh circuits.

Touch Sensitivity   The sensitivity of a capacitance sensor at which the alarm device will be activated only if an intruder touches or comes in very close proximity (about 1 centimeter or $1/_2$ inch) to the protected object.

Trap   (1) A device, usually a switch, installed within a protected area, which serves as secondary protection in the event a perimeter alarm system is successfully penetrated. Examples are a trip-wise switch placed across a likely path for an intruder, a mat switch hidden under a rug, or a magnetic switch mounted on an inner door. (2) A volumetric sensor installed so as to detect an intruder in a likely traveled corridor or pathway within a security area.

Trickle Charge   A continuous direct current, usually very low, which is applied to a battery to maintain it at peak charge or to recharge it after it has been partially or completely discharged. Usually applied to nickel-cadmium (NICAD) or wet cell batteries.

Trip Wire Switch   A switch which is actuated by breaking or moving a wire or cord installed across a floor space.

Trouble Signal   See *Break alarm*.

Twist Connectors   See *Wire nuts*.

UL   See *Underwriters Laboratories, Inc.*

UL-Certificated   For certain types of products which have met UL requirements, for which it is impractical to apply the UL Listing Mark or Classification Marking to the individual product, a certificate is provided which the manufacturer may use to identify quantities of material for specific job sites or to identify field-installed systems.

UL-Listed   Signifies that production samples of the product have been found to comply with established Underwriters Laboratories' requirements and that the manufacturer is authorized to use the UL Listing Marks on the listed products which comply with the requirements, contingent upon the follow-up services as a check of compliance.

Ultrasonic   Pertaining to a sound wave having a frequency above that of audible sound (approximately 20,000 Hz). Ultrasonic sound is used in ultrasonic detection systems.

Ultrasonic Detection System   See *Ultrasonic motion detector* and *Passive ultrasonic alarm system*.

Ultrasonic Frequency   Sound frequencies which are above the range of human hearing; approximately 20,000 Hz and higher.

Ultrasonic Motion Detector   A sensor which detects the motion of an intruder through the use of ultrasonic generating and receiving equipment. The device operates by filling a space with a pattern of ultrasonic waves; the modulation of these waves by a moving object is detected and initiates an alarm signal.

Underdome Bell   A bell most of whose mechanism is concealed by its gong.

Underwriters Laboratories, Inc. (UL)   A private independent research and testing laboratory which tests and lists various items meeting good practice and safety standards.

Vibrating Bell   A bell whose mechanism is designed to strike repeatedly and for as long as it is activated.

Vibrating Contact   See *Vibration sensor*.

Vibration Detection System   An alarm system which employs one or more contact microphones or vibration sensors which are fastened to the surfaces of the area or object being protected to detect excessive levels of vibration. The contact microphone system consists of microphones, a control unit containing an amplifier and an accumulator, and a power supply. The unit's sensitivity is adjustable so that ambient noises or normal vibrations will not initiate an alarm signal. In the vibration sensor system, the sensor responds to excessive vibration by opening a switch in a closed-circuit system.

Vibration Detector   See *Vibration sensor*.

Vibration Sensor   A sensor which responds to vibrations of the surface on which it is mounted. It has a normally closed switch which will momentarily open when it is subjected to a vibration with sufficiently large amplitude. Its sensitivity is adjustable to allow for the different levels of normal vibration, to which the sensor should not respond, at different locations. See also *Vibration detection system*.

Visual Signal Device   A pilot light, annunciator, or other device which provides a visual indication of the condition of the circuit or system being supervised.

Voltage (or Volts)   A unit for measuring electric power. Watts equal volts times amperes.

Volumetric Detector   See *Volumetric sensor*.

Volumetric Sensor   A sensor with a detection zone which extends over a volume such as an entire room, part of a room, or a passageway. Ultrasonic motion detectors and sonic motion detectors are examples of volumetric sensors.

Walk Test Light   A light-on-motion detector which comes on when the detector senses motion in the area. It is used while setting the sensitivity of the detector and during routine checking and maintenance.

Watchman's Reporting System   A supervisory alarm system arranged for the transmission of a patrolling watchman's regularly recurring report signals from stations along the patrol route to a central supervisory agency.

Wire Nuts (or Twist Connectors)   Plastic caps with metal threads inside, used for connecting two or more wires together.

Zoned Circuit   A circuit which provides continual protection for parts of zones of the protected area while normally used doors and windows or zones may be released for access.

Zones   Smaller subdivisions into which large areas are divided to permit selective access to some zones while maintaining other zones secure and to permit pinpointing the specific location from which an alarm signal is transmitted.

Index